Abiding with God

© 2015 Forward Movement

Forward Movement
412 Sycamore Street
Cincinnati, Ohio 45202-4194

800.543.1813

www.forwardmovement.org

Psalm passages are from the Psalter in *The Book of Common Prayer.*

ISBN 978-0-88028-416-5

Printed in the United States of America

Forward
Movement

Abiding with God

"Abide in me…abide in my love…" These words of instruction, given by Jesus in John's Gospel, invite us to do more than just walk, talk, or live with Jesus. To abide means something altogether more full and fulfilling than simply hanging around. By inviting us to abide with him, to abide in his love, Jesus is offering us the chance to crawl in, curl up, and be willing captives to restoration, redemption, and renewal.

This book of daily meditations offers suggestions to help you find your way to abide with God. We've selected twelve spiritual practices and themes. Each month, you'll find a short introduction highlighting the spiritual practice for the month as well as some helpful hints to engage and deepen your experience. Our hope is that by year's end, you will learn new ways to pray and to enjoy your daily devotional time—and that you will be encouraged to share some of those new experiences with those you know and love.

I'm fortunate to remember crawling into the laps of my parents and grandparents and feeling encircled by their arms and love for me. When I think about abiding in Jesus and his love for me, I think about those moments of being cradled, of time standing still, of feeling fully loved and accepted. My hope and prayer is that as you spend time with this collection of meditations, you will find your own ways of understanding what it means to abide with Jesus and in his love.

Forward Movement is happy and humbled to offer this resource to the glory of God, to inspire disciples and empower evangelists by encouraging us all to practice our faith daily. We hope that this offering of *Abiding with God: Day by Day* offers you refreshment for your continued journey.

—**Rachel Jones, editor**

JANUARY

Meditation
&
Mindfulness

Be still, then, and know that I am God.
—PSALM 46:11

Be Still and Know

Being still, the idea of undertaking intentional mindfulness and meditation, doesn't come easy for most of us. This month, we are invited to spend a little time each day undertaking this practice. Stillness and quiet are a luxury for many of us; when we can achieve peace in our hearts and minds for even a few minutes, God can fill up that space with creative quiet, contentment, and joy. Consider setting aside a prescribed amount of time this month just for your devotional practice. Set a timer if that helps. It's OK if you struggle to sit still or clear your mind—remember the good advice your coaches, teachers, and parents may have given you when trying a new thing—practice makes perfect. And don't worry too much about the perfect part. Be still, and rest in the confidence that a mighty God loves you very much and is waiting to meet you in those still, small moments of your daily life.

WAYS TO ENGAGE

If you're new to the ideas of mindfulness and mediation, try running a quick Internet search. Spend a while familiarizing yourself with these ideas.

Pick a word on which to focus your meditation time—peace, love, hope, healing, light, etc.

Memorize a verse or passage in the Bible.

Use a chime, bell, or particular piece of music to provide a sound cue for beginning and ending your quiet time.

Set aside space in your home or office to use just for quiet time. Try to practice your quiet time at the same time every day.

It's the very first day of a brand new year. Some of us face this new year with gusto, excitement—chomping at the bit to get into this new and limitless territory. Others of us may find ourselves looking at the new year and wondering how the last one passed so quickly; we may be reeling from hard knocks or difficult transitions and wishing we could put a two-week delay on all things new. All of us are going to need generous portions of grace and mercy to get us through the next twelve months—not to mention the next twelve minutes.

Psalm 46 reminds us to be still and know that God is God. Too many times, we get caught up in our own busy-ness, strategic plans, and life goals. We forget to be still and to remember that the Living God, this Creator, this Love is both the deep root and sweet fruit of all our work, no matter how large or small our tasks may be.

May the God of Peace, who calls us each to be still and to know, find you, fill you, and abide with you today and every day.

—Rachel Jones

ꭓ

O God of peace, who has taught us that in returning and rest we shall be saved, in quietness and in confidence shall be our strength: By the might of your Spirit lift us, we pray you, to your presence, where we may be still and know that you are God, through Jesus Christ our Lord. Amen.

—*The Book of Common Prayer*, p. 832

Children raised in churches are taught to pray from a very young age. From the Lord's Prayer to "Now I lay me down to sleep," it seems like I have never known a time when I didn't know how to pray. But meditation? That's a different story. I've studied meditation as an adult many times, in many different forms, and I'm still not very good at it. I'm not very good at silence in general. Even in group gatherings, when silence descends, I am the first to try and shatter it. Silence is scary. When I try to meditate, my mind races with my to-do list, my fears, lyrics to the song I heard in the car yesterday, the parts of my body that ache, and on and on and on.

But even in the small spaces between the words of my racing mind, there is a grace and a peace. There is a comfort in not doing but simply being in the presence of the indwelling Spirit. Knowing that I can stop the chatter and still be a beloved child of God is beyond freeing. And Jesus himself tells us that God knows what we are asking before we ever even say the words (Matthew 6:8). Meditation doesn't have to be sitting cross-legged on the floor for hours on end; it can be simply sitting for a few moments, doing my best to keep my mouth and my mind silent, listening for the still, small voice of God.

—**Holli Powell**

I first read the words, "Be still, and know that I am God," when I was fifteen. Standing outside on a summer evening, staring up at the stars, there I was, feeling overwhelmed, frustrated, weighed down. As I stood there, staring up at the stars, I was alone, with nothing but a book of psalms to keep me company.

My mother had given me that Psalter only a few days before. Those timeless prayers and songs meant the world to her, were part of her. For me, they had always been just…words. Still, I had grabbed that book of psalms when I stormed out of the campsite that night, so I decided I might as well flip through its pages and see if there was anything in there for me.

And that is when I first read those words, "Be still, and know that I am God." In the version of the Bible I had, it read, "Stop fighting, and know that I am God." I froze in my tracks. I had been fighting for some time, it seemed, always trying to be strong enough, clever enough, anything enough to force things to go my way. "All right, God," I said out loud, "I'll stop fighting. So where are you?"

In one sense, nothing happened. My problems were still there, still weighing me down. But in another sense, deep in my soul, I suddenly knew. God was indeed present, and God was God, so I didn't have to try to be. So "be still, stop fighting." Through prayer and meditation today, I just might find once again that blessed stillness that filled my soul those many years ago and that can fill it once again.

—Chuck Robertson

God shows up in the middle of our lives. It is messy. The presence of God rolls us around in the mud of existence and calls us to walk into the muck and mire of what is—without ever knowing where we will land.

Be still and know. Be still. And know. God asks us the hardest of things in the midst of the hardest of times—the act of presence in the midst of our lives on most days seems a task too difficult to handle.

God calls us to find moments of stillness, silence, and breath. The most mindful act is that of breathing. The first and last act as an expression of humanity and divinity that we do on this earth is breathe—we breathe in the presence of God in our midst; we breathe out all that is not serving us in this moment, place, and time.

God is our waking breath, at the dawn of life. God is our last exhale, the dying breath of a life lived with intention. Every inhale is God. Every exhale is God. Everything in between is our attempt to live out the destiny of sacred breath. May God offer us the strength and resilience given to us, inherently, in breath, each and every day of our lives.

—Teresa Pasquale

In today's fast-paced, instant-gratification, always-updating-and-trending world, we often forget to take time to stop. Stop to smell the roses, stop to look around, stop to take a breath. It's often when we stop and pay attention to those around us that we feel awe at God's creation. When our worries and concerns aren't always at the forefront of our mind. When we engage in intentional conversation and intentional listening instead of thinking about how to respond. When we declutter our hearts and minds of worries and sorrow, and remember that God is there to help us bear our burden.

Meditation has been viewed as something of a new age experience. It has often been seen as a strict regimen of sitting with your legs crossed, eyes closed, and palms to the sky. But how often we forget that when we drop to our knees, close our eyes, and clasp our hands tight, we are meditating. Regardless of how we do it, we all are seeking a deeper and closer experience with God.

When we slow life down a little, we are able to enjoy the blessings we have in our lives. When we take some time to pray, we are able to experience God's nearness to us. But when slowing down and prayer find the perfect harmony, we feel the limitlessness of God's care and love.

—Longkee Vang

Most cities of any size in the US provide opportunities for enjoyment: art museums, restaurants, concerts. People privileged enough to afford these activities are willing to sacrifice valuable money and time to enjoy them. We think of ourselves as going to places like these for the things they provide (art, food, etc.). I believe that we also desire the chance to focus on the experiences. Art museums use careful lighting and quiet rooms to focus our attention completely on the artwork; music venues make choices about volume and seating that encourage people to throw themselves into the musical experience. Good venues provide people not only with high quality products but also with atmospheres that bring mindfulness to people's experiences. Our spending practices indicate that we value the opportunity to pay that kind of attention.

Bringing this level of focus into our daily routine is more difficult. My first cup of morning coffee tastes as good as anything in a high-end restaurant because in the quiet of early morning, I pay wholehearted attention to those blissful sips. Then the day starts, I become distracted, and the coffee fades into the background.

Mindfulness practices, at their best, give us the discipline to bring the focus that we give to restaurant food or concert music into our ordinary lives, where our attention is being constantly funneled away from our experiences instead of toward them. We become more aware of our blessings when we give ourselves the space to pay attention to them.

—Elizabeth Brignac

S everal times a month I wake at 4 a.m. Email isn't checked. No tea is brewed. The phone stays off—a huge challenge. There's no early-morning news about war, hate, or injustice to anger or sadden my heart. Like good diet, physical exercise, or nurturing relationships, keeping quiet requires commitment. Sometimes lots of it. If you have pets or children, you may need extra planning to make this work for yourself.

It's easier getting up at 4 a.m. during spring, summer, and autumn than in the unforgiving throes of winter in the Northeast. At this hour, I may begin my morning with reflection, meditation, or standing before a small, dedicated worship space with soft, spoken prayer before icons.

It's what follows, however, that is most elusive and what I hunger for most—stillness.

Sitting quietly as the first rays of hope break in the east to awaken the earth is often when I experience something transcendental. Without the morning buzz of street traffic or noise from folks in my building, there is something mystically intangible for a few moments.

If I'm especially blessed, time stands still for several minutes, and I catch my spiritual breath, feeling strengthened to sojourn again in a cold, unjust, complicated world to make positive, incremental change.

—Paul Jesep

I don't often feel that I am good at mindfulness and meditation. I am easily distracted. I haven't tamed what Buddhists call the "monkey mind." There are many monkeys clamoring for my attention in my head all the time. Thoughts, song fragments, images. For many years, I tried to accept that this is just the way I am. Or at least I tried to accept it when I wasn't beating myself up over it. Because secretly I believed that all those serene contemplative people out there, who clearly did not have monkeys of their own, were vastly superior to me, both as people and as Christians.

And so I seesawed. I'm OK. I'm a failure. I went from defending against suggestions that I try meditation to signing up for contemplative prayer class to feeling bad that I failed at it. Not everyone has to meditate, I declared. I wish I could be more meditative, I whispered.

Finally, I gave up this inner battle. I just let it be. And I discovered that in fact, now that I'm not struggling over it, I often am mindful. I notice things. I'm really good at noticing things, both inwardly and outwardly. It's actually one of the gifts of my monkey mind. I started practicing yoga again. As my kids left home and my daily life started changing, I discovered that I often have silence in my life, and it is good. I've become mindful of that.

If you struggle with meditation, let it be. It is good to spend some time in silence with God, and everyone is not the same in how they can do that. And that's OK.

—Penny Nash

In another life, I was a television news producer. It's imperative that producers book guests who understand that when their lips stop moving and they go quiet for even a nanosecond, viewers start clicking their remotes to another channel. In television news, you must be mindful that silence is never golden.

My survival as a producer hinged on possessing a preternatural revulsion to silence and mindfulness. Then divine intervention changed that. I suffered the equivalent of a traumatic brain injury when a doctor bungled a medical diagnosis and drug treatment. My body and life got pushed off a cliff, and there was no architect, contractor, or toolmaker who knew how to put Humpty Dumpty back together again. I had to become my own DIY designer, engineer, and project manager for a complete rebuild.

Sitting alone for many months, trying to come up with plans and actions I could make and take to recover and get my life back didn't work. Every plan fizzled, and every action ended in the spinning of wheels. Then a new doctor suggested a radical course of treatment: Do nothing. Be still. Wait for guidance to come from the silence.

Moment by quiet moment, my mind stilled, and the answers I needed to rebuild my body and reclaim my soul quietly came. Today, I am fully recovered.

—**Charlotte Chere Graham**

My Blackberry froze on me as I was using an app during Morning Prayer at my parish. I tried all four tricks:

1) Soft Reset/Press ALT + RIGHT SHIFT(CAP) + DELETE; 2) Double-Soft Reset/Press ALT + RIGHT SHIFT(CAP) + DELETE & When the screen comes back on, immediately press ALT + RIGHT SHIFT(CAP) + DELETE again; 3) Hard Reset/ take battery out for thirty seconds and then reinsert; and 4) leave battery out overnight. Alas, none of that worked; and next I tried rebooting the entire software suite.

I even went to my service provider to see if they could fix it. They offered me an insurance plan at $6.95 per month so that I could replace the bad one with a new Blackberry. I said that I thought I would try laying hands on it and praying over it first. The salesperson was not too happy with my response.

I think God was a little annoyed with me for checking my Blackberry during prayer when I heard it buzz. OK, God, I hear you. Be still and know that I am.

—Westina Matthews

⟡

The LORD will fight for you,
and you only have to keep still.

—EXODUS 14:14

Two months ago, during my morning commute through New York's Grand Central Station, I saw the thing I fear the most: a backpack with no one around, leaning against a wall.

I wasn't the only person who saw it, of course. All around me, people were stopping in their tracks, some visibly shaken, turning in the other direction to get away as fast as possible. Years of daily reminders to keep an eye out for bombs in backpacks, of being told to say something should we see something, had taken their toll. We were afraid.

And thank God, it was for no good reason. Moments later, as I watched the tourist who'd left her backpack return to pick it up, oblivious to how many people she'd startled, I realized how quickly fear had overtaken me—us. What, then, does it mean to "be still and know that I am God" when we are afraid?

Oftentimes when people think about meditation, we tend to imagine serenity: the breathing exercises in a yoga class, the minimalism of a Zen temple. In contrast, the phrase "Be still, then, and know that I am God" comes from Psalm 46, a tumultuous reflection on taking refuge in God during times of heightened fear. Though "the nations make much ado, and the kingdoms are shaken," we learn that God is the one remaining place of stillness and that God's version of desolation "breaks the bow, and shatters the spear, and burns the shields with fire."

God is that place of stillness and peace in the midst of frightening times. Let's all breathe and draw near.

—Miguel Escobar

"Don't touch it."

My friend's father had bought a theremin and was showing his son and me how to play it. He moved his hand up and down beside—but not touching—the antenna on the electronic instrument, producing the sort of tremulous, spooky tones that haunted many horror movies of the 1940s and 50s.

I often think that meditation is a bit like playing the theremin. As a person with way too many words bursting to be spoken, written, or at least, thought, I find contemplative silence difficult. I want to "touch" it, to poke at it with questions and demands, when what I need is simply to come near the holy, to be, as a former rector always reminded us, "in the Presence." Trying to touch won't make music.

> A theremin you play by standing back,
> moving your hands across the empty air.
> It must be difficult to learn the knack
> of just not touching, with exquisite care.
>
> Bodies learn early: Music's made by touch
> fingers that strike the keyboard, pluck the string;
> lips that enfold vibrating reed with such
> a firm embrace that even wood must sing.
>
> Now this contrary instrument confounds:
> Grasp, and it groans complaint discordantly,
> but lift your hands, and sweet, ethereal sounds
> rise from your new restraint in harmony.
>
> Perhaps, with practice, one might come to know
> how to make music out of letting go.

—Mary W. Cox

Every year I have the same New Year's resolution. It is not to eat breakfast or exercise more. It is not to be more organized or to avoid procrastination, although all of these things would be worthy pursuits for me. No, my resolution, year in and year out, is to be more mindful, to pay attention.

I don't want to skim the surface of all life offers each day. I want to wake and taste that first breath, to recognize and give thanks for another day of God's animating grace. I want to truly see the people I encounter each day: the barista, the bank teller, the colleague, the kids at the bus stop, the messenger on the bike, my husband, my friends.

I want to notice the change in the winter light, the lengthening of each day, the glacial blue in the crevasses of white snow shoveled off the driveway, again. I want nothing to go unheralded, unnoticed, unappreciated.

The spiritual life tempts my thoughts heavenward. But God made the earth and called it good. Made the plants and the animals, the birds and the fish, and called them good. God made you and me. And called us good. I don't want to miss that, any of it, any of you. I want to taste and see it all. I want to pay attention.

Lord, make me mindful, literally. Fill my mind with all your wonders that my heart might be exceedingly thankful. Above all, keep me mindful of you. Amen.

—Susan Wyper

I'm nursing an imaginary knot the size of a tennis ball that sits on the top of my head. This knot is the result of the two-by-four boards that God is constantly beating me over the head with. I'm stubborn, which is why the knot is so large. I have no hope of living without it but I long for a day when it will shrink. When I tell people my two-by-four theory on relationships with God, I usually find I am not alone in this approach.

In an effort to shrink this knot, I've been trying to be more present with the Holy Spirit. I'm more open to the things being offered to me, trying to follow my gut more and act accordingly. It takes me on wonderful adventures; I feel more complete. I think the Holy Spirit speaks to and guides us daily. We only have to be quiet enough to hear it. It can lead to some beautiful places but most importantly, it keeps God from having to swing that two-by-four so often.

—Lauren Caldwell

"This battle is not for you to fight; take your position, stand still, and see the victory of the LORD on your behalf, O Judah and Jerusalem." Do not fear or be dismayed; tomorrow go out against them, and the LORD will be with you.

—2 CHRONICLES 20:17

January takes its name from Janus, a Roman god. Janus possessed two heads looking in opposing directions, the past and the future. January reminds us to reflect on the past, not in an obsessive way or by being possessive of the past. Mature Christians who seek the time to meditate offer the past to God. They ask only one thing: how may I know God more deeply and serve God more faithfully because of the activities and experiences of my past?

The past can catapult us into a more prophetic, compassionate, and Christ-like living. As Socrates reminds us, the unexamined life is not worth living. When we examine our sins, the evil powers that worked against the good news of God, and when we examine our selfishness, our lies, and our choices of ego over the cross, we open ourselves to a more abundant life.

When we bring our sins of racism, sexism, unloving thoughts, words, or actions to God, God calls us to recommit to a life that respects the dignity of every human being. Reviewing calls from God we heard over the past year, we are challenged to live lives that make a difference. We are challenged to live out our belief that all lives matter.

January reminds us that God's call for us to know and do the will of God requires mindfulness. We are called to be still and know Jesus Christ by serving others and loving our neighbors as God loves us.

—Mark Bozzuti-Jones

He felt badgered in his mind, writing, "Call off thoughts a while...leave comfort root-room." English poet and Jesuit priest Gerard Manley Hopkins expressed in the 1800s what people have needed across time: to allow mental room for comfort to take root, instead of permitting worry to thrive, undisciplined.

John the Baptist needed comfort too. After his empowered introductions of Jesus the Savior, the one who would bring salvation, John landed in prison; meanwhile, Jesus was performing miracles all around. With limited root-room for comfort, John sent others to ask, "So—are you the Messiah, or not?"

Haven't most of us asked God some "why" questions? "I'm struggling with this diagnosis, with finances, with this dilemma, this relationship. If you are God, do something dramatic here." Or we might beg, "Jesus, free me from imprisonment in my own thoughts." Jesus' response to John applies to us all: Blessed is the person who isn't tripped up in the walk of faith. Take another step. Keep coming to me.

To the overburdened, he says: Come. Come, sit with me. I will give you rest. Learn from me. Jesus might ask if you are carrying weights placed upon you by yourself or by others. Instead, he says, accept my expectations that are lighter. Give comfort root-room, and find rest for your souls (Matthew 11).

—June Terry

When I was a teenager, Master Lee, my martial arts instructor, taught us how to meditate. Focus on your heartbeat, he would say. We knew that meditation was intended to clear the mind of all thoughts. Master Lee knew, however, that just jumping into such a thing was nearly impossible, especially for a bunch of teenagers. So we started off small, by focusing on just one thing, our heartbeats. Keeping that as the sole object of my attention was hard.

Later, I learned about Buddhist monks who attempt to achieve enlightenment through meditation. They spend years clearing their minds of thoughts and worldly desires. I can only keep my focus on one thing for about fifteen seconds; the feat these men achieve boggles my mind. When I met a Buddhist monk in person, he told me that he didn't try to erase every thought. Instead, he tried to be "in the now." He seemed to say, "Focus, instead, on everything, from the stirring of air currents to the light of the sun, the buzz of insects to the pressure of our blood vessels." This, too, I found nearly impossible to do.

As a Christian, meditation has taken on a new facet for me. When I meditate, I try instead to take the focus off of myself and my surroundings and think only of God and of those in need.

—Spencer Hixon

X

He makes me lie down in green pastures
and leads me beside still waters.

—PSALM 23:2

"Noah, do you have ants in your pants?" He instantly froze. He looked at me with dumbfounded confusion, which gave way to juvenile panic. I stifled a giggle as he jumped to his feet, while simultaneously dropping his pants to his ankles. I heard a whispered, "I hope not!!" as he checked to make sure. I spent the rest of the morning talking about figures of speech and treating our house for an ant infestation that existed only in his five-year-old imagination.

Lately, I have been fluttering between tasks, chores, appointments, responsibilities, and locations so haphazardly that I've been making myself dizzy. There never seem to be enough hours in the day, money in the bank, or gas in the tank to get the jobs done. Yet, I spin my wheels as fast as I can, trying to make it all happen anyway. I have developed a bad case of ants in the pants!

Sometimes it's hard to hear anything above the noise. Jesus whispers while my to-do list screams. The Holy Spirit beckons, but my toddler demands. God pursues, but sometimes the only thing that overtakes me is sleep. My soul has grown weary, and my spirit is parched. What I truly need is quiet rest and a few moments each day where my undivided attention is set on God, who sees me through the tumultuous whirlwind of chaos.

Today, I will choose a retreat. It won't be on a glorious beach or among majestic mountains. In fact, it will most likely be a stolen moment hiding in the closet or waiting in the carpool line after school. But I will choose to be still for a brief respite and listen only to the God who made me. For just a few moments, I refuse to let the ants rule my pants!

—Bree Combs

Where I live, it gets very cold in the winter. Getting out of a warm bed in the middle of January is a pretty miserable experience. I venture out each morning in expectation of two things—the inevitable arrival of spring and the hot cup of coffee waiting in the kitchen. The hot cup of coffee happens because I set the timer on the coffee maker every night before I go to bed. I am diligent about this. If I don't set the timer, the wait for the hot cup of coffee makes the cold morning all that much more miserable. There is absolutely a cause and effect to this daily discipline. Spring, however, comes without any effort on my part. It is a miracle that unfolds around me and I am reminded that God really can make all things new. The seasons change.

Warm weather comes and cold weather goes and the cold weather comes again. Week in and week out, through it all…the good and the bad…God, in whom we live and move and have our being, is not only present but also sustains us and everything around us. Perhaps when I set the timer every night on my coffee pot, I should take a moment to be mindful of who really gets me through the day and who does more for all of us than we could ever ask for or imagine.

—Jason Leo

Whenever I have a chance, I try to be mindful and responsive to what my dad exhorts and encourages every Sunday in his sermon—"Read the Bible!" I know that we all want God's promises fulfilled. We all want to obtain the promise, whatever promise that might be, tailored to our needs and utterly fulfilled. The only way to know what the promise might be is to read God's Word.

When I read and meditate on scripture, the love letter God inspired, I can see one more promise that I want and to which I will hold. I will write it out and post it where I can see it daily. And I will wait—sometimes patiently, sometimes crying, sometimes screaming, sometimes doubting. But I will wait. I can be impatient. But when I know I will get something if I wait, it's easier.

When I waited almost nine months for my son to be born (and to find out if he was going to be a girl or a boy), I knew that the promise was worth the patient wait, because shorter than that time wouldn't be good for my baby! It's the same with the promises God has for us. They might take a few days, weeks, hours, or even years, but they are worth the wait.

—Sandra Montes

My grandson goes through his usual ritual: turning off the canned music playing in the lobby of his apartment building, propping up the lid of the baby grand piano, and extracting his music books from his bag. After a series of scales, he begins playing increasingly complex and beautiful music.

Recently, my grandson has added an additional practice. He has begun using a new set of junior golf clubs given to him as a gift. He spends an hour or two at a nearby driving range while we patiently wait under the shade of a nearby live oak. He listens to advice and encouragement and then asks the person who gave him his clubs how soon it might be before he can begin to play on a "real course." He knows that the quality of his practice will hasten that experience.

One of the things that strikes me is how joyfully my grandson practices what he loves. He rarely pays attention to the clock. We who profess faith are also invited to practice—through prayer and meditation; through attention to nature, to others, and to that guiding inner voice; through active works of creativity, kindness, and justice. I ask myself: am I as unselfconsciously joyful in my spiritual practices as my grandson is at the piano and the driving range?

—Joan Bowers

The machines are anything but still; they clang and clack, swoosh, and, in the case of the MRI, thump loudly and rhythmically. The disembodied voice of a technician comes through headphones or over speakers: "Take a breath, and hold it…hold it…Now you can breathe." Eventually the scan is done, and the mechanized gurney slides me out of my narrow tubular tomb.

The first cancer, stage 3 inflammatory breast carcinoma, was diagnosed in November 2010; IBC is nasty and aggressive and so is the treatment. I beat the odds. The second, discovered with a mammogram in November 2012, was early stage. Surgery eliminated that one. In November 2014 (I have grown nervous about that month in even-numbered years), scans revealed that the first cancer had returned as Stage 4, attacking my sacrum and eating arches into the bone.

Post-radiation, I pop a pill, take part in a clinical trial involving another pill, have a monthly infusion of a bone-builder, and get scanned every quarter. Last time, there was good news: the spots found on my lungs during the initial Dance of the Seven Scans were gone. (Maybe I have the real drug; maybe it's all the prayer offered up for my healing; maybe it's a combination thereof.)

The machines are not still, but I am still lying within them, listening, waiting, hoping. I am freed to be open to God and to all that God is and was and shall be to me, now and for eternity.

—Sarah Bryan Miller

If we choose to practice meditation, it's good to remember that God's time is not our time.

I was first jarred into realizing this at a party some years ago. When someone spoke of a friend who'd just come back from a meditation retreat, some listeners nodded in empathy. Comments ranged from "That's really cool!" to "I wish I had the time to do that!" And then one person said, with a laugh, "Yeah, but what if she spent all that time and then nothing happened?"

His cynicism shouldn't have surprised me. We live in a fast food culture, bombarded by ads trying to persuade us that instant gratification is our natural right. Even if we know better, it's easy to let this mindset affect our attitude toward meditation—or any spiritual practice, for that matter. But whether we are snatching fifteen minutes before work or settling into a week-long retreat, we are on God's time, not our own. The times we struggle, the times we wonder what the point of it all is, may be the very times God is doing the deepest work within us. And that work can change us so subtly that we may not recognize it till much later.

It can be a real challenge some days to find time to meditate, let alone to make time for a quiet day or weekend retreat. But if we are faithful and let God set the agenda, we can relax—and trust that something is happening.

—Kathleen M. Flanagan

I am "trapped" in one of those happy marriages you sometimes read about. One of the few negative things I can say about my husband is that he insists on driving every time we go somewhere. Every time.

When we drive in our big, red, Texas pickup truck, I'm relieved that he's behind the wheel. My skill set and depth perception are far more suited to my much smaller car. Sitting in the passenger seat of the big truck also affords me the opportunity to use that invisible passenger side brake and horn. You know the ones… moms and dads use them when they are teaching their kids to drive. My fifty-three-year-old husband loves it when I employ those invisible devices.

It finally dawned on me one day that my perspective in the passenger seat was different than his in the driver's seat. On occasion…I was wrong! There, I admit it, and it's in print. (My husband will order 100 copies of this book now). He wasn't (always) too close to the dividing line or a motorcyclist. From where I sat, it looked like we were headed for trouble, but it was a false perception on my part.

That revelation made me think about God…and the big picture… and where we, finite creatures, sit. It is my prayer in this new year that I can remember "my place" in God's universe—and that I can trust…

—**Rhoda Montgomery**

Stare into the quiet spaces of your home: the nooks and crannies of daily life that your amazing brain glosses over and fills with the knowing of memory and familiarity. A vase, a picture frame, a rug, a pillow: when was the last time you held it in your gaze, remembered where it came from, noticed its imperfections and character? When is the last time you filled your house with your looking, peering around and appreciating everything as though it were new, as though you had just moved in?

There are moments when I am struck by the visual world around me, the colors and movement, shape and line, moments when I know I should pay attention: a sunset, a formal occasion when my partner dons his best suit, a walk through a flower garden or an art museum. But for each of these, there are countless others when I fail to pick up on the beauty and complexity of the visual world that constantly surrounds me. I'm just too busy.

I've read that, depending on the study, our brains are only capable of processing between 60 and 110 bits of data per second. That means if we're trying to carry out any complex task, if we are multitasking or carrying on a conversation, we barely have enough processing power to make sure we keep breathing, walking, chewing. We crowd out the stimuli from the world around us with the busy-ness of the world inside us.

And the truth is, sometimes God doesn't knock. Sometimes God just surrounds us with a wondrous and complex reality and waits for us to look up, to be still, to see, and to marvel.

—Jason Sierra

If you are like so many of us today, your life gets busy and your energy scatters. You might benefit from some kind of mindfulness practice, you hear it is good for you, but you think you can't settle down long enough to do it. A practice that works for me uses what I call "mindful moments," short spans of time of being still, of deeply paying attention. One practical way I like to experience this is in the shower.

First, I'll confess that sometimes there is a lot of chatter going on in my head. I'm thinking about what I need to get at the store, what I'm going to wear, or how the shower needs a good scrubbing. There have been a few times my mind is so busy I've nearly completed my shower and wondered if I washed my hair. When this happens I'm abruptly reminded to practice a mindful moment.

In this brief practice of mindfulness, I pay attention to the water. I notice how it feels on my skin. I notice the temperature, whether the spray is light or pulsing; I feel the water on my face and the back of my neck and head and let it run down my body. My breath deepens when I focus totally on the sensation of the water, and for this brief time, I am not scattered. If I have a couple more minutes in the shower, I like to think of water as a gift, giving thanks for the stream of water, for the plumbing that brought it to our home, and offering thanksgiving to the Source of all water.

—Linda Gelbrich

S peak peace to the chaos, Lord, where the madness continues to swirl. Speak peace to the chaos, Lord, whether within or outside of me...Let it cease to be. Call back order to the world, my world, our world, your world!

Where reason lies sleeping, with weary ones weeping, mend the brokenness that is so very much in need of repair...Breathe fresh breath upon us and clear the air that we might b-r-e-a-t-h-e again! Renew our hope; dispel our despair. The world and all that's in it are in your hand. Make what's upside down right-side up again, as only you and you alone can!

Speak peace, O Lord. Speak peace to the chaos, within us and among us, and in the whole world, lest it consume. Don't let it consume us. As you did in the beginning, speak your "Let-it-be" to the chaos and let it be so. Let peace resume. Peace, we know, does not mean that all around us is still, but just as the eye in the midst of the storm is where peace is found, may your peace surround. And may it fill. May we find ourselves in the stillness, amidst the calm at the center of your will. Help us to find and let us be...still...and know that you are God!

—Kathy H. Culmer

When I read the portion of the morning collect that says, "You have brought us in safety to this new day," I sometimes can barely finish the rest. And on some days, that is enough for me. There is so much to be mindful of in that one sentence.

We have been brought.

Everyone has seen the ubiquitous poem "Footprints in the Sand" hanging on the wall of a doctor's office or sitting on someone's desk. I think the sentiment is true, though it has been used so many times that I am afraid those footprints are about seven feet deep by now. Through the night, for those of us who get to rest (God bless the emergency responders and new parents), the secret inner workings of our bodies cycle in and out of REM sleep. The systems that keep us alive pump blood, send electrical impulses to neurons, and breathe in oxygen and exhale carbon dioxide. This symphony (or cacophony if you snore like I do) is conducted without us knowing a thing about it as we lie vulnerable in our beds.

This morning, know that you have been brought. Breathe in the safety of the new. The fulfilling of your unique part of God's purpose is right here, right now, right where you live. Thanks be to God.

—Charles McClain

God's stillness comes from within God's changeless nature. God is "the Father of lights with whom there is no variation or shadow due to change" (James 1:17). God's existence has no beginning and no end. The very name God gives Moses to use says it all, and says it with such beautiful economy of word, "I AM." But even as CEO of all creation, God still took a day off and blessed the sabbath as a time of special stillness—for God and for us.

Our stillness is pausing to reflect on the fact that we are merely created beings. It can be the stillness of a meditation at sunrise, or the stillness of waiting upon God, praying to God, and believing that God is working in an omniscient manner to help us in ways we could never envision. It is the stillness of having faith to believe that even before our petitions leave our lips, God is busy knitting us blessings with an endless supply of invisible and miraculous yarn.

—Susan Taylor Block

Jesus stood still and called them, saying,
"What do you want me to do for you?"

—MATTHEW 20:32

In the morning, I get up already thinking about the demands of the day. I wake with plans, the tasks and challenges of the day on my mind. My mind is filled with how I will meet those challenges. I often turn on the news and hear the challenges and difficulties in the community and the world. In the distance, I hear the sounds of birds singing their morning song. The bird song invites me to be still for a moment and listen.

That invitation calls me to notice the different songs. Some are close by and some seem to answer from far away. Their song invites me to savor the moment. What is the true song that the morning brings? So I begin the day in another way. What delight! The invitation is to still my internal urgings and to turn to listening, to be still.

In those few moments of listening, my mind finds a sense of quiet. I want to spend more time like this. My breathing slows. I can hear the great opportunity the day brings in the songs of the birds. Periodically during my busy day, I hear them again. Perched on a tree above my head or in the distance, I am reminded. I am filled with the calming voice of God in birdsong.

—**Karen Montagno**

Psalm 122 speaks of the unity and strength of Jerusalem. This unity has benefits for those in Jerusalem and those outside. Mindfulness meditation works similarly, providing unity within oneself.

I have engaged in martial arts training for several years, and an important part of the training is meditation. My teacher fosters in his students the ability to cultivate unity in the mind, body, spirit, and emotion. The whole of the program works to improve your breathing, blood flow, mental clarity, and emotional maturity. My pain tolerance is higher than when I began. My weight is better, and my blood pressure is great.

These are the first fruits of mindful meditation. We begin to feel the flow of blood and air through us. Our health (emotional and physical) improves. We begin to know ourselves better as we cultivate unity within ourselves.

The second benefit is an exterior one. We share and manifest our unity of self with others. A mindful person can share their peace, their unity with others. As Jesus said, "Peace I leave with you; my peace I give you" (John 14:27).

—Carl Fosnaugh

Ж

[Jesus] woke up and rebuked the wind,
and said to the sea, "Peace! Be still!"

—MARK 4:39

FEBRUARY

Intercessory Prayer

Ask, and it will be given to you; search, and you will find; knock, and the door will be opened for you.
—Matthew 7:7

A Little Talk with Jesus

Intercessory prayer, along with prayers of adoration, confession, and thanksgiving, provide the Christian experience with four distinct and historical examples of prayer. Praying for another person is one of the joys of being a Christian. When we intercede on behalf of another person, or on our own behalf, we are asking God to do something—help, save, heal, hurry, etc. When we gather in corporate worship, offering up the Prayers of the People is one of the non-negotiable elements of our liturgy we do every single time.

This month we will focus our reflections upon intercessory prayer—offering our deepest longings, needs, and hopes to God, who is always in the business of doing more than we can ask or imagine.

Praying for our own needs or those of others can sometimes feel daunting. We may not always feel like we know how to pray. Below are some practical applications for this spiritual discipline.

WAYS TO ENGAGE

Create your own prayer list.

Pray along with your church or congregation's prayer list.

Use the various forms of the Prayers of the People, found in *The Book of Common Prayer.*

Use the various prayers found in the back of *The Book of Common Prayer.*

Consider reading the particular Psalm appointed for the day in connection with your quiet time.

Of all the people we meet in the Bible, Moses is among the most prayerful. He spends so much time in deep conversation with God that his physical appearance is changed.

But Moses does not pray only to God about his personal concerns over shepherding those rascally children of Israel into the Promised Land. Moses prays with urgency—a deep understanding of the thin line between life and death that only comes when we are pushed into hard, dry places; he prays constantly because he knows that his life, and the lives of his people, depend on those prayers.

Moses grows tired and weary, and sometimes that tiredness is impossible to overcome on his own. In a beautiful example of intercessory prayer, Aaron and Hur physically hold up Moses' hands, their prayers helping secure a pivotal victory against the forces of Amalek (Exodus 17:11-12).

There are no words from Aaron or Hur—they see the need, and with their hands and their hearts, they lift up their own hands to offer help—and to ask for it on behalf of their beloved leader. Whether we find ourselves in tough spots like Moses did or find ways we can be like Aaron and Hur, may we keep praying for and lifting up those we love.

—Rachel Jones

*A*lmighty God, to you all hearts are open, all desires known, and from you no secrets are hid: cleanse the thoughts of our hearts by the inspiration of your Holy Spirit, that we may perfectly love you, and worthily magnify your holy Name; through Christ our Lord. Amen.

We say this prayer at the start of every celebration of Holy Eucharist Rite II in The Episcopal Church. At this point in my life, I know the prayer so well, I can say it without flipping through my bulletin or *The Book of Common Prayer*. And yet, until I sat down to write this meditation, I had never really thought about what I was praying.

Intercessory prayer is one of the primary types of prayer (along with adoration, confession, and thanksgiving), and this prayer is a perfect example of it, because in this prayer, we are asking for something as a community. Cleanse the thoughts of *our* hearts. That we may perfectly love *you*.

Whenever we talk to God about someone outside our own selves, we are practicing intercessory prayer—even if we include ourselves in said prayer. We are praying for purity for all people, not just ourselves. We include ourselves in that great human family, full of blessings and hurts, and we ask God to grant our desires through Jesus, who "is at the right hand of God, who indeed intercedes for us" (Romans 8:34).

—**Holli Powell**

As a child I would spend at least twenty minutes every night on my bedtime prayers, even after my parents had left the room and presumed me asleep. Silently I would pray against the worst-case scenarios—listing every person and thing I cared about. In my head, my prayer was a protective spell that had to be said just right, guarding against every calamity. It was my responsibility to invoke the protection.

As a teenager my prayers became less fear-driven and reflected my uncertainty. These (mostly one-way) conversations would wind and circle around heady topics like friendship, vocation, acceptance, identity, and love, leaving me either in an emotional pool of uncertainty and confusion or with a sense of certainty and clarity that only the egotism of youth can sustain.

During my twenties, my prayers fell silent. My prayers had no words; they were simply moments of stillness, of listening to my own heart and hoping to hear some wider, deeper, rumbling heartbeat of God, to find in the silence some direction, some longing or pulling that would help me navigate the possibilities and heartbreak of life.

How will I pray in this new decade of my thirties? Will it be with focus and intention? Will it be in the ancient words of a chosen community? Will it be from exhaustion and desperation or from peace and hopefulness? May God find my ears and my lips ready to speak or to listen, however prayer comes in this phase of life.

—Jason Sierra

We live in a time when we are called, as people of God and reflections of Jesus, to wake up to the world as it is. The prayer we are called into is one that asks more of us than to just show up to our own lives—we are asked to transform and be transformed in the act of prayer. Then, we are called to be the act of prayer in the world.

In this place and time, intercessory prayer asks more of us than to just call out the names of the needy but rather to live in the midst of the needy, the homeless, the helpless, the broken, and those who have no voice. Our call to God on behalf of others means we have to do more than just internalize intercession. We have to live a life that intercedes.

We have to be the intercession of God in the world.

Our lives are intended to be intercessory prayer for the world. We must pray for the world, not only in the pews of Sunday worship but also in the streets, in the middle of suffering. Let the prayers we say now, in the quiet, express themselves in our lives in the world, breath after breath, day after day. Let us be the justice-seekers and the change-makers born of our intercession in silence, shouted into the world each and every day.

—Teresa Pasquale

Oftentimes during group prayers, we are given an opportunity to offer prayers for people in our lives. In any setting, this moment can often be intimidating. What if you say something dumb? Or if you have something you don't want to be public knowledge but still want prayers for? More often than not, we would rather keep our prayers silent and to ourselves than share them out loud to a group. And there is nothing wrong with that. However, we should remind each other that being able to pray and to ask for prayers for a loved one or a stranger is an incredible gift.

When we offer prayers on behalf of someone, we must remember why we are doing it. We are doing it because we love that person. We want them to know that God loves him or her as well. Intercessory prayers are serious and important matters in a person's prayer life. They are important because we see the love of Christ present in our prayers on behalf of one another.

—Longkee Vang

𝄪

Likewise the Spirit helps us in our weakness;
for we do not know how to pray as we ought,
but that very Spirit intercedes with sighs too deep for words.

—Romans 8:26

Intercessory prayer has been tough for me at times. I have gone through periods of feeling that God is going to do what God is going to do without helpful advice from me. And I have wondered if it is right to pray for God to fix things—for God to improve the health of my friend, for example, when she faced cancer. If I prayed and she got better and I thanked God for it, wouldn't it make sense to blame God for letting her die if she died? Was it better to pray just for God to guide her and her family through their terrible trial? But that prayer seemed weak; what I wanted was her healing, and God and I both knew it.

My friend died of her illness. So it may seem strange that at this point in my life, I am more committed to intercessory prayer than I have been since childhood. My friend may not have been healed, but I believe that my prayers for her were somehow good and useful actions. I wonder if intercessory prayers come from God rather than moving from us to God. Perhaps the prayers themselves are, to some extent, God's answer to our prayers. Perhaps our prayers are a way that God acts in the world rather than just our blind requests to make bad things go away. I do not know. But I do know that I have been refreshed; I have been given the understanding that intercessory prayer is in some way a gift from God to help us help one another.

—Elizabeth Brignac

As part of my prayer life, I've developed a personal set of devotions. Some are standard and several I've written and customized to suit my faith journey. Sometimes we overlook the opportunity to craft our own prayers while using and arranging those authored by others in an individualized way.

As time passes, prayer requests from my family and friends have increased. Often, I don't speak their names out loud when I pray. I visualize the people I'm praying for, and sometimes their families. My best friend in Kentucky, for example, is pictured at the dinner table with his spouse and two children. They flash before me and then another face or family comes to mind.

"Oh Lord," I begin, "for all those who have touched my life directly and indirectly, positively or negatively, for the short-term or long-term, and for those I remember and those I've forgotten, bless them, guide them, bring joy, happiness, and good health to them, and let their actions be pleasing to you with each passing day so that when you call them from this earth, they are welcomed into your kingdom." It's a prayer for friends, family, acquaintances, the homeless, folks I knew long ago, people who challenge me as a Christian, and dejected strangers I see on the street.

Sometimes I visualize faces for whom I pray while looking at icons of Christ, Mary, Holy Sophia the Holy Spirit, and photos of men and women of mature faith that hang in my worship space. I try to see holiness and the face of God in those I visualize during my prayers.

—Paul Jesep

Sometimes I wonder, who and what is it for, this business of praying for folks? Is it to remind God of those in trouble? Doesn't God know about this already? Is it for the ones for whom we pray, to help them feel supported? Is intercessory prayer about trying to change God's mind, like Abraham did when he talked God down from destroying the righteous people in Sodom and Gommorah? Is it for us, to keep us mindful of the needs of others?

We gather for daily morning prayer at our church, and I have noticed that for many people, the part they love best is when we are invited to offer our own intercessions. Immediately, voices begin to murmur, lips begin to move. Some pray silently, others voice concerns and thanksgivings distinctly.

Similarly, in our small groups, we ask that each participant pray for the others in the group every day because we believe that praying for one another daily is at the heart of Christian community. These prayers bind us together in a way that nothing else does.

In the end, I believe that talking with Jesus about those we love, situations about which we are concerned, and those we don't love as we should, changes us. Praying for someone we have difficulty with helps us soften our stance toward them, opens our heart to them. Asking for Jesus to help, heal, comfort us and others, and to make awful situations right keeps us connected both to God and to our neighbors.

And praying honestly for our own needs—our hurts and disappointments especially—cracks us open so that God's healing love can come into our broken hearts.

—Penny Nash

I am writing this at a time when many members of my family are gravely ill, and the veil between this world and the next is about to be lifted. Usually when I see a problem, my reaction is to look for a solution. Sometimes that reaction is more knee-jerk and less helpful than I would like. I am now fighting my nature to scan the horizon for earthly solutions and cures to suggest because I really don't have any to offer. Now is the time for prayer.

To honor this moment in each family member's life, I have created a prayer book. The cover is a joyful pink. I rise at 5:30 a.m., go to my patio, and face east toward the morning's sun. For one minute, I stand before its force. I then go inside and take out the book from a special place and turn to the next fresh blank page. I write down the name of each member of my family who is ill. Then I follow the advice of Jesus about how we should pray: I recite the Lord's Prayer....Thy will be done.

—Charlotte Chere Graham

※

First of all, then, I urge that suplications, prayers, intercessions, and thanksgivings be made for everyone.

—1 TIMOTHY 2:1

As a child, I was forced to wear those ugly Buster Brown shoes—the kind that went up over your ankle bones and laced up tightly. I had to wear them through the first grade to strengthen my ankles. I hated those ol' brown leather shoes, but my parents explained that I had to wear them or I would need surgery, which they absolutely could not afford. At night, my mother used to stretch out at the foot of my bed, rubbing my feet and ankles, having a little talk with Jesus, praying for the healing of my ankles. I must confess that I too was praying: "Lord, please fix my feet, so I can wear pretty shoes like my sister and all the other little girls. Amen."

Yesterday, I hobbled over to the urgent care facility in my neighborhood to determine if I had broken the middle toe of my right foot. I know better than to walk around barefoot in my home around heavy furniture but seemed to have forgotten. As I waited to be called for an X-ray, I was having a little talk with Jesus about my feet: "Lord, please fix my toe so that I can wear a shoe…any shoe, even an ol' leather brown shoe. Amen."

—**Westina Matthews**

I hate to admit it, but growing up, my grandmother—whom we called Mamá Grande—frightened me. Incredibly devout, serious, and silent, the volume of a conversation naturally lowered when she walked into the room.

Years later, I learned that my grandfather had a goal of making her laugh at least once each day. And my goodness, did he have to work for that!

My strongest memories of my grandmother are of her in a rocking chair, praying the rosary over me and my siblings as we desperately tried to play quietly. I see her sitting silently off to the side as the rest of the family had a boisterous conversation and her formally kissing and silently blessing her grandchildren each time we left her home.

Time and distance have made me see my formidable grandmother in a different light. More and more, what remains with me are the prayers she said over me and my siblings, both in her rocking chair and before we'd leave each night for home. I imagine her intercessions as having a life of their own, a sort of enduring gift that crosses time and space, still speaking to a God who has watched us grow and mature into imperfect, yet beloved, adults. Lord knows we've needed those prayers!

—Miguel Escobar

When we were growing up, my brother and I usually played quite amiably together, but sometimes he'd poke at me till I'd lash out and hit him back. Then he'd shout, "She hit me!" and I'd wail, "I'm sorry, I'm sorry, I'm sorry!"

He'd glare at me, sticking out his lip in an unforgiving pout, and snarl, "Sorry doesn't help!"

I hate to admit it after all these years, but he had a point.

We're very good at apologizing; the scripted "I didn't really do it, and besides, I'm not doing it anymore," apologies of various public figures regularly go viral on social media. Like the ancient Israelites who needed to be told by the prophet Joel that God wanted them to "Rend your hearts, and not your clothing," we often find "I'm sorry," along with public displays of contrition, to be convenient substitutes for making amends or changing our behavior.

In our prayers of confession, especially during Lent, we do say "I'm sorry," but we also ask for strength and guidance to repent, to change direction, and to turn away from the patterns of behavior that estrange us from God and hurt our neighbors. Saying "I'm sorry" is an important first step—we can't repent if we don't admit our faults and failings and ask for forgiveness—but it's easy to get stuck there, feeling sorry for ourselves for being such sorry people. Repentance moves us outward and forward. Repentance changes relationships. Repentance helps.

—Mary W. Cox

Today is my dad's birthday. My great galumph of a father, my very own oak of righteousness, the biggest tree in my landscape. He has been gone seven years now, and I still miss him every day. Happy Birthday Bubba!

At the time my father was sick, our youngest son was in his eighth-grade confirmation year. This child adored his grandfather and was adored in return. In the eight weeks my dad was in the intensive care unit, I made daily trips back and forth to the hospital to see him. His young sidekick kept the faith. "Don't worry, Mom," my son would text me. "I spoke to God; I've got Bubba covered."

But the "covering," to our disappointment, wasn't in the healing of Dad's body as my son had prescribed. It was rather in the love of my family, the inherited strength my dad passed down to us all. The covering was the gift of a good death.

It took the entirety of that confirmation year for our son to stop being mad at God. But, by grace, when he knelt before the bishop, his faith was stronger than ever. It had been tried and tested and still it held.

God answers our prayers, in ways as unsearchable as God's love is big. When we trust that God loves us, we can better let God be God. That's daring. But by daring to pray, we also dare to discover God's absolute power, which through Jesus is our power too.

—Susan Wyper

When my son was born, and they laid him on my chest, he looked at me and with his best duck face said, "Meh." It was in this beautiful sing-songy voice, and my husband and I cooed over this precious first expression. Almost immediately, the nurse came and took him, telling us that this beautiful noise was in fact a sign of distress. He was born early and was having trouble breathing.

As they whisked him away, the emptiness of the room overwhelmed me. For anyone who hasn't experienced this, it feels really lonely and awful to be on a maternity ward with no baby. Our baby was never in any danger that he wouldn't survive but he had to be in the neonatal intensive care unit. I can't imagine how much worse it is for the mothers of babies who are in critical condition.

Soon text messages began to arrive asking how things had gone and telling me that people were praying for us. The thought of those prayers surrounded us and made the room feel less empty. The act of praying for us and with us made things seem less awful. Sometimes knowing that there are people out in the world asking God to watch over you and hold you can make all the difference. Sometimes it makes the most important difference.

—Lauren Caldwell

ꭓ

We will shout for joy at
your victory and triumph in the Name of our God;
may the LORD grant all your requests.

—PSALM 20:5

A friend of mine has a game she plays. Whenever she sees herself in the mirror, she whispers, "It is not about me."

Every so often, I have to remind myself that it is not about me. It is why I practice deliberate acts of kindness, compassion, and prophetic challenge. I pray for others; it is an important spiritual practice to offer intercessory prayers. However, true prayer always requires that we do the will of God, which is to live our lives in God's justice and love.

Prayer, our required daily talk with Jesus, gives us the assurance, courage, and vocation to be men and women of compassion. When Jesus talks with us, an invitation goes out with extreme clarity: "Go and make disciples of all nations." This is Jesus' way of reminding us to love the world with all our heart, mind, and soul.

When next we pray, may our prayers imitate the prayers of Saint Francis and all the holy women and men who prayed that they might have the courage to see God and serve God in all. Let us pay attention today as we talk to God, and as Jesus talks to us, that we might do something to serve others. The Christian life demands that we daily live our lives in service of others. Our life in Christ is an intercessory way of living.

—Mark Bozzuti-Jones

"The flight will be delayed overnight." Fearing that several reservations might collapse if a later connecting flight left without me, I began two conversations: arranging a new airlines schedule and asking God to order my thoughts. Awaiting confirmation of the next-day flight and reading a "whodunnit," I also prayed for a woman standing interminably in line.

Separated by yards of carpet and dozens of churning travelers, we didn't meet that evening. But the next morning at the gate, she beamed, saying: "I'm so glad you're here! Last night, I wanted to ask you to pray." We exchanged prayer requests. We will probably never meet again on earth.

Even in our travel anxieties the night before, God had wordlessly communicated something across the space. I'm well-experienced in anxiety, but Mother taught me in childhood to pray about everything. Back then, prayers centered on getting my own way. In adulthood, I began to pray for openness to God's agenda and for others' needs, but frankly, that night at the airport, I still wanted my own way more than a surprise gift in the form of a woman who now lives among my dearest memories.

Archbishop of Canterbury William Temple said that when he prayed, coincidences happened. When he didn't, they didn't. Through conversations with God, meaningful recognitions and encounters occur. The most valued gift is God's presence, behind-the-scenes or within God's followers, even during our muddled moments.

—June Terry

It happens about once a week. Someone on my Facebook feed asks for prayers. Sometimes they tell the story of a baby fighting for life, a friend with depression, or an upcoming test. Sometimes the problem is so personal they cannot bring themselves to be specific about their need. Whatever the reason, they've asked for help. I make a concerted effort to include them in my prayers that week.

All too often, these requests are forgotten within a few minutes. I get distracted by Facebook, work, or my toddler, and my mind fills with things more immediately demanding. This usually lasts until Sunday. There, in the corner of our church, a table is covered in votives. When I see the candles, the symbol of the prayers other people are making for their friends, neighbors, or people they hardly know, I am reminded of the hardships of those around me. I remember the requests of my friends. When I think about all the people I meant to pray for, it can be overwhelming. Waiting for my "prayer time" or church isn't enough. When I see needs, I should help—and pray right there and then.

—Spencer Hixon

))(

*He sets his heart to rise early to seek the Lord
who made him, and to petition the Most High;
he opens his mouth in prayer and asks pardon for his sins.*

—Sirach 39:5

I listened as people offered their support, kind words meant to bring encouragement and inspire peace. The newly divorced man graciously received the sentiments, but his demeanor seemed unchanged, tense, and tired. One perceptive friend sensed his restlessness and refused to ignore the obvious tension in his face. His question was straightforward and sincere, "What do you need, friend?" The man didn't hesitate. His need was as clear, as his heart was shattered. "Please, just pray for me...I'm finding it very difficult to pray for myself right now."

As the Body of Christ, we are called to be many things. Jesus taught us to intercede. He asks us to carry those who can't carry themselves. In a sense, we are meant to be wheelchairs and strollers. We are surrounded by wounded, hurting, struggling people. And sometimes, we are the ones who need carrying—a sea of sojourners traveling from grief to joy, pain to wholeness, and spiritual infancy to maturity. Parts of the journey are too difficult to traverse alone.

If you look to your left or your right along your life path, chances are you will see people struggling to take the next step. Refuse to look the other way. Carry them for a while. Praying for others is a supreme act of selflessness.

—**Bree Combs**

My youngest son is five years old. He wakes up very early in the morning and always wants to play, and I always say no and try to go back to sleep. This is hard to do because he will sit on my head or pry open my eyes. Always with a smile. "Come on, let's play." This happens every day. It gets old sometimes. My wife has the patience of a saint, and she always says yes and figures out some way to entertain him until the rest of the house is awake.

Sometimes I listen to them play. One morning they played "fire truck." He pretended his pillow was a house that was on fire. He yelled, "The people were afraid so God sent the firemen to save them." He made lots of siren and engine noises and gave directions about climbing down the ladder and then declared, "The people are saved! Thank God!"

Sometimes I have a hard time having conversations with God. Maybe you do too. I find myself in circumstances where it just seems impossible. Perhaps you have found yourself in similar circumstances. If you do, try listening to someone else's conversation with God. These conversations are happening all around us and all the time. You will be amazed at what you hear and then be wonderfully blessed.

—Jason Leo

I met a woman when I was sixteen who taught me that I could pray day and night. She taught me that I do not have to bow my head or close my eyes. I don't have to wait for the right posture or even the right words—just pray.

I am in a constant conversation with my best friend—I laugh, cry, argue, and thank God all day long. God knows the purpose of my heart and knows the needs of those I am praying with, for, and about.

I have found a power in praying on my knees and with my hands stretched up to God, humbled before my Creator. I have seen God's power happen instantly when God's people pray. I have seen miracles occur, and dreams tucked deep within my heart have been fulfilled when I pray on my knees. It is not magic, but I feel it is mystical. I have felt God's power as I pray and know things are somehow changing, even if I don't say one word, because God knows my heart.

If you want to have conversations with God all day long, start simply. It might seem a little forced at first, but it does become easier. And soon, you will be in a daylong conversation—silent or aloud—with the One who knows your heart.

—**Sandra Montes**

For almost twenty years, I have belonged to a vowed community of Episcopal women who take seriously the ministry of intercession. Whether through local and national prayer chains connecting hundreds of women or through slips of paper prayed over all summer long at two prie-dieux in our chapel at Adelynrood in Massachusetts, we join our voices together in supplication and thanksgiving. The results can be both humbling and awe-inspiring.

When I find myself beginning to doubt the necessity of intercessory prayer, I turn to the last chapter of biblical scholar Walter Wink's *The Powers That Be*, where he states: "Intercession visualizes an alternative future to the one apparently fated by the momentum of current forces…It changes the world and it changes what is possible to God…History belongs to the intercessors, who believe the future into being."

Wow! What could be more current, more necessary? With these powerful words resonating in my heart, I renew my own personal commitment to prayers of intercession and vow to expand my own range of what I pray for—for nations as well as my family, for the health of the earth itself as well as the health of individual friends.

—Joan Bowers

I talk to Jesus all the time. Every time I start the car, I say, "Lord, please get me there and home quickly, safely, and without incident. Lord, guide my thoughts, and guard my words. Help me to see your face in all I meet, and to do your work in the world. I ask this in your name. Amen." It seems to work, although I have to make a serious effort with really bad drivers.

I thank Jesus in the morning for bringing me to the new day and its possibilities and at night for getting me through the day and its challenges. Sometimes I thank him for prayers granted. Sometimes I yell at him about all kinds of calamities, personal and global: "Why won't you just fix this, Lord?" I know the answer, of course. I just don't like it.

Each day I pray for a long list of family, friends, coworkers, friends of friends, myself. I often borrow a concept from my mother: pray for healing, and let God decide what form that healing should take. Sometimes I receive an answer; sometimes I don't. But I know I'm always heard.

—Sarah Bryan Miller

☼

Hear, O Lord, the prayer of your servant,
and give ear to the petition of your creature;
attend to my words.

—2 ESDRAS 8:24

When we intercede for those we love, we are like the men who were determined to bring their paralyzed friend before Jesus, even though it meant lowering him down through the roof. They were willing to do anything because they loved their friend so much. Yet, during our Lenten walk with this same Jesus, we will hear him call down from the cross, "Father, forgive them; for they do not know what they are doing."

How can we pray for those who have hurt us, for those for whom we can't feel any love at all? How could we possibly intercede for them?

The prayer "For our Enemies" is one of the shortest in *The Book of Common Prayer* (p. 816), perhaps because it is so hard to say. First, we're reminded that Jesus taught us to pray for our enemies. Then, we pray not just for them but for ourselves as well. We pray that we each will be led "from prejudice to truth" and are delivered from "hatred, cruelty, and revenge." It doesn't say anything about not being angry, or even outraged, at whatever might have been done. What it does say though is "in your good time enable us"—both our enemies and ourselves—"to stand reconciled before you." Wherever we are on the journey toward forgiveness, whatever hurt or anger we still feel, we can pray to let God work in both of us, in God's own time.

—**Kathleen M. Flanagan**

I grew up in a denomination that very much emphasized "name it and claim it" as the approach to prayer. The church of my childhood loved using Matthew 18:19: "if two of you agree on earth about anything you ask, it will be done for you." My elementary school friend and I are still waiting for our ponies.

My desire for a pony was, of course, a great distortion of prayer and of what the adults in my church meant. It's hard work to pray, really pray, because it involves a lot of listening and attentiveness and pushing through those times where we feel completely ignored. It's easy to think of prayer as simply the card we swipe in the great cosmic ATM hoping that there's still something in the "account" that will be delivered to us in a neat little envelope.

The fifteen years I spent working at a children's cancer clinic and then as the manager of a Ronald McDonald House taught me more about intercessory prayer than any seminary course I attended or book I read. I saw moments that can only be described as miraculous: a suddenly clear CAT scan or a child pronounced dead at the scene of an accident who later skipped into an intensive care unit reunion party. Folks around those families would be quick to say, "That's the power of prayer." And I had no reason to argue.

I saw families crumpled over in such agonizing grief that I didn't think they or I would be able to draw another breath. But they did. And that too is the power of prayer. Not always getting the result you want, not by a long shot, but holding onto the hope that prayer matters and connects us in ways that are miraculous.

—Rhoda Montgomery

No one likes to be talked about, to be the subject of a gossiper's loose talk: "Hey, did you hear about Chuck?" We keep a low profile around some people, guard and protect ourselves from what might be said.

Now, don't misunderstand. It's not that we don't enjoy gossip—far from it! An entire industry has been created with cover stories about celebrities we love and (even more) celebrities we love to gossip about. Gossip sells quite nicely, thank you. We just don't want it to be about us.

No one likes to be talked about.

There are exceptions to this, however. For example, it is very nice indeed to have someone talk about us in a positive way to a potential employer.

This is what intercessory prayer is like. We talk with God about someone we know, someone we love, perhaps someone we just met.

To intercede is to care enough to bring another person to the Holy One's attention: "God, let me tell you about Mike. I care about him, and he could really use your help right now." Not that God doesn't already know more about that person than we ever will. Intercessory prayer is caring enough to get involved, to make a connection between someone in need and Someone who is ready to listen and stand alongside.

—Chuck Robertson

Now that I am retired, I like to spend time in prayer before I get out of bed in the mornings. It still feels like a luxury. I picture in my mind the people I am praying for; this time spent praying for them is centering and healing for me.

When we hike in the Southwest, we often notice cairns, stones placed one on top of the other, often in protected areas alongside the trail. We've built these kinds of cairns, too, as an act of prayer and remembrance.

A few years ago, two friends back home were dealing with cancer and one had ALS. I prayed for them often during the day and found that building a cairn for each of them took me deeper into the prayers. The rocks I used were primarily reddish sandstone. I looked for ones flat enough to stack, then prayed as I set each stone in place.

I've built a little patio in our yard, and I think I'll build a cairn there. Maybe it will be for peace. I will pray as I stack the stones and pray each time I see it.

—Linda Gelbrich

X

Regard your servant's prayer and his plea,
O LORD my God, heeding the cry and the prayer
that your servant prays to you today.

—I KINGS 8:28

Two raindrops sat above the earth, looking down on the farmer's drought-stricken corn. The first raindrop felt compassion for the farmer and said, "I wish I could do something to help that poor farmer." The other said, "You're just one little raindrop. You can barely cover a kernel of corn; you certainly can't save a whole field."

The first raindrop responded, "You're right, but there must be something I can do to help. I'm going to do what I can." With that, he leaped over the edge of a cloud. Inspired by the first raindrop, the second one followed. Other raindrops heard, came running and joined them. Soon, there was a great downpour. The field was saturated, the corn revived, and the farmer's livelihood restored.

While we may not think of it as doing very much, intercessory prayer lets us be like those raindrops that watered the field. It begins with realizing another's need; then out of compassion, acting upon the desire to see their situation improved, we make our requests known to God on their behalf that they might have their needs or desires met. It is our seeking God's blessing for another and, in turn, realizing blessing for ourselves.

—Kathy H. Culmer

P rayer is about orientation. We practice it in a real and tangible way during worship. We stand, kneel, and sit (affectionately known to some as pew aerobics) at the appropriate times. We orient our bodies differently when we pray. These exercises are common even among our brothers and sisters of other faith traditions. Why do human beings engage in this curious practice?

We practice prayer so we can practice reconciliation. The Christian life is deeply concerned with reorientation. Moses said, "I have set before you life and death, blessings and curses. Now choose life" (Deuteronomy 30:19). Jesus' speech often takes the form of, "You have heard it said…But truly I tell you…" Paul says in his letter to the Romans, "Do not be conformed to this world, but be transformed by the renewing of your minds" (12:2). We are in the process of reorienting ourselves toward friendship with God and the restoration of the world.

—Charles McClain

Ʌ

Almighty God, who has promised to hear the petitions of those who ask in your Son's Name: we ask you mercifully to incline your ear toward us who have now made our prayers and supplications known to you; and grant that those things which we have faithfully asked according to your will may effectually be obtained, to the relief of our necessity, and to your glory; through Jesus Christ our Lord. Amen.

—ADAPTED FROM *THE BOOK OF COMMON PRAYER*, P. 834

Advice is now easier than ever to find. A Google search will cough up over a billion answers to a million questions. Human guidance can be very helpful, but it only goes so far. Recently, I have tried to ask for God's recommendations more often and in more categories. This exercise, tougher than I anticipated, became a tad easier after I kept pondering these familiar words: "For my thoughts are not your thoughts, nor are your ways my ways, says the LORD. For as the heavens are higher than the earth, so are my ways higher than your ways and my thoughts than your thoughts" (Isaiah 55:8-9).

"But just how high are the heavens?" I wondered. Current measurements of what is visible indicate the heavens are ninety-two billion light years large. Since one light year equals about six trillion miles, the known heavens' size is the number 552 followed by about two-dozen zeros. Such knowledge drops heavy like a humility hammer, something similar to the ringing Peter may have heard in his ears at the Transfiguration, after the voice of God interrupted the disciple's proposal to build temporary festival booths. God, the heavens. This love is bigger than any of us are able to grasp.

—**Susan Taylor Block**

MARCH

Praying with
the Saints

*Therefore, since we are surrounded by so great a
cloud of witnesses, let us also lay aside every weight
and the sin that clings so closely, and let us run with
perseverance the race that is set before us.*
—Hebrews 12:1

*A Great Cloud
of Witnesses*

INTRODUCTION   *A Great Cloud of Witnesses*

E very Sunday, as we gather around the table, we are reminded that the hosts of heaven join with us in our prayers—and that means all the people who have gone before us are with us in those tender moments of communion and community. This month, we are exploring the discipline of praying with the saints. For some of us, that may mean picking our favorite person from the Calendar of Saints, or it may mean picking through some of our favorite stories of people who have entered the nearer presence of Jesus. It's also helpful to remember that the saints of God are not only the ones in stained glass windows, but they are also the people who sit next to us on the bus, or live down the block. You may think about these folks (or even yourself) when you think about praying with the saints. However you choose to engage this aspect of daily devotion, know that you are deeply loved and fully accepted, and that you never walk alone.

WAYS TO ENGAGE

Visit www.lentmadness.org for a substantive and refreshing look at the lives of the saints.

Research and study the life of your favorite saint.

Make a calendar of saints using the birthdays or special occasion days of people you know and love.

I belong to a very unique online women's community. We refer to ourselves as "the sisren." Some of us know each other in real life, and some of us will likely never lay hands on each other in person. We celebrate. We mourn. We kvetch. We encourage. We check in. And even when we don't understand what one of the sisren may be struggling with, we always meet each other with a deep, nonjudgmental love.

When I think of these women—when I stop and ponder the wonders that have brought us together from diverse backgrounds, different theologies, radically divergent life choices and lifestyles—I can only marvel at the variety God creates and loves. We believe that our scars are part of what makes us beautiful and that our broken places are cracks where the grace and mercy of God shine through. The sisren are part and parcel of the great cloud of witnesses who believe and hope with me each and every time we meet in prayer. They are saints to me—spiritual super-friends who help me stumble through the valleys and dance with me on the mountaintops.

My hope and prayer for you today is that you may find and be found in such a great cloud of witnesses, and that like my own sisren, they will sing the songs of peace and joy you need to hear, reminding you that all things shall be very well.

—Rachel Jones

On page 250 of *The Book of Common Prayer*, there is a collect designed to be used to commemorate saints who do not appear on the official calendar of the church. The prayer reads:

Almighty God, by your Holy Spirit you have made us one with your saints in heaven and on earth: Grant that in our earthly pilgrimage we may always be supported by this fellowship of love and prayer, and know ourselves to be surrounded by their witness to your power and mercy. We ask this for the sake of Jesus Christ, in whom all our intercessions are acceptable through the Spirit, and who lives and reigns for ever and ever. Amen.

This prayer reminds me that I am supported by love and prayer, surrounded by witnesses, one with the saints of God. Not only Peter, Paul, and Mary Magdalene, but also my grandmother, Mother Teresa, my fourth-grade teacher, and writer Anne Lamott. It is powerful for me, not only because it helps me remember the love and prayer surrounding and supporting me as I continue to walk through this earthly pilgrimage, but also because it reminds me that I am an integral part of the communion of saints.

I have been made one with all of them, a necessary and vital piece of the puzzle. How many people read this prayer and think of me, just as I think of the people I've mentioned (and so many more)? And how can I live my life in such a way that I'm worthy to be named in such a group? I don't know. I try my best. And I keep praying, knowing the saints are praying too.

—Holli Powell

Dan had traveled the world, mastered a trade, been a change agent in one of the globe's leading corporations, and came to rest at the school of business I called home. But the man I saw seated before me in that moment was a spiritual guru, on his own journey of hypotheses and tests, chasing his own bright sun. "Treat your career as an experiment," he told me, "and once you've learned what you came to learn, design the next experiment and chase it."

He encouraged me to know my "theory of change," his words for how I believed change happens in this world and how I saw myself participating in that change. When I think about praying with the saints, I think about aligning my theory of change with the theory of transformation and reconciliation that has united Christians for millennia. Francis thought change would happen through asceticism and prayer, Benedict through work, Martin through nonviolent resistance.

Whose theory speaks best to you? Whose bright sun will you choose to align your own with? Whose tests can you build upon? When I pray with the saints, I look to my professor Dan, to my parents, to my mentors, to all the saints and their commitments, not to copy but to test and fortify my own.

—Jason Sierra

And God, who searches the heart,
knows what is the mind of the Spirit,
because the Spirit intercedes for the saints
according to the will of God.

—ROMANS 8:27

I was named after Teresa of Avila, twice. First in an orphanage in Colombia by Grey Order nuns who could not ignore the sainted date of my birth—the feast day of Teresa. Then again, I was named by my adoptive parents [of British and Anglo-Hungarian origin] who had prayed for seven years in the pews of their local Catholic church in New Jersey—Teresa of Avila Catholic Church.

I joke regularly that I could not avoid my fate as someone who delves into the mystics because Teresa breathed me into being before I had an option to choose another fate.

We call out to our sacred ancestors; they are the origins of our faith, lived out in the world. This is no small calling. When we ask for them to be by our side, we ask for the boldness to live out a life of faith in its fullest possible potential. When we call into the expanse of the saints, we ask for the strength to live out the lineage of courage and hope that was divined to us by those who came before.

I call on Teresa in my life regularly, if not daily, and out of the depths of those prayers comes the deepest, most ancient calling to be more than I think I can—bellowing from the ages into the present—asking me to live into the legacy of sainthood. Let us remember that each and every time we call on the saints to be in our midst, what we are calling for is a transformation of ourselves to be more than we ever thought possible.

—Teresa Pasquale

When I first became a youth minister, I was driven—driven to reinvigorate a new group of youth, to inspire the young adult volunteers who were going to help, and driven to succeed. I wanted to prove everyone wrong—that this youth group could thrive and I could be the one to help them. I had come off a period of great loss in my life and was still feeling its effects.

One weekend, our priest took us to her family cabin to plan out the program year and to reflect on where God was calling our youth group.

In her loving way, our priest began to talk about how the great cloud of witnesses is the way God sees us: through eyes of love and encouragement. That the cloud of witnesses is full of voices of joy and gladness.

There are always going to be doubters. There are always going to be tough obstacles to overcome in life. But supporters and friends can drown out the voices of discontent, anger, panic, and shame. Love can help conquer the hate we see in the world. Through God's love, we remember that no matter the obstacles or hardships, we are always in good company, surrounded by witnesses to grace and mercy—the communion of saints.

—Longkee Vang

Most families have a few noteworthy individuals who appear in stories long after they have died. My husband's family has Great Aunt Eunice, renowned for her warmth and kindness. My family has my mom's Great Uncle Dixie, renowned for doing things like buying an elephant once when he was drunk.

The other day, I heard someone refer to the writers of scripture as our ancestors in faith, our spiritual family tree, and this metaphor can extend to Christians throughout the ages. Silently, they remind us that they remain with us, that our understanding of God has been shaped by theirs. The saints, to my mind, are the Great Aunt Eunices (and sometimes even the Great Uncle Dixies) of our spiritual families. Their extraordinary lives help us to define what it means to be Christian. My ancestors' behavior has trickled down to me through their children; their genes have shaped who I am; their stories have given my family character. Likewise, the faith of the saints has been essential in shaping my spiritual existence and faith.

Because prayer is not bound by time, however, my relationship with the saints doesn't stop in the past. In prayer, I can feel close to the saints, especially when I use prayers that have been attributed to them—Saint Patrick's Breastplate, for example—that Christians have passed down through the ages. At those times, I feel like I am praying along with the saints, following their lead with the rest of God's people toward that bright center that we have all identified as what we want—or what wants us.

—**Elizabeth Brignac**

"And justice will be done," Theodore Dostoevsky wrote in *The Brothers Karamazov*. "Believe that, never doubt it, for therein lies the hope and the faith of the saints."

There is an invigorating spiritual freshness in walking with saints (formally designated or not), especially when you find several among the thousands who speak to you soulfully and cerebrally. It's like being aware for the first time of a crisp, energizing spring air with a hint of hyacinths.

There's Mother Maria Skobtsova, an Orthodox nun who hid French Jews and died in a death camp. She never doubted her faith, believed in humanity's goodness, and exemplified forgiveness and unconditional love.

Others like Father Pierre de Chardin, a Catholic priest and paleontologist, wrote of the regal elegance of unfolding creation, sharing greater divine truths and our role as co-creators with the Creator and the Holy Spirit.

Dostoevsky taught, "Have faith to the end. Even if everyone else on earth goes astray, give your life to your faith…even if you are the last of the faithful left on earth. And if you find another being who preserved his faith, there will be a world of living love…" It's with the saints that we can find strength to have faith.

—Paul Jesep

I did not grow up thinking much about saints. Saints were not a part of my tradition. But one time I had a kind of mystical experience when I visited Durham Cathedral in England and viewed the coffin, vestments, and a pectoral cross of Saint Cuthbert, a seventh-century bishop and hermit originally buried on the Holy Island of Lindisfarne. I was amazed by his story, not only in life but also after his death, when his faithful brothers took his body away from Lindisfarne to safeguard it in the wake of Viking raids.

Seeing Cuthbert's relics and hearing his story suddenly connected me with a sense of tradition that expands across time, backwards and forwards, a tradition in which all Christians swim together. We are indeed one body. We are on the same team, Cuthbert and I, along with Francis, Brigid, Mary Magdalene, Matthew, Mark, Luke, and John. The stories of saints began to interest me as touchstones to this vast universe of people across time and space who love God, who follow Jesus as best they can. The saints show me different ways to follow.

And so while I don't necessarily pray to any saints, I certainly feel that I pray with them. I pray with Joan of Arc for courage and perseverance. I pray with Benedict for balance in my life. I pray with Brigid for generosity. Indeed, I am very comforted by the knowledge that I am surrounded by such a great cloud of witnesses and that I am not doing this faith business alone.

—Penny Nash

I go to Emmitsburg, Maryland, when times are trying and when all is well. My connection is with Sister Elizabeth Ann Seton, who founded the Sisters of Charity there. Her moxie and the joy she found in God, even during hard times and crushing grief, has been an inspiring foundation for my faith in God.

This is where I go to be with the saints…a tiny chapel and modest glass church. A grotto where holy water runs freely for anyone in need. And a statue of Saint Bernadette placed in the middle of a pond, built just for her.

I learned about this sanctuary among the trees and silence of Emmitsburg from my mother. When life left her mute with no answers to a problem, she and my father traveled several hours to stand and pray with the saints honored there. Saint Bernadette granted Mother a miracle when a degenerative eye disease threatened to take her sight. She was in her fifties. Today, on the sunny side of 100, she still drives, plays bridge, and lives alone in the home she loves.

I know miracles are possible, especially at Emmitsburg, when I pray with the saints.

—Charlotte Chere Graham

)(

Greet one another with a holy kiss. All the saints greet you.

—2 CORINTHIANS 13:12

Pedro Claver (1580-1654) was a Spanish-born monk who was called the "Apostle of the Blacks" or the "Slave of the Slaves." He spent all his life in Colombia ministering to the slaves brought from Africa, and in 1888, he was the first person to be canonized in the New World. One evening, I found myself having dinner across from a church that has a bronze sculpture named Saint Peter and the Slave, composed of two standing figures, created by the sculptor Enrique Grau. I could hear the tolling of the church bells—its own call to prayer.

As Cartagena is one of the two oldest Colombian cities, I am certain that over the centuries many prayers were offered up within these walls—on bended knee and with bowed head (or perhaps with head up to the heavens in desperate cry) by the buccaneers, heretics, slaves, and foreign immigrants. That evening, I joined my prayers with the communion of saints, and with those on their way to God. "For the saints of God are just folk like me, and I mean to be one too" (*The Hymnal 1982*, p. 293).

—Westina Matthews

One of my favorite Bible passages is when the wandering Israelites, hungry and weary from their recent exodus from Egypt, begin dreaming of "the fish we used to eat in Egypt for nothing, the cucumbers, the melons, the leeks, the onions, and the garlic" of their former lives (Numbers 11:5). Of all the bitter complaints that the Israelites make during their forty years of wandering, this is the one I identify with most—perhaps because it's about food but also because it reveals how often we can wax nostalgic for even the most brutal of pasts.

While I haven't ever experienced the acute hunger that the Israelites were suffering from, there have certainly been moments when I have experienced an acute loss of faith, a loss of memory over where all of this is going, and despair about the value of the path I've chosen. I've found that it is in moments like these that I've most needed the witness of the saints.

As anyone who has ever had to preach on feast days knows, the saints are not perfect people. Their lives include fear, despair over setbacks, quick tempers, and many forms of insanity. Yet what I have found in studying and preaching on their lives is that the saints are remarkably clear about the direction we, as a people, are headed and the value of the sacrifices the journey of faith entails.

As someone who is occasionally prone to forgetfulness, I've found such clarity to be refreshing. Time and time again, the saints have helped me to put aside such dreaming, get up, and press on.

—**Miguel Escobar**

My husband and I often say of our meager efforts at gardening that what grows in our yard is what God intended to grow there, because the Creator is getting little or no help from us.

We moved into our home in Charlotte, North Carolina, at the end of February, so we raked leaves and scraps of mulch from the unpaved half of our fenced patio and waited to see what would appear.

By April, visiting friends looked at the red shoots barely visible above the dirt and exclaimed, "Oh, you have peonies!" Sure enough, only a few weeks later, there were huge, lush, pink blooms falling over as the stems bent under their weight. This year, there are even more blooms and more buds; I look out my back door every morning at beauty that someone else imagined and brought to reality.

The woman who lived here before us was a widow, mostly housebound in her later years; she died a month or two before we came looking for a new home, and we bought the house from her children. Her name was Kathy, and she is my patron saint of peonies; she planted, or had planted for her, these flowers that have outlasted her in this life.

When I look out at the peonies, I thank God for the sheer exuberance of creation—and then I say, "Thank you, Kathy." I think she's smiling.

—Mary W. Cox

The advent of wireless technology, the iCloud, and cyberspace have opened up a whole new way of visualizing an ancient scene of the cloud of witnesses who surround us. As a kid, I'd always thought that somewhere along the way, "crowd of witnesses" had been transposed as "cloud of witnesses." But now cloud makes complete sense. And I love that cloud of witnesses, those folks whose lives, however long past, inform and bless my present reality.

We are surrounded by a great cloud of witnesses. And they inhabit a zone with full, four-bar coverage. There are no bad cell zones. During a recent confirmation class, we looked at the creeds of our church and specifically the Nicene Creed. As a way to get the kids to think about and understand what the creeds were really saying—how often do they become for us an unthinking exercise in muscle memory?—we asked the class to rewrite the creed in their own words. One group came up with a simple, succinct, and apt description of the Holy Spirit. The Holy Spirit, they wrote, is our wi-fi.

Who resides in your cloud? Who modeled forgiveness for you? Whose story is the inspiration for your own? Whose love warms your days, strengthens your steps, and keeps you connected?

—Susan Wyper

Being a person of faith is challenging. As our society becomes more focused on the individual, it is increasingly important that we focus on the collective. For me, that is easier when I imagine the centuries of support I have in Christianity. With each moment that passes, we add another beam to the foundation of our collective faith. The challenges of our commitment to God are made easier by this support system. I can know that what may feel new to me has been laid out before me by generations of the faithful.

I'm drawn to the practices of The Episcopal Church mainly for their history. I get energy from the tradition and symbolism that enhances my connection with Christ. I find value in standing in a building where generations before have prayed and experienced the sacraments. I feel power from thinking that people have practiced these same common prayers for centuries, that apostolic succession binds me to them, and that we are connected not only to each other but also to two millennia of Christians. Quite often I can feel the weight of what that means, and it is invigorating.

—Lauren Caldwell

I believe there is a saint for every season and experience in life. Saints, by their very nature, invite us to pray with them. Saints invite us to follow their examples and enter into what is holy with them. When we pray with the saints, we seek to live lives that reflect the teaching and actions of Jesus.

All Christian witness begins with desire. To pray with the saints is to seek and desire to be like them. When Jesus prays that all his followers be one, Jesus desires that we encourage each other to be united in our efforts to do and reflect what is good, true, and beautiful.

We need more witnesses to the truth, more witnesses for economic justice, and more witnesses who wash each other's feet. The saints remind us that we, too, form part of a great cloud of witnesses. To be surrounded by a great cloud of witnesses is to desire to be in that number when the saints go marching in.

—Mark Bozzuti-Jones

𝄂

So then, whenever we have an opportunity,
let us work for the good of all,
and especially for the family of faith.

—GALATIANS 6:10

A large cast of characters populate the eleventh chapter of Hebrews—people who demonstrate faith in excruciating situations. Then, the twelfth chapter pictures them witnessing our lives and cheering us on throughout our earthly journeys.

I envision being introduced to the cloud of witnesses upon arrival in heaven. I want to thank them along with other believers who lived much later in history—people like Julian of Norwich, Adelyn of Connecticut, and Jim of Rhode Island. The whole throng is joyfully captivated in worship. When you and I finally join them, we'll be immediately caught up in praise, enjoying God gloriously, without delay.

Maybe, freed from bodily limitations, we'll multitask, simultaneously greeting others and praising Christ, without missing a beat. Yes, I'm imagining heaven, but the author of Hebrews was writing based on past facts, remembering faithful people who had endured, with the towering example of Christ who endured the cross. The lesson: endure as he did, as they did.

—June Terry

"Give to the departed eternal rest; let light perpetual shine upon them." Every week we pray this, or some variation of it, in church. I go through the list of loved ones who have passed, my grandparents, my uncle, my friends, and my sister. My sister died when I was just a baby, so I never really knew her. She was eight. My parents never talked about her; it was always up to me to ask questions.

It wasn't until my thirties that I realized that if I didn't ask questions, I would never have answers. I found out that my sister was a remarkable person who tried to cheer up the other children in the hospital even though she was weak and in pain. She had great faith and an even greater capacity to love.

She is one of the saints praying with me. Our loved ones whom we see no longer may very well be our intercessors to Christ. I know she may be a witness to all my shortcomings, but she also sees the good deeds. I am proud to have her as my witness before the Lord.

—**Spencer Hixon**

Several years ago I ran a half marathon. It was 13.1 miles of sheer and utter torture. The only thing that got me through the race was the promise of the finish line. I knew the end was coming, and my sweet husband would be waiting there for me. He couldn't see me push through tears and exhaustion mile after mile, but he was cheering me on anyway, praying every step of the way.

We all need to know we aren't alone in our journey of faith. Christianity isn't always easy. In fact, sometimes it can be really hard. Hebrews 12:1 reminds us that a great cloud of witnesses can attest to suffering far greater than ours. These men and women now stand in solidarity of faith with us, though they are now with our heavenly Father. They ran races similar to those we embark upon. Legions of faithful Christ followers suffered, persevered, and endured. Knowledge of their fortitude spurs us on toward our own finish line. Sometimes the journey seems too treacherous, but we must keep working and keep running. Jesus is the author and perfecter of our faith and our greatest ally as we fight the good fight.

A host of saints are cheering for us. I believe they are anticipating our arrival and celebrating with each sojourner who finds his or her way home. The end will come, friend. Let's run every step of the race with determination, grit, and grace.

—**Bree Combs**

This past summer, the city where I live hosted the All-Star Game for Major League Baseball. People filled the sidewalks downtown with the hope of catching a glimpse of some of the players. Admittedly, these were some of the very best players in the game, from every team in the sport. I was surprised at how big the crowds were. The majority of the people crowded into downtown didn't even have a ticket to see the game. Just seeing the players was enough of a thrill.

When I attend church on Sundays, I look around at the people, and I am surrounded by the all-stars in my community. They are the followers of Jesus in our own day and time. I get to see them up close and personal and hear their adventures from the previous week and their hopes for the future.

They don't hit a ball with a stick, but they serve meals at the soup kitchen, make beds at the shelter, lead prayers, sing in the choir, teach Sunday School, and perform miracles on a regular basis. To me, they are stars. All of them. And the best part is, I not only get to see them, but I also get to watch the game. And more often than not, I'm invited to play as well. They are the saints among us.

—Jason Leo

When the principal calls you into his office, you know it can't be good. I have never been called into the principal's office to be encouraged or congratulated. My principal had questions; I was nervous. Why all the questions? A parent complaint.

Thankfully, the principal knew my work ethic and had observed me with my students. He was confident in me and came to ask me before judging me. Although I felt my principal's support, I was concerned. I knew I had to pray—I needed to be on my knees as I do when things are too much to bear. But how? When?

As I walked into the office, I dropped my car key, and as I knelt to pick it up, I offered a plea to my helper, to my advocate, to my God. I felt my dad, mom, brother, and all the people who love me lifting me up. I believe in the power of prayer and in the power of "two or more." I know situations change, and people's attitudes shift when people pray. The principal sat me next to him, showing his support.

—**Sandra Montes**

〉〈

Pray in the Spirit at all times in every prayer and supplication.
To that end keep alert and always persevere
in supplication for all the saints.

—Ephesians 6:18

We had left behind in the Great Hall the chatter and giggles of Harry Potter fans visiting Oxford. Now, in the quiet of Christ Church Cathedral, I was standing in front of an unusual object—an irregular black wooden cube—and trying to figure out what it was. A black-robed verger materialized beside me and began to talk about the Bell Altar and the man for whom it was named, George Bell, Bishop of Chichester (1929-1958).

Tears began trickling down my face as I listened to the verger tell me about this courageous man who in the very midst of World War II vigorously opposed the wholesale Allied bombing of German cities and the slaughter of innocent civilians. An example of loving inclusiveness, Bishop Bell had been a pioneer in the ecumenical movement and, it is thought, might have been named Archbishop of Canterbury had it not been for his unpopular and unequivocal moral stance during a time of war.

It seems fairly easy in our own culture to stand up for what we believe in the face of radically hateful opposition, but the hard thing is to stand for or against something in the face of our closest friends and fellow believers. For me, ever since that time spent in front of a black, modernist cube in Christ Church Cathedral, Bishop Bell has been my patron saint of moral courage.

—Joan Bowers

A couple of years ago, I began making it my conscious practice to try to see Jesus in everyone I meet and to treat them all accordingly. The results are sometimes startling. It turns out that the saints of God aren't hard to find at all. I meet saints every day, from the friendly checker at the grocery store to the kind nurse at the hospital to the first-time visitor at church. All that's needed to find them is to be open to the possibilities of Christ's kingdom.

When I think of the "cloud of witnesses" who surround us, I don't think so much of the ones who've been vetted and canonized and presented to the world in stained-glass windows (or on mugs) wearing halos. I think a lot about the ones I've known, with all their human faults and failings: my mother and father, my great-aunt Eleanor, friends, both living and dead, priests and teachers who helped to form me, and many others.

When I sing my favorite hymn, Ralph Vaughan Williams's setting of "For All the Saints," to his great tune *Sine nomine*, these are the saints who come to mind. For that matter, when it's time for "I Sing a Song of the Saints of God," with its saints in shops, that is my theme as well.

—Sarah Bryan Miller

In the cathedral of Our Lady of the Angels in Los Angeles hang several marvelous tapestries created by artist John Nava. Within the walls of this sparse, modern cathedral, worshipers are surrounded by two long rows of figures, all with hands poised in prayer, their gaze directed to the altar and the great cross. There are men and women from widely different centuries, cultures, and countries, people from all walks of life—farmers, scholars, missionaries, teachers, children. Though I've never been there in person, I can guess what it must feel like. I would be very literally standing in the midst of a crowd—a cloud of witnesses, in fact. The tapestries represent the communion of saints.

When I first saw images of the tapestries, I was able to understand in a whole new way that we are part of a living stream. Time doesn't separate us from those who have gone before us. We all stand together, looking to Christ.

It's startling at first to see people from very different time periods standing together in the beautiful way only art can portray. If you look more closely at some of the tapestries, though, you discover something even more startling. Scattered among the saints, each of whom are identified by name, are nameless people dressed in contemporary clothing. These people look like you or me, like people you'd pass in the street. They are a part of this communion, too.

—Kathleen M. Flanagan

In March of 2015, I was diagnosed with liver cancer... actually two kinds of liver cancer. Mama always said I was an overachiever. Like most devastating things, this hard news came suddenly and unexpectedly. One day I had a stomachache, and a few weeks later, I was tethered to my first round of chemo.

I presided at our parish's Maundy Thursday service two days after that first round of chemo. I knelt on wobbly legs to wash the feet of a high school student. Later in the service, as the daughter of our parish's founding member knelt to wash my feet, I was overcome. Serving and, often more difficult and humbling, being served through the foot washing always brings tears to my eyes. I thought about the saints, and on the countless days that followed, I thought about the saints in my parish and in my circle of friends. Those saints would be the hands that would comfort me and the arms that would carry me through the most difficult time of my life.

Thanks be to God for the saints that surround us...famous... infamous...anonymous...."and I mean to be one too."

—Rhoda Montgomery

They lived not only in ages past, there are hundreds of thousands still, the world is bright with the joyous saints who love to do Jesus' will. You can meet them in school, or in lanes, or at sea, or in church, or in trains, or in shops, or at tea, for the saints of God are just folk like me, and I mean to be one too.

—The Hymnal 1982, #293

Images of saints with halos around their heads, with hands raised in blessing, may lead us to forget that they are people just like us, complete with resentments, regrets, and anxieties. But they found a way to say, "Yes," to God. Sometimes this yes would mean a monumental task of starting a new movement, preaching before thousands, or facing a martyr's death.

This day, the Feast of the Annunciation, marks the traditional commemoration of the announcement of the angel Gabriel to a young Jewish girl named Mary that she would have a child, though she had not yet been with Joseph to whom she was espoused. This child, the angel said, would be the Son of God. It is perhaps even more noteworthy that Mary, laying aside any incredulity or personal fears, accepts this remarkable news: "Let it be with me according to your word" (Luke 1:38).

Those who have dared to follow Christ have likewise stepped out of their comfort zones, sometimes with grim smiles of fortitude and sometimes with trembling hands and weak knees.

But many more times following Christ means speaking a word of encouragement to someone, reaching out to someone in need, asking forgiveness or offering it. It is not the size of the task that is remarkable and life-changing; it is the simple but profound decision to say, "Yes," each time.

—Chuck Robertson

I have collected quotations that are meaningful to me for a very long time.

One is attributed to mystic Meister Eckhart, "If the only prayer you ever say in your life is 'thank you,' that would suffice." Saint Patrick's prayer for protection includes, "Christ within me, Christ behind me, Christ before me, Christ beside me..." Words attributed to Julian of Norwich read, "All shall be well, and all shall be well, and all manner of things shall be well." Repeating these lines connects me to these saints and others in a timeless way, helping to reorient me in my journey, bringing the presence of Christ closer.

I think of a man who used to make a bag of sandwiches every day and walk twenty-seven blocks to feed homeless people who gathered at midday. I think of a woman in our congregation who tirelessly works for universal healthcare for all. They are among the multitude of people volunteering time, talent, and energy to meet the needs of others. To pray with the saints is to open ourselves to the spirit moving through them in their work. Saints are all around us, and I want to join my prayers with theirs and with their work, remembering Meister Eckhart and saying, "Thank you."

—Linda Gelbrich

I offer a workshop called "Family Reunion: Telling the Stories of God." Much like a family reunion, it is a time of sharing stories. When asked why stories are told at family reunions about the scoundrels as well as the saints, participants often answer, "to keep them alive."

Family reunions remind us that we belong to something bigger than ourselves. We are connected to, and in some ways held accountable by, those with whom we share the story. When we come together in worship and to study God's word, it is the family coming together once more to witness (and to bear witness to) God's involvement in our lives. It is a family reunion.

As our ancestors in the faith witness to us through their stories and as we grow in knowledge and experience with God personally, we are likewise called upon to be witnesses for others, that they may know as we have known.

—Kathy H. Culmer

X

And may he so strengthen your hearts in holiness
that you may be blameless before our God and Father
at the coming of our Lord Jesus with all his saints.

—1 THESSALONIANS 3:13

*A*nd one was a soldier,

And one was a priest,

And one was slain by a fierce wild beast...

The first time I heard the words to "I sing a song of the saints of God," I immediately knew it would be my all-time favorite. I'd like to share a few stories of the saints I know.

One was a deacon who fed the food-insecure people of an isolated mountain community,

One was my best friend in kindergarten who drowned in a lake during our sophomore year of high school,

One was a preacher who never took a pay raise so his parish could pay off the new church building,

One stormed the beach at Normandy and cared for his wife who had Alzheimer's,

They were all of them saints of God—and I mean,

God helping, to be one too.

—Charles McClain

My mom and I fell apart in my fourteenth year. At that age, I couldn't imagine ever respecting her or looking up to her again. That kind of maternal admiration was for little kids. Obligatory love was all I could do for a long time.

Then, as often happens, our spirits reconnected when I got married and grew even stronger when I had my first daughter. Suddenly her words made sense. I sought her wisdom constantly. She was a nurse, so she had much to teach. More importantly, I respected her again.

When my second daughter was a baby, my mom had a heart attack and then was diagnosed with colon cancer that had spread to her liver. No one wanted to say how much time she had left. We just made the most of it by being with her as much as possible. Sponging it up, we called it. I wanted to absorb all that I could.

At her funeral, I learned how many people's lives she had touched. As a public health nurse in our city's clinics, she cared for the poorest and neediest. Mom was a five-foot fighter. She made a way when people had no way. She advocated for the rights of her nursing staff. She was proof that saints walk among us, and sometimes we don't even see them until they're gone.

—Miriam McKenney

Each day I walk past my neighbors' yards. I see statues of young Jesus crowned, his mother robed in blue, Saint Francis with animals, and angels. Most are lovingly attended to, with nearby bird feeders, ribbons, lighted enclosures, and flowers. I find myself noticing them and saying little prayers.

Saints are scriptural personalities, pioneers of the faith. Jesus, Mary, Francis, and others were saints. Their stories are ones we can read and take heart. The statues, lights, flowers, and containers are signs of devotion.

On the way to church on Sunday, I pass them again. As service begins, we are greeted with, "Good morning, saints!" As I look around the room, I see many whose daily struggle and faith give so much encouragement. Saints are all around us. We need to notice.

—Karen Montagno

X

And the smoke of the incense,
with the prayers of the saints,
rose before God from the hand of the angel.

—REVELATION 8:4

I admit: I had some confusion about praying to Mary and the saints. But praying to Mary and the saints has become easier and easier over the years. My confusion was whether it was Jesus or the saint who did the answering. At Cana, it was Mary asking, and Jesus doing.

When I asked a friend why he prayed to the Virgin Mary, he responded that sons do what their mothers ask them to. At the wedding in Cana, Jesus' mother notices that the wine has run out and informs her son of this. Jesus, against his better judgment, turns the water into wine, even after needling Mary for asking.

What son doesn't do what his mother asks? Mary and the saints are never silent. Ever are they singing and praying before Jesus, for us and with us. Amen.

—Carl Fosnaugh

)(

O God, the King of saints, we praise and glorify your holy Name for all your servants who have finished their course in your faith and fear: for the blessed Virgin Mary; for the holy patriarchs, prophets, apostles, and martyrs; ...and we pray that, encouraged by their examples, aided by their prayers, and strengthened by their fellowship, we also may be partakers of the inheritance of the saints in light; through the merits of your Son Jesus Christ our Lord. Amen.

—THE BOOK OF COMMON PRAYER, P. 504

APRIL

Being
in Nature

*The heavens declare the glory of God, and the
firmament shows his handiwork.*
—Psalm 19:1

In the Beginning

INTRODUCTION *In the Beginning*

For those of us who live in the Northern Hemisphere, April is the month when spring really shows up. Some years, April also plays host to Easter, so it's a great time of year to consider the wonder of the created world around us, to watch the flowers and trees wake up from their winter rest. Seeing the changing colors, the baby animals, and the lengthening daylight reminds us of all the ways God is doing new and beautiful things in our lives. This is also a reminder that God looks at all of creation with great love and calls it good. Whether you observe the spiritual discipline of being in nature by adding a walk to your daily devotional time, spend some extra time gazing out your favorite window, or take a camping trip with someone you love, we hope that you find yourself in awe of the Creator and the creation.

WAYS TO ENGAGE

Take a walk before or after your devotional time, as you are able.

Plant an herb garden or pot some flowers. Before or after your devotional time, take care of your garden plot or potted plants.

Drive to work using a different route. Keep your windows down, and enjoy the new scenery!

My herb and lettuce garden at our house in Houston was one of the delights of my life. Started from tiny plants and seeds, the two-foot square plot sat in the middle of our backyard. Three kinds of mint, three kinds of rosemary, chives, sage, thyme, two kinds of oregano, and a big beautiful basil plant all complemented the bed of mixed lettuces, collard and mustard greens.

I babied that little spot of dirt and hope. Underemployed and bored, I spent many hours in my garden, fussing with just the right way and time to water, picking over just the right leaves for our dinner salad, making a bouquet of herbs for a roast or a vase. I worried about bills, about learning how to be a wife, about finding a job I would love, about the health of my family, while I pulled weeds and introduced 10,000 ladybugs to my little plot.

As I worked over my garden and my worries, I found myself relaxing—breathing in the smells of the earth, the plants, and the life springing up under my hands. I could hear God telling me that a garden was a good place, and maybe the best place, to start life.

—Rachel Jones

I love the idea of the great outdoors. I love flowers and trees and birds and secret gardens. They do not love me back. Ever since my childhood, I have been extremely allergic to grass and pollen and trees and basically everything that grows in the ground. When spring comes and things begin to bloom, my eyes swell, my nose runs, and my skin itches. I desperately want to lounge in the thick grass and read a book all day, but instead I look out the window with longing.

Thanks to the miracle of modern medicine and some very committed doctors, I am now able to be outdoors in the spring (as long as I don't touch the grass). Yesterday I went for a walk with my daughter, with blossoming trees and plants all around us, and we picked those little flowers that lots of people think are weeds but she and I think are beautiful. We took our time, stopping at each yard to marvel at the size of a particular leaf or how two red tulips looked exactly the same on the outside but one was purplish-black on the inside and the other a bright sky blue. We left our home hunting for joy, and we found it.

—Holli Powell

𝕏

*He gives rain on the earth
and sends waters on the fields.*

—Job 5:10

What is it in nature that draws the breath from our lungs, widens our eyes, and silences our hearts? Sometimes I think it is fear (absolute terror) of the unknown and untamed. Other times, I experience nature with a deep sadness, a feeling of separation from a wild and joyous mother to whom I can never return. And still other times, I find a deep peace of belonging, an anti-anxious freedom from everyday realities that suddenly seem distant and insignificant.

There is a prayer in this rhythm of experience, from fear and trembling to heartbreak and repentance to reconciliation and belonging. It is the story of our human relationship with the divine.

In encountering nature we have the opportunity to confront the arc of the biblical story on an immediate and emotional level. Surrounded by the mighty mountains and trees, we can re-encounter the joyous possibility of wholeness amid the fear and loneliness in our lives. Beside a river, looking out over an ocean, we can be reintroduced to the transformative power of the gospel and find ourselves re-energized for the work of reconciliation to which we are all called.

—Jason Sierra

In the beginning, God reigned down on the earth all that was good and whole and possible—breathing into existence everything we might be and everything we were intended to be.

And then we found our way, like most mythic stories, into a world of limitation, shame, and impossibility. Rather than living from a place of abundance and wholeness, we began a human history of less-than and scarcity. We believed we could not be all things in all places and all times, and so we weren't.

Since that time, we have lived into the myth of scarcity and impossibility. There are moments we believe in the impossible and stretch beyond the limits of our understanding, but we are often called back into the myth of not-enoughness. We have spent most of our human existence convincing ourselves of our own not-enoughness. What we never realized in the process is that this is the myth.

My home is full of five dogs (don't judge), and the barn is home to several horses. I am reminded daily of the presence of God in each and every earthly moment. When I see a dog wriggle in the grass, fully living into the bliss of earth and greenery, or when I hear the whinny of a horse after dawn, stretching its legs or messing around with a playmate in the paddocks, I am reminded of the presence of God in everything. I am reminded by the creatures in my midst of the smell of earth, the joy of grass, and the presence of God in every single ray of sun that offers itself to us each day. The bliss animals exude in these moments reminds me of God, alive, in every blade of grass, every breeze, and every single sunrise.

—Teresa Pasquale

The Bible offers us many great illustrations of tough beginnings. The Jews wandered the desert for forty years before they came to the Promised Land. Jonah was swallowed by a whale before he converted the people of Nineveh. Jesus was born while Mary and Joseph traveled from Nazareth to Bethlehem. But the greatest tough beginning has to be the very beginning.

God creates a perfect world, only for humankind to betray him. Then the first murder happens, and God punishes Cain. Then the people multiply in the world, only for God to wipe them out with a flood. It goes on and on like this, like a cosmic wash-and-rinse cycle.

Through beginnings and endings, God is always present, always forgiving, and always loving. When we fall and fail, we are always given the opportunity to try again. Sometimes it's difficult for us to comprehend how deep God's love really is. But it's not our job to comprehend the expanse of God's love, only to comprehend that it is there from our beginnings to our endings, and everything in between.

—Longkee Vang

In 2010, Dr. Frances E. Kuo at the University of Illinois reviewed many medical studies that examined interactions between exposure to nature and human well-being. She discovered that across the board, with startling consistency, the results agreed: human beings thrive in nature. Exposure to the natural world reduces aggression, relieves depression and anxiety, enhances community life, and helps us in dozens of other ways.

The results of this study make sense within the Christian tradition. Scripture emphasizes our connection with the natural world. In Genesis, God makes Adam's body from the earth. Adam and Eve rule and name the animals, but they also live with them and work with them. Scripture emphasizes repeatedly that we are made from earth and return to earth; our lives are short because we are part of the ebb and flow of the natural world.

We recognize our need to interact with nature. Wealthy people spend money on gaining access to nature, buying houses with big yards and vacationing in beautiful outdoor areas. Even people who aren't super wealthy try to find living spaces with grass and trees and to take trips to the beach. All of these data points indicate that we don't just fund parks and nature preserves because they are pretty. We maintain them because we know we need them and that our children need them.

God created us to be intimately connected to the created world. We require access to nature to be physically and mentally whole, and we need to make sure other people have access to nature to make our communities whole.

—Elizabeth Brignac

Holy Sophia (Divine Wisdom) is the Holy Spirit. In art, culture, and nature, I see creation and witness Sophia.

In the "wind from God" that "swept over the face of the waters" (Genesis 1:2), Sophia is God's co-creator, present in the beginning when the Giver of Life created angels, the heavens, and earth (Proverbs 8:22-31). Sophia is the breath the Holy Author breathed into clay, creating humankind.

In the mist, mountains, budding leaves, and blossoming flowers, Sophia invites us to feast, cleanses us in the rain, and blesses us in snow. Wisdom speaks to us in the ballet of swaying tree branches caressed by the wind.

Wisdom does not suffer fools, but offers intuition, common sense, and creative expression to those who ask. What is it we do when praying to the Holy Spirit? We seek wisdom, guidance, and revelation. Sophia empowers us to create solutions for the challenges in our lives and those of others.

Creating and creativity, like nature itself, is holy and organic. It is sacred, constant action. Nature teaches through its cycles to be mindful, patient, present, observant, and to believe during winter in the rebirth to come and to be mystified in the wonders of autumn's fiery colors.

—Paul Jesep

The Bible is an outdoor book. In the beginning, we see the earth and sky and the sea, plants and animals—we see that these are good. Most important stories in the Bible happen outdoors: Adam and Eve, Jonah, Jesus. Abraham and Sarah are usually on the road. Moses leads people through the Red Sea. Jacob and David spend time with sheep. John baptizes in the Jordan. Jesus walks through Galilee to Jerusalem and on lakes and engages people on a mountain, a plain, and on roads.

I never feel so small as when I stand on a beach at night, gazing up at the Milky Way. But it is a good kind of small because I understand completely that God is bigger than the universe and all encompassing. I want my God to be huge, creative, life-giving, and even incomprehensible, rather than small and tamed.

Standing on that beach looking at the stars also makes me feel as if the power of the universe is inside me too, that I am connected to it, that I am made of stardust too, along with the earth, the flowers, whales, foxes, and the ocean. That makes me love God and all of this sacred creation.

—Penny Nash

*For the L*ORD *your God is bringing you into a good land,*
a land with flowing streams, with springs
and underground waters welling up in valleys and hills.

—DEUTERONOMY 8:7

When I was three years old, I sat in the tiny mimosa tree in our front yard. An only child in a neighborhood with no other children, on a summer morning, under the white-hot Texas sky, I perched on one of the tiny branches. But I was never alone.

The pink feathery blossoms nestled amongst the spiny leaves were friends to my eye. The clouds weren't shapeless puffs. They were parades of animals or skies full of flowers. Other days the clouds turned green and bilious, becoming the trumpeters of a bad storm. Then there were the days when there wasn't a cloud in the sky. Those were the days when a miraculous Light appeared and embraced me in its care and comfort. It was love at first sight. Even when I couldn't see the Light, I could feel its presence and offerings of love and safety when I sat in the mimosa.

When I grew too big to sit in the little tree, I thought I might be too big for my friend to come see me. I was wrong. From the first sighting, the Light has been my friend for life. Always showing up when needed and always bringing me hope, renewal, and profound moments of transformation. This is the nature of the Light.

—Charlotte Chere Graham

I was part of a small tour group led by Ahmen "Kathy" Kathrada at the Liliesleaf Farm in northern Johannesburg, South Africa. This farm was the secret convening place for many liberation leaders in the early 1960s in the struggle for freedom. Evidence found on this farm led to the famous Rivonia Trial and convicted Kathy and his other comrades (including Nelson Mandela) to Robben Island, the infamous South Africa prison.

Kathy would stand on a stool in his cell and look over to Capetown, only five and a half miles away, longing to be able to enjoy flowering gardens and indigenous trees and to wade in the choppy water. Kathy lamented, "No one has asked me what I missed most, children...the laughter of a child, the crying of a child, the singing of a child. I did not see a child for twenty years; and when I did, I began to cry."

Back in the United States, strolling freely in the gardens and parks, watching children play happily with one another, I am filled with gratitude for God's grace in tasting Kathy's tears and for his answered prayers.

—Westina Matthews

I recently read about a problem that's taking place in newly built homes. In order to create energy-efficient, draft-free homes, newly constructed buildings are now as nearly sealed off from the outside world as the Vatican was at the beginning of the Second Council. Consider that in some newly constructed homes, studies show that the rate at which indoor air is exchanged for fresh air is now ten times lower than it was thirty years ago, with significant increases in humidity and concentrations of indoor pollutants and airborne allergens. Being sealed off quite literally makes us sick.

"Open!" Pope John XXIII is said to have proclaimed, and all the windows of the Vatican were flung wide open. It was his symbolic way of beginning the Second Vatican Council, which sought to open the Roman Catholic Church to the outside world, welcoming a fresh Spirit into the mustier corners of Roman Catholic theology.

In our own lives, and on a much smaller scale, each of us needs our own chance to declare ourselves "open" to change.

Let's take a page from Pope John XXIII and proclaim our own opening and openness. This month is a perfect time to open a window, allowing the wind and sun to bring fresh air—and a fresh Spirit—into our homes and into our lives.

—**Miguel Escobar**

"It's something to do with—uh—the sugar in the leaves?" I asked my sister-in-law, who has a doctorate in biology. We were riding through the countryside of western Massachusetts on a gray, chilly October afternoon, and I was marveling at the fall colors, so much more intense than the hints of autumn I'd left behind in North Carolina.

Elaine shook her head. "The colors are in the leaves all along," she said, explaining that chlorophyll makes the leaves green through the summer, but when cold weather comes, the tree pulls the chlorophyll back from the leaves to nourish the branches, the trunk, and the roots through the winter. "True colors revealed," I said. "I like that—it's a good image for getting older!"

This spring I've looked carefully as the new leaves begin to unfold on trees and shrubs—and sure enough, those buds and tiny, curled leaves are red, and the new growth comes in gold or pale yellow. Robert Frost got it right: "Nature's first green is gold..." Or crimson, or burgundy.

Like the trees, we are made for beauty in every season.

—**Mary W. Cox**

ᛉ

The earth brought forth vegetation: plants yielding seed of every kind, and trees of every kind bearing fruit with the seed in it. And God saw that it was good.

—GENESIS 1:12

In the monastic tradition of praying the hours, a bell tolls to call the members of the order to prayer. In my day, out in the secular world, it is the song of the northern cardinal that tolls for me. The cardinal's distinctive, "What cheer, what cheer, teew teew teew!" is my call to prayer. Red, as I've come to name my divine friend, finds me throughout the day, catching my eye on the feeder outside my kitchen, darting in front of me as I drive to work, singing from the cedar tree, calling to friends across the way, calling to me. As I wrote this, he landed in the red maple outside my window. Thank you, Red!

Not long ago, I officiated at the funeral of a man whose name was Red. I offered to his grieving widow my experience with the cardinal. I hope that she hears Red's call and in it, the promise of eternal life for her husband, the presence of God in her life now, and the love of all those who walk with her.

Choose for yourself a piece of nature, a piece you love. It needn't be the cardinal. It could be a constellation in the night sky or the daily "good morning" of the sunrise; it could be the sparkle of dew or the hush of evening color; it might be the sound of the tide or the rustle of wind. Let nature call you back to God. Deep calling to deep. One holy creation to another. All in praise of our shared Creator.

—Susan Wyper

I'm a Christian who believes that science and faith are compatible, not irreconcilable. Does the path set out before us in the beginning exclude the idea that things evolve as time passes? I find it more beautiful when I think of the delicate hand that was there when everything began. It's hard to create something and then have the strength to let it go, knowing that it will move on without you. Will people remember who was there in the beginning and the love that was shown in those first moments of creation?

While God doesn't have ego involved the way I do, God still longs for us to see God in all things. Sometimes seeing God is easy, and other times it takes a strong resolve. I think seeing God in science is easy; I am surrounded by its visual and tangible beauty. Seeing God in people is much harder because sometimes I have to look deeply to find God. The question is: am I willing to open my eyes to what God is putting before me? I can't open my eyes without seeing God in everything I encounter. That is God's love for us, and in my opinion, it is undeniable.

—**Lauren Caldwell**

I love to watch the trees, flowers, and grass come back to life. I love the cherry and the pear blossoms. April showers often knock the gentle blossoms to the ground. I like to notice the way the rain causes the petals to fall soundlessly to the ground. Every spring, I say the same thing to my wife, "Falling blossoms teach me to let go and let God."

The creation stories we read in Genesis emphasize our connection to nature. We are created to be in nature and to be good stewards of nature. I believe this is another way of saying that all of nature should see God in us and we should see God in nature.

When the beauty of nature takes on new life during spring, we are reminded that God is calling us to new life. Pick up a stone, observe a leaf or flower, and try to notice the sun when it rises or sets. The beauty we see in nature is the beauty we are called to be. From the beginning of time, God has wanted us to bloom and be beautiful. Pay attention to everything and practice saying, "It is good."

—**Mark Bozzuti-Jones**

The LORD *God took the man and put him in the garden of Eden to till it and keep it.*

—GENESIS 2:15

Waking early, I drank coffee and read, looking up later to discover that sunlight sparkled brilliantly around ice-layered twigs and branches. Fog, covering everything, had frozen, and I'd missed a dazzling dawn, my mind elsewhere. Temperatures rose, icicles dripped, and the trees appeared to rain.

In my bookish preoccupation, I'd missed the dawn's beauty, and of all things, I'd been reading about those of us who offer a "preoccupied presence" to nature, events, and people. Haven't most of us been caught in conversations when our thoughts had wandered and we were asked an unheard question?

Openness relates to an out-of-fashion word, "surrender." Surrendering my mental agenda to God, I am more free to temporarily set aside my own stuff throughout the day. Trusting God with our concerns, becoming more aware of God's attentive presence, we become more "present tense" with others; and over time, we may become more mentally and spiritually still, peaceful and hospitable.

I could go on, but at the moment, a chickadee is flying nearby. Daffodils are opening now. And my neighbor wants a listener— a present-tense listener.

— June Terry

A few weeks ago, I walked my first trail in over thirty years. That first trail flipped the switch: I've been on twelve hikes in the last three weeks. Even I can't believe it. That's how I know it's Spirit-led.

See, I'm not the type of person that I'd ever think would own a hydration backpack. I've been a large person most of my life. Even when I was active, I kept things civilized and walked on the pavement. Nature kept its distance, like a gentleman. Then various injuries and arthritis forced me off the pavement and onto soft tracks and the treadmill.

Trail walking answered my prayers. The ground and gravel forgive my joints their aches and pains. Now, I take spiderwebs to the face in the name of my health and well-being. Exercising in the woods in the rain, in the heat, is the most empowering thing I've ever done for myself. I marvel at God's ever-changing creation. I take lots of pictures, because it's never the same when I return.

Try taking a walk today, or one day soon. Don't plan it too much—find someplace close to you and just do it. God has so much to reveal to you out here. Get out there so you can see for yourself.

—**Miriam McKenney**

The sky was painted a glorious pink, with streaks of purple and yellow hues. The sun retreated beneath the rolling horizon, like a child barely peeking above a temporary hiding place. The scents of spring danced in the air as a symphony of cricket songs accompanied their production. Peace seemed to flood my soul as I walked outside that evening burdened with life, the worries and pressures of the world weighing heavily on my mind. I stepped into nature, focusing on my little corner of the world. But, my senses were bombarded by the colossal canvas that surrounded me. Suddenly, my problems seemed small. My worries seemed small. In fact, I seemed small. But the earth…it felt big. God's creation felt enormous. I was instantly saturated by this awareness: my God is big.

We serve a God whose scope is limitless, with influence beyond our wildest imagination. God paints delicate feathers on the tiniest hummingbird, wraps the daintiest caterpillar in a perfect cocoon, and gifts the occasional shamrock with an extra love-shaped leaf. But our God also orchestrates the spectacular samba of the stars. Nothing exceeds the bounds of God's control, and nothing cowers beneath the threshold of God's love.

I type this devotion being serenaded by a nest of baby birds chirping outside my window. My God knows them by name. Nature calls us out of fear, helplessness, boredom, anxiety, complacency, worry, and selfishness to acknowledge the creator of everything. The God who knows your name wants to remind you of this love and the scope of love's influence in your life. May the God who calms the oceans calm your heart today.

—**Bree Combs**

A lot of people see the presence of God in the natural order. I'm right there with them...most of the time. Sunsets. Sunrises. Rainbows. Beautiful mountain ranges. In the places that make it on the postcards, I see the hand of God at work, and I am sure you do too.

Jesus pointed to nature time and time again as a sign of God's presence: the lilies of the field, the blowing wind, the birds of the air, branches, vines. Surely the connection between God's presence and nature is strong. For me, pollen is an exception.

Seasonal allergies leave me struggling to breathe. I know pollen is part of God's plan to make all things new, but I am not friends with pollen. I cough. I sneeze. My eyes turn red and burn and itch.

I like to breathe, and it is hard for me to breathe in April. If it were up to me, pollen would not be part of the system. A friend of mine saw my suffering and said, "What a wonderful reminder that you are not the center of the universe." I thought about that for a while and concluded that she was right. There is a God, and it is not me, and it is not you. Thank God for that. Eventually June comes and the beauty of new life and growth continues to unfold all around, and I am thankful, especially as the pollen subsides, and God continues to make all things new.

—Jason Leo

I was looking forward to spending spring break with my son. Somehow, I decided we should visit Niagara Falls. I had heard the Canadian side was more beautiful, and we decided to take a road trip from his home in Chicago, Illinois, to Niagara Falls, Canada. We began the trek so excited.

Because I love social media, I kept checking us into every place I could, posting pictures on Instagram, exclaiming that this trip was amazing. As we passed customs to enter Canada, I asked my son to check us into Canada. Suddenly I received several texts saying we were entering Canada and our mobile carrier was going to charge us an arm and a leg for texts, calls, and (gasp!) data. I immediately froze and pulled over because I needed the GPS for directions before we turned off our data.

When we made it to the falls, I didn't see them. All I saw were people walking and traffic. The glorious falls were in front of me, and I asked Ellis (my son), "Where are they?" He looked at me incredulously; after focusing my eyes, I realized they were right in front of me—and had been the whole time. We laughed, but when I meditated on that, I realized that God's glory is often right in front of me. Big. Beautiful. Overflowing. But I say, "Where is it? Where is God's glory?" I ask God to show me God's glory, but I sometimes don't focus on it and instead get distracted by all the noise and buzz around me. God, help me focus on you and your glory.

—Sandra Montes

My husband and I have just pulled into a small parking area off one of the dirt roads winding through the Ritch Grissom Memorial Wetlands in Florida.

We quietly extract our binoculars from their cases and exit the car. Between us and the edge of the water, we notice a couple crouched in the back of their large SUV, using the side of the vehicle as a bird blind. It's obvious from the size of their huge lenses, thermos bottles, and pile of sandwiches that these people are here for the long haul.

We catch a glimpse of what they are watching.

There, absolutely motionless in the reeds, is a great blue heron waiting to spear an unlucky frog or fish with its long beak. The heron doesn't move. We don't move, and any motion of the photographers is hidden by their vehicle.

All of us wait. The heron makes one failed stab at something, and we all wait some more. Fifteen or twenty minutes go by. Finally, a car moving on the main road frightens the bird away.

The heron's endless patience serves as a lesson when I find myself becoming impatient with myself, with others, with God. Fortunately, birding provides a spiritual discipline in strengthening that virtue.

—**Joan Bowers**

I moved two years ago from a big house with a big yard and big maintenance to a much smaller affair more suitable for someone with unreliable supplies of physical energy. I find I hardly miss the house, for all its amenities; what I do miss is the view from the back windows.

The ridge at the top of my yard was a wildlife highway; I might glance out and see deer or a family of foxes. The trees at its back sheltered a multitude of birds in their season: woodpeckers, brown thrashers and doves, house finches, goldfinches, and chickadees by the dozen.

This is the time of year when hummingbirds return from beyond the Gulf of Mexico to their northern breeding grounds, their iridescent colors flashing in the springtime light. Although the feeders on my deck brought indifferent trade, the hummingbird buffet on the window fetched feisty little jewels hovering on impossibly fast-moving wings.

I observed them through the glass as they ate and challenged one another for possession. (The word "share" is not in the hummer's vocabulary.) With each encounter, I caught a precious glimpse of God's creation and the endless variety with which it is filled, and I knew in my bones that it is very good.

—Sarah Bryan Miller

A few years ago I journeyed to Iona, an island steeped in holy history. Arriving after a long day's journey through the rugged, wild highlands of Scotland, twilight was falling. I walked the narrow, quiet road to the abbey for the evening service, carrying the flashlight the hostel owner had warned me to take.

When I stepped outside an hour later, I walked into a darkness I'd never experienced before. On Iona there is almost no artificial light, with only a few scattered houses beyond the abbey. The only light came from the stars. Instead of the scattered pinpoints of light my suburban self was used to, the stars stretched above me in massed glory, like a canopy spread between the low hills and the sea. It was almost too beautiful to believe.

When I reached the hostel, I walked out to the adjoining field and lay down, stargazing for I don't know how long. I could hardly bear to go inside even when the autumn night grew cold. I had seen how the heavens declare the glory of God.

I believe that whenever we feel awe at God's creation, we are praying, without realizing it, a prayer of attention, gratitude, and praise. We can't explain why the beauty moves us so—it is simply a pure gift from the One who loves us. God is present to us in all of nature, and when we feel awe, we are fully present to God.

—Kathleen M. Flanagan

Yesterday was one of those days with Doug during which the harder I tried to help him feel happy and relaxed, the less he seemed to feel happy and relaxed. We tried my old reliable remedy, but even a few bites of ice cream (which always makes him happy) couldn't hold his attention or spark his joy. I finally decided to ask Doug if he wanted me to take him back to his house. In the past, this would have been the last thing he would have wanted. To my surprise, and slight relief, he said, "Yes, please."

I wondered, as we were driving back to the house, if Doug would remember he'd just asked me to take him home, whether or not he would be upset when we pulled up in front of the building. I bent over to kiss him, and he said, "I know you have to go." I wanted to cry, but I held back my tears and said, "I do, but I will be back." He nodded, and responded, "I know…"

I woke this morning at 2:30 to the sound of a pair of owls outside my window, calling back and forth to each other in the night. I lay awake for some time, listening to them before falling back to sleep. My alarm went off at 5 a.m. and I got up, hoping I might hear the owls again from the patio. Sure enough, with my coffee in hand, sitting in the stillness, I heard them calling—a sound that was magical and mysterious.

I think about that pair of owls that came to call this early morning. Love calls out to love, and they find each other, even in the shadows. Love calls out to love, and even on days when Doug and I struggle to understand each other through the fog of Alzheimer's, we find each other.

Allison Zent Blankemeyer

Saint Francis is well-known for his love of nature. Pictures and statues usually depict him surrounded by birds or animals. Centuries before the circle of life became part of our musical vocabulary, this poet from Assisi sang of the sun, moon, and stars as his brothers and sisters. Nature was not something separate from him; it was part of him, and he was part of it.

The world around Francis was changing rapidly. His attempts at reform to point others to the beauty of a simple Christ-like life all too often led to hostility and opposition. In all of it, God's nature renewed his spirit and gave him joy. To Francis, "a single sunbeam is enough to drive away many shadows."

At times we might feel as if our lives—our very souls—are in danger of being swallowed whole by our own increasingly complicated and exhausting twenty-first-century world. When the shadows around and within us threaten to rob us of our joy, perhaps it is time to step outside—even for a few minutes in the middle of a busy day—to look and listen and feel the miracle of a single sunbeam, then lift our arms toward heaven and raise our voices in song.

—Chuck Robertson

)(

My beloved has gone down to his garden, to the beds of spices, to pasture his flock in the gardens, and to gather lilies.

—Song of Solomon 6:2

S everal years ago I traveled to the Grand Canyon by tour bus, leaving from Tucson, Arizona. The bus carried us up the freeway, then turned off toward Sedona, where we were to spend the first night. We rounded a curve, and it was as though we had driven into the center of a geode. I could barely catch my breath as we passed one massive red-stone formation after another, until they were on all sides of us. The afternoon sun bore down and illuminated this landscape, burning the images into my mind. I'd never even imagined such a colorful, majestic scene. I was ecstatic. I knew I'd be back.

I've been to Sedona numerous times since then, and each time, I gasp as we enter the red-stone landscape. I'm eager to put on walking shoes, grab a walking pole, and set out with my husband on one of the many trails we have come to love. We walk around the top of the airport mesa in town and look out over the rock formations, a creek, and the busyness below. We see clouds thickening in the distance, hear the raven's throaty call, feel the sun's heat, and taste the dust.

Each time we are there, I am filled to overflowing with gratitude and wonder. I carry that awe with me as I return home and feel a renewed appreciation for the wonders in our own yard— the rhododendron blooming, the doe in the backyard resting while her spotted twins chase each other in circles, and the smell of damp earth.

—Linda Gelbrich

Mountain climbing is not easy. The mountains, massive rocks with steep sloping sides and sharp ridges, might seem impassable. Our feet were not made for climbing big rocks or scaling mountains, at least not on their own. The heights are too great, the terrain too rugged, the conditions unbearable at certain altitudes, and the risk of falling too much a possibility.

Most of us will never climb an actual mountain, but we will face many metaphoric mountains throughout our lives—obstacles that seem insurmountable and summits that seem unreachable, our footing too unsure. But the promise of the One who inspired the psalmist is that, "He makes me sure-footed like a deer and lets me stand firm on the heights" (Psalm 18:33).

It is no accident that the mountains are part of God's creation, God's plan, God's divine purpose. They remind us of our dependence on a power greater than ourselves, of the vastness of our world. As daunting as they may appear, the mountains were placed to take us to greater heights. Though the terrain is rugged and the climb steep, we must dare to climb. God has promised to be there to make our footing sure from valley to peak.

—**Kathy H. Culmer**

I 've seen some beautiful sights along the backroads of Middle Tennessee. I am struck by the blankets of purple clover that covered the cotton fields of Franklin County in two short weeks. My thoughts turn to one of my favorite hymns, "O love, how deep, how broad, how high." As we sing, we tell the story of Jesus' life, death, and resurrection, "For us to wicked hands betrayed, scourged, mocked, in purple robe arrayed" (*The Hymnal 1982*, #449).

They put Jesus in a purple robe to make fun of him and to pronounce the end of an illegitimate kingship that threatened the Jewish establishment and worried the Roman governor. As I drive, I am confronted with the ways I want to limit the kingship of Jesus, to deny the pull and demand it makes on my life.

"He bore the shameful cross and death; for us gave up his dying breath."

I am pulled out of myself, and I see the clover again. The fields of Tennessee cannot hold their peace. They are erupting with the true kingship of Jesus. For a minute, I consider pulling over and lying down in the field. I think better of it and decide to wait... at least until Easter.

—Charles McClain

Children know the color purple is significant because it comprises one seventh of God's rainbow. Saint Lydia made her living brokering it. She sold fabric colored a lustrous shade of deep purple by dye that was harvested in and near Thyatira, a city known today as Akhisar, Turkey. The natural dye, first recorded when a dog's mouth turned purple after biting a murex sea snail, is fade-proof. The price of this commodity reflected that permanence and the labor-intensive process of harvesting the dye from murex secretions. The expense and engagement of such beautiful color earned it the name, "royal purple." This tone tinted robes for many rulers.

Lydia was a devout and steady worshiper of God even before she met Saint Paul. Her adoration and patience were rewarded when God chose to open her heart completely. After hearing Paul's message, she and her whole family were baptized. Come and stay at my home, Lydia insisted to Paul, Luke, and the others who were with them. And what an interior they must have seen: beauty laced with purple.

Through her faith in the forgiving, redeeming power of Jesus' death and resurrection, Lydia was granted her own fade-proof purple robe for eternity.

—**Susan Taylor Block**

Cities may not seem to be a place to enjoy nature. However most cities have green spaces, a river, or some parkland. Community gardens are springing up in the midst of the hustle and bustle of urban and downtown areas.

Finding green in the heart of the city is a secret treasure and a refuge. Turn a corner—creation cannot be denied by green spaces. People are growing flowers, and community gardens are sprouting. Green things growing in the heart of the city with the voice of creation saying, " Yes, yes, yes!"

Cars slow a bit to see the green space, parents push strollers, and bikers soak in the beauty of flowers and vegetables growing in the midst of pavement.

—Karen Montagno

))(

Almighty and everlasting God, you made the universe with all its marvelous order, its atoms, worlds, and galaxies, and the infinite complexity of living creatures: Grant that, as we probe the mysteries of your creation, we may come to know you more truly, and more surely fulfill our role in your eternal purpose; in the name of Jesus Christ our Lord. Amen.

—The Book of Common Prayer, p. 827

Anglican Rosary

*Rejoice always, pray without ceasing,
give thanks in all circumstances;
for this is the will of God in Christ Jesus for you.*
—1 THESSALONIANS 5:16-18

Pray Without Ceasing

INTRODUCTION   *Pray Without Ceasing*

P rayer beads are an important devotional tool in many faith traditions. Anglican rosaries, or Anglican prayer beads, are one way that many Episcopalians have chosen to engage the discipline of praying without ceasing. Made up of a series of thirty-three beads and composed of several simple prayers that are easy to commit to memory, the Anglican Rosary is a way to literally hold your prayers in your hand and lift up your worries and concerns to God. However you choose to think about praying without ceasing during this month, know that your prayers are heard and felt in the very heart of God, even on days when you may not be able to find the right words to say.

Ways to Engage

If the idea of the Anglican Rosary is new to you, spend a few minutes on your favorite search engine finding some additional information on this way to pray.

Consider using your rosary before or after your devotional time.

Pick a particular prayer request to hold as a special intention during your rosary practice.

Carry your beads with you throughout the day.

Make a set of beads (there are many, many suggestions for making your own set of Anglican rosary beads online) for a friend or loved one, and introduce them to the practice.

My grandmother is fond of the phrase, "Tell the truth, and shame the devil." One of my truths is that I struggle with anxiety. There are days when it yells loud enough to make my face tingle and to make my heart wonder if I am really beloved, really OK, really enough. Learning to pray the Anglican rosary, especially the Jesus Prayer, has been one of the ways I have confronted this truth about my anxiety and one of the ways I have found to help control it.

When I find myself feeling stuck, starting to spin into scary or hard places, even if I can't get my hands on my beads, I start praying...*Lord Jesus Christ, Savior, Son of God, have mercy on me, a sinner...your beloved...your servant...your friend.* I roll that prayer around in my head and heart, like a little ball of healing fire, losing myself in the wonder of a Jesus who hears all our prayers with equal urgency and equal response. I find my breath again. I can hear the birds singing louder than the pounding in my ears, and I stay with that prayer, letting Jesus love me, save me, rescue me, restore me, and remind me of the wholeness he brings to my brokenness.

My hope and prayer for you, as you cultivate your own way to pray without ceasing, whether using the Anglican rosary or some other discipline that works for you, is that you hear the words of your prayers mixing with the prayers of Jesus in an endless chorus of peace, plenty, and providence.

—Rachel Jones

Almost ten years ago, I was visiting Austria on a business trip and attended Roman Catholic Mass with a coworker. When we walked into the church and took our seats a few minutes early, it took a second for my ears to adjust to the silence enough to hear a soft murmur. When I finally attuned to the sound, I wasn't quite sure what I was hearing. Were these older ladies whispering to one another? No…that wasn't quite right…it seemed to almost be a pattern or a chant. I looked at my coworker, who was Catholic, with a question in my eyes. "The rosary," she whispered. And then I heard it. *Heilige Maria, Mutter Gottes. Hail Mary, Mother of God.* These women gathered together before the Mass to say the rosary together, quietly, reverently.

It wasn't long after that when I discovered that there was an Anglican rosary as well, and began adapting it into my own spiritual practices. When I had a baby, my silent prayer time became counting down the Hail Marys on my fingers during nursing sessions or while rocking my daughter to sleep. Mother to mother, I prayed.

Blessed are we among women, blessed is the fruit of our womb. I started saying it on airplanes, during takeoffs and landings, rising above the clouds as I prayed silently. When I kneel at church and can't find any words to express the longing in my soul, I drop right back into the rosary prayers, just like those women in the darkened church in Austria. *Have mercy on me, a sinner. Have mercy.*

—Holli Powell

My dad taught me to body surf when I was growing up. We would take weeklong vacations down to Padre Island off the Texas coast, just outside Corpus Christi. The gulf in that area didn't create waves big enough for actual surfing, but they would crash with enough weight to carry you (minus the board) twenty or thirty feet. It was an exhilarating feeling, flying through the water toward the shore, the wave pushing at your back as though you were just more water displaced by the might of the sea.

Of course, you had to wait for the right wave. Sometimes a dozen would crash just before or just after where you were standing before the right one came along. But they always kept coming, kept crashing, regular and reliable, and the wait was usually worth it.

I try to build a routine in my prayers, to create a cycle of prayer as reliable and mundane as breathing or eating or waves. I try to find myself awash in awareness of the Spirit around me, such that I can count the waves crashing around me as I go through my days. And when I do, I find myself also ready and more likely to catch the larger waves of the Spirit's movement, those waves that send me flying through the world, my prayer as much a part of God's work as the birds or the trees. It is these moments when I become aware of all that God is accomplishing in and around me, but only because I was listening to the waves in the first place.

—Jason Sierra

Once upon a time, in a lifetime far away, when I had forsworn myself against all things Christian (as many of us pre-millennial Christians do), I found myself breathing and moving and holding space for the sacred on a yoga mat. In the midst of yoga culture, I found my way back home and one of those breadcrumbs came in the form of the rosary. If we seek it out, we can find a lineage of rosary in most every sacred tradition. Exploring the ritual of rosary prayer, helped me remember, with sacred nostalgia, the rosary experiences of my youth.

My grandmother was a devout Roman Catholic, and she carried her rosary wherever she went and prayed the rosary daily. She had a deep and powerful connection with the maternal nature of Mary. While this is intrinsic to Catholic tradition for many, for her it was a connection through time, history, and tradition from one mother to the prophetic mother. I still have the rosary beads she gave me for my first communion, and throughout my apathy and agnosticism, all the way back to the Catholic [and Anglican] rosary of my origin, they have never left my bedside— connecting me to my grandmother and to the great ritual of prayer without ceasing.

As I pack my bags for my trip to the Camino in Spain, I will carry my grandmother's rosary every step of the way. I can imagine my hands rolling over the beads on the hard and painful pathway—a pilgrimage back into my soul and into my own familial lineage of prayer that never ends.

This is true pilgrimage, and the rosary is the constant reminder that life is meant to be the lived experience of prayer without ceasing. Every step. Every mile. We move into ourselves and forward toward our promised land. We are called to God, to the maternal nature of the sacred and into the rhythm of life, an offering of embodied prayer without end.

—Teresa Pasquale

I've never been a "drop to your knees and clasp your hands" prayer guy; it's not how I saw my parents pray when I was growing up. Don't get me wrong; we prayed when we were in church or when we ate dinner. But we never prayed when we went to bed or when we were out in public; again, it's not how I saw my parents pray.

How did my parents pray? They talked to God. They talked when they were driving, when they were cooking, and when they were doing work at their desk. They were always talking to God, thanking God for a great day, for good health, or asking for some reassurance. Sometimes they went silent while working; this was when I knew they were talking to God. Through these actions I learned to constantly pray, at all times. It didn't matter if I had a million thoughts on my mind or just wanted to say thank you. I knew the Lord was willing and available to hear me.

God always has an ear out for us. Sometimes we feel we can only turn to God when times are tough. But it's also important to remember God wants to be with us in good times as well. Turning to God during our times of strife and struggle are important but so is rejoicing and celebrating with God. It allows us to better understand our relationship with God and God's love for us.

God is ever present and willing to listen to us. And by continuing to reach out to God through prayer, God abides with us.

—Longkee Vang

As a parent of young children, I find that people push an exhausting kind of mindfulness upon me. No matter what is going on, if we are in public, some nice lady is sure to wander over to me, pat me on the hand, and remind me to appreciate these moments because all too soon, my birds will have flown. These people are kind; they mean well, but I sometimes think that there is no situation that someone can't make sadder by reminding me that my little ones are leaving someday and that I need to appreciate them instantly. This type of pressure doesn't draw appreciative attention to the present; it draws mournful attention to the future.

At first I feel a similar pressure in response to the demand that I pray without ceasing. It seems like it would make prayer an annoying obligation that would interrupt real prayer. If I can't enjoy a moment in life without obligatory prayer, how can spontaneous prayer from the heart ever happen?

But really, praying without ceasing is sort of like appreciating my children without having strangers remind me to do so. I don't appreciate them out of obligation; like most parents, I love them as naturally as I breathe. Likewise, people who pray without ceasing bring God into their lives like air. They don't consciously form prayers all the time; instead, they move prayer and sing prayer as instinctively as they breathe or walk around.

I want to pray unceasingly the same way that I love my family—in everything that I do, without obligation, or even conscious thought, coming into it.

—Elizabeth Brignac

The beads are worn. The wooden cross is darkened with dirt and sweat. The rope has broken several times over the years with loss of beads. It's now kept together with the original tattered fabric string, reinforced with fishing line.

I've kept a prayer rope of red, wood beads with a three-bar cross in my left pocket for many years. It is with me every day. Sometimes I reach into my pocket during the day to recite a short, silent prayer.

The prayer rope isn't a talisman. It's not a magic charm protecting me from lightning, falling pianos, or drivers with a lead foot. It is, however, one way to stay connected with a divine force, challenging me to identify daily opportunities to grow spiritually and make a positive difference for others.

—Paul Jesep

Ⅹ

The LORD has heard my supplication;
the LORD accepts my prayer.

—PSALM 6:9

One summer, our Vacation Bible School theme was "All the ways we pray." We walked a big labyrinth, we constructed prayer journals and prayer boxes, and we put together a prayer chain to adorn the altar at communion. My job was to lead the craft of Anglican rosary making.

We gathered around a table laden with string and wire and beads of all shapes, colors, and sizes along with some "silver" crosses. I showed the children the two Anglican rosaries I own—both were made for me by others—and explained what the parts of the rosary meant and how we use it to pray. We talked about the two funny words: the cruciform beads ("Look! They form a cross!" several children exclaimed), and the invitatory bead ("What the heck does that mean?"), and we counted out the week's beads.

And then everyone got to work. This was serious business, and I witnessed universal concentration—a minor miracle in VBS! With increasing appreciation, I sensed the Spirit moving among these boys and girls as they put together not just beads but also something they knew was holy. It didn't matter how the rosary turned out, whether it was mismatched or professional looking. My sense was that whether or not any of them ever used the rosary to pray in the future, the children were having a religious experience making them now.

After my last group left, I rifled through the beads to find some that spoke to me, and I made my own rosary. The children were right. I was making something for prayer, and it was very much a holy activity. In fact, it was prayer.

—Penny Nash

The circular symmetry of humanity, nature, and God comes alive for me when I move my fingers around the Anglican rosary. The words I've prayed and the prayer-filled energy that's embedded into each round bead ground me in the soothing, smoothing grace of God. This is a holy opportunity to come to God with our joys, our hurts, our transgressions, and our hopes.

The Anglican rosary is like God's help and forgiveness—a circle that never ends. As I deepen my spiritual practice, the rosary teaches me the wisdom of connecting with God's essence in ceaseless, circular prayer, even when my hands are otherwise busy with the work of my day.

—Charlotte Chere Graham

The LORD grants his loving-kindness in the daytime;
in the night season his song is with me,
a prayer to the God of my life.

—PSALM 42:10

On Sunday, September 14, 2001, I went to church. It was the Sunday following 9/11, and it was standing room only at my church. People came searching for meaning, for comfort, for reassurance, for prayer, and for answers. I liked to think of myself as a prayerful woman, and that I answered Apostle Paul's call to "pray without ceasing," but to my dismay, I had not been able to pray since I had run for my life from the World Financial Center Tuesday morning.

I slipped into one of the back pews of the church, journaling, not really paying attention to the service, when I heard my name being called. I was being asked to bring prayer. As the hymn was being sung, I slowly began to make my way up to the front, holding tightly to my rosary, shaking my head and thinking, "God, you are something else. I haven't prayed since Tuesday, and now you want me to pray with, for, and in front of this entire congregation."

I don't remember all that I prayed but it ended with: *Now, in the quiet and the stillness of this hour, let us draw our ears close to our hearts, take a deep breath, listen closely, and hear God call out to each of us by name, saying: keep praying.* Amen.

—Westina Matthews

Of the twelve reflections I've written for this collection, I must admit that I found this practice—to pray without ceasing—to be the hardest to write. I can certainly reflect on praying regularly, even frequently. But ceaselessly?

I suppose the real reason I struggled with writing about this practice is because this is a legitimately daunting thing to consider. My mind turns to all those parts of my life that I've conveniently separated from my faith and even to those tendencies that can only be described as far-from-God. How on earth would my faith reach all the way there?

What strikes me about this practice is its all-encompassing nature—the way it sets out to consume and transform the height, depth, and breadth of our lives—and I must confess that the prospect of singling even one of these areas out and reorienting it toward Christ is more challenging and more interesting than previously thought possible.

So, yes, it's daunting—but it's also exciting.

—**Miguel Escobar**

I am inundated all day with spam. I get emails and texts from causes and organizations I've supported, telling me that the bad guys will win and people will suffer and die if I don't text 10 dollars immediately. And there are messages from businesses, trumpeting sales and coupons—if I act NOW!

All day long, I bombard God with messages too, and I have begun to suspect that much of what I believe to be unceasing prayer is also spam: I whimper, "Please, please, please! I'm so scared—what's going to happen? Why is this happening?" I tell Jesus I need him to act NOW, or all will be lost. I rant on at length with my ideas about how the universe should be governed.

Using Anne Lamott's description of the types of prayer—"Help! Thanks! Wow!"—I find myself fully engaged with the "Help!" variety (with a number of "Whys?" thrown in), and light on the "Thanks!" and "Wow!"

I'm hoping Jesus doesn't have a spam folder, or that's where many of my prayers would end up. If I want real communication with God, maybe I need to start with the kind of message I like to get from a friend or family member: "Hi—thinking of you this morning. Want to have lunch? I love you." Maybe I need to remember to begin and end each day with, "Thank you." Maybe I just need to turn off the phone—and my worrying thoughts—and listen.

—Mary W. Cox

Over and over as we read the lessons of our scriptural ancestors, we discover that prayer is about nurturing and building our relationship with God. But I began to wonder, why does Jesus pray? He is God, after all. What, I ask myself, does prayer do when it is God speaking to God?

That's when it hit me. Prayer is not just about getting to know God better; it's about getting to know myself better. Yes, prayer develops my relationship with God, helps me to know God. But it also helps me to know me. And just as getting to know God can be eye-opening, so can getting to know myself. Knowledge is power, and self-knowledge powers my best self. I get to know God as I pray, and I get to know me. Blessing upon blessing.

When I include in my prayers thanking my red cardinal for his morning song, nodding to Jupiter as it approaches the moon, and encouraging the brave little snowdrops in my garden, my landscape of spirituality opens up. When writing a condolence letter becomes as prayerful as writing in my journal, when walking with a friend is as prayerful as kneeling in church, when listening to someone's story is akin to hearing church bells, suddenly Paul's direction to pray without ceasing seems possible. Suddenly I don't want to do anything outside of that; suddenly prayer becomes as natural as breathing. Prayer in, prayer out.

—Susan Wyper

Our young adult group made Anglican rosaries as a fundraiser each year. It was one of my favorite things we did as a community. We taught new people to make them, and one rite of passage was that a rosary would fall apart while making it. It happened at least once every time we got together to make them.

There was one rosary pattern we called the devil rosary because every time we made it, it would fail for one reason or another. We tried everything, different stringing materials, different people stringing it, different tactics to secure it. Nothing worked. Sometimes it would stay together, then break when we took it out to sell it. It was a running joke within our community and became a challenge to us.

When making a prayer aid, it's customary to pray while your hands work, and we prayed over this rosary like we had never prayed before. Feeling guilty that our prayers were never nice, we decided to keep it as a reminder of our struggles and the bonding that happened while we made it. It was a sign that anger and disappointment were also a type of prayer. God hears the angry prayers too. Any healthy relationship has its trials, and our relationship with God can be no different. We need to pray without ceasing, and it's OK if those prayers aren't always pretty or perfect.

—Lauren Caldwell

I grew up as a Roman Catholic in Jamaica. My favorite month as a child was May. We had what were called May processions. We would take the six-foot statue of Mary from the church and parade around the neighborhood, as if the circus had come to town.

The procession always ended back at the church, with us crowning the statue of Mary with a garland of fresh flowers. We would have said at least 150 Hail Marys along the way. For the faithful, singing songs about Mary and saying the rosary as we walked was a special time. To this day, the Hail Mary is one of my favorite prayers.

The rosary is a great spiritual practice and gift; the repetition of a prayer, a spiritual thought, or a spiritual desire is a powerful way to remember who we are and whose we are. Repeating prayers offers us a chance to go deeper and deeper into the mystery of prayer and deepens our desire to love God. Repetition is indeed the mother of intention. May is a good time to spend praying the rosary.

—**Mark Bozzuti-Jones**

※

Hail Mary, full of grace, the Lord is with thee; blessed art thou amongst women, and blessed is the fruit of thy womb, Jesus. Holy Mary, Mother of God, pray for us sinners, now and at the hour of our death. Amen.

She'd ask, "How are you?" Having known her briefly, I was surprised at the words coming out of my mouth, more revealing than intended. Later, I said, "Pardon me, I'm telling you more than expected," and she responded, "There's something understood." Something understood…beyond acquaintance. She and I had jumped over small talk and landed in friendship.

Perhaps you've known a relationship in which understanding quickly felt full grown.

In her reply, my friend helped me comprehend something I had reread over several years. Fifteenth-century priest George Herbert wrote that prayer is the "heart in pilgrimage." Perhaps Herbert sensed the impossibility of describing prayer, concluding with prayer as "something understood" between the soul and God.

God asks, "And how are you?" Small talk with a scripted formula is not required. Once we perceive God's voice brimming with warm heartedness, there's no threat; freedom is total: from laughter and joy to tears, or from peace even to anger and back. At last, we feel at home. We may say more than we intended, but not more than God embraces. Our Creator awaits us, and finally in our space and in our time, we know profound acceptance. Something is understood.

—June Terry

We supplicate, we thank, we ask forgiveness, and we adore through our prayers, even though at times it can seem like a one-sided conversation. Some monks try to pray every minute of their waking lives. My mind gets distracted too easily: my attention is stolen by anything shiny or new.

This is where structure becomes important. Memorized prayer lets me focus on what it is I am praying, not on how I want to say it. It is almost like muscle memory.

The rosary is a good way for me to habitually pray. I am still not good at constant prayer, but at least I can use this series of memorized prayers to get a good chunk of prayer. The structure of the rosary makes it like a sonnet, something with concrete structure that allows the beauty of our deepest, most liminal thoughts to shine through.

—Spencer Hixon

)(

Please, please, God of my father, God of the heritage of Israel,
Lord of heaven and earth, Creator of the waters,
King of all your creation, hear my prayer!

—JUDITH 9:12

When my daughter was little, she had a stuffed animal we affectionately called "Huggy Puppy." Huggy Puppy went everywhere with Grace...and I do mean everywhere. The ratty, worn toy was her constant companion. He was Grace's best friend and confidant. Sometimes she talked to him, sometimes she interacted with him, and sometimes he just hung by her side. His constant presence was never a burden to her; it only brought peace and joy. She was always aware of his location and in the rare instance he had been misplaced or forgotten, she had an acute sense of urgency to find him again.

One day, I was watching Grace sleep with Huggy Puppy tucked under her arm, when it occurred to me the real meaning of "pray without ceasing." Paul isn't saying we are supposed to sit with our heads bowed in fixed conversation with the Lord every minute of the day but rather to live every day with a keen awareness that Jesus is with us. His constant and abiding presence is meant to bring us peace and joy, and even help when the need arises. He is there to guide. He is there to hear. He is there when we need to talk and when we are silent.

Don't get me wrong, I am not implying Jesus is like Huggy Puppy that we carry around for our own enjoyment. But Paul reminds us that acknowledging Jesus as our constant companion unleashes a power in our lives that is unimaginable.

—Bree Combs

There was a time in my life when I got so busy that I didn't have time to pray. Job, family, kids…the result was that I usually felt guilty. "Am I so busy that I can't take a little quiet time to be alone with God? Is my schedule so heavy that I can't take a moment now and again to offer prayers for friends and family and neighbors in need? Am I so important in the whole scheme of things that I can't take the time to thank God for all of the many blessings in my life?"

Well, the answer to all of those questions was a resounding "No," but my prayer life was still awful. So, I presented my dilemma to a friend whom I consider a spiritual mentor, a powerful example of someone who lives her Christian faith in an inspiring and meaningful way.

She smiled and told me that her prayer life had been pretty much reduced to two basic prayers that she repeated throughout the day. Life for her had also become very busy, very complex. "Please, share with me these prayers." I was so hopeful that I too would be able to pray them without ceasing and that my walk would become more meaningful, more centered on God's constant and abiding presence.

She smiled and said the first prayer is "Help." And the second one is "Thank you."

My prayer life still isn't all that I wish it would be, but it's a whole lot better.

—Jason Leo

My mom loves. She knows how to love. She has taught us all to love. And I think her greatest act of love is prayer.

She prays daily for each one of us in the family. She uses many methods—she wears different colored bracelets depending on our favorite color. I know that when she's wearing orange, she is praying for my son. I call these her prayer beads. She makes her prayer bracelets herself.

If you were to ask her to pray for you, she would! She will immediately make a prayer bracelet for you depending on your favorite color. I don't know how she can keep them all in order, but she does.

I also know that any tenth of any month or the time 10:10 will trigger her to think of me because my birthday is October 10. She does this for family, friends, and loved ones (and total strangers).

I have seen her kneeling at the foot of my bed, praying for God's favor and protection. I have seen her praying over items of clothing, food, gifts—all specifically for someone. She prays with her grandchildren who live with her—and anyone who has spent the night at her house, before they leave. She is the epitome of praying without ceasing.

—**Sandra Montes**

Be pleased, O God, to deliver me;
O LORD make haste to help me.

—PSALM 70:1

I learned something of the power of praying with a rosary in a small Roman Catholic chapel down the hall from where my mother was dying of cancer. Those who took care of the chapel had thoughtfully provided prayer cards and several rosaries, and I discovered that the traditional crucifix gave me unexpected comfort. "You knew suffering...be with my mother in her suffering," was sometimes the only prayer I could muster as I fingered the beads in my hand.

Later, as I became acquainted with Anglican prayer beads, I appreciated their versatility both in adapting to traditional rosary prayers and in constructing my own. I have even learned how to make my own prayer beads, not just the prayers. There is joy in choosing personally meaningful beads, stones, and crosses and in creating special rosaries for liturgical seasons or special events.

Several years ago I witnessed how a prayer bead workshop could bring together people in a congregation. Those who usually enjoyed book discussions strung their beads next to those who usually preferred crafts. Head, hands, heart, and spirit joined in the final prayers.

"Jesus...mercy...thanks..."—an intention, even if inarticulate or silent, on every bead.

—Joan Bowers

I'm comfortable with the idea of the Trinity. I don't mean to say that I could explain it theologically without (almost certainly) lapsing into heresy, but I do think that it's the only logical way to explain the different faces, facets, and characteristics that God presents to the world, without either going polytheistic and heretical or denying that Jesus is a part of the Godhead.

I'm comfortable with the concept of the Spirit, of Holy Wisdom, demonstrating the feminine side of the Godhead, a counterpoint to the oft-cranky God the Father (so swift to smite in the Hebrew Bible). I'm comfortable with Jesus, our brother, our friend, the approachable God in man made manifest.

With the three persons of the Trinity, to pray without ceasing becomes as seamless as shifting gears on my old Toyota. The Spirit guides us into truth, and we pray (if we have any sense at all) for wisdom. Jesus joins us on the road as our best companion and helper. God the Creator is all around us. I don't worry too much about the specific address. I just offer my prayer to God and know that it is heard.

—Sarah Bryan Miller

As a Benedictine oblate, I am encouraged to reflect on the Rule of Saint Benedict regularly. One of my favorite chapters of the Rule is 52, "On the Oratory of the Monastery." The monastery chapel is to be kept, Benedict says, as a sacred place, used only for its intended purpose as a place to pray without distractions.

Considered less literally, this chapter becomes a meditation on the challenge of creating our own sacred space for prayer. How do we find ways to pray that don't depend on a dedicated physical place? For many people, the answer is to simply use whatever quiet corner they can find at home, perhaps lighting a candle or using an icon to create an atmosphere of prayer.

Reading this chapter again recently put me in mind of another practice. The use of beads as a tool of prayer is part of a long tradition stretching far back through Christian history and through many other faiths as well. There is good reason why so many people have found prayer beads useful. You can pull them out anytime, anywhere, and the intention to pray in itself creates your sacred space. The act of carrying them with you can remind you to pray. We can make a chapel in our hearts and also with our hands.

—Kathleen M. Flanagan

Let my prayer enter into your presence;
incline your ear to my lamentation.

—Psalm 88:2

The honest and heartbreaking truth is that Doug doesn't know if I've been to see him today, yesterday, or last week. He no longer asks for me at all, much less the constant requests that characterized his early days at his new house. He is in transition, moving between sets of symptoms that define the stages of Alzheimer's. His disease is in constant motion. The most loving thing I can do for him is to allow that transition, to recognize the motion, and not fall into the temptation of trying to pull him back into a world to which he cannot stay connected, even when he tries desperately. It is hard not to drive over and see him.

Other than when Doug moved to his new house, this has been the hardest transition I have had to face. I didn't see this change coming the way I saw the move coming. Grasping to understand this change, wrestling with the abruptness of this move from one stage to the next has been profoundly hard. In spite of this bone-deep hurt, I keep finding comfort in the collected wisdom of caregivers and family members of other residents. They see Doug smiling, happy, at peace. It is a huge leap of faith to trust others to help him find those smiles, that happiness, a sense of peace, and to come to terms with knowing that he's OK without me, right now. It is hard knowledge, but it is also full of truth and love. Thanks be to God.

—Allison Zent Blankemeyer

I t is difficult to overestimate the power of touch.

In the first chapter of the Gospel of Mark, there is the wonderful tale of Jesus being approached by a leper begging to be healed. Lepers were shunned by all. They were, in every sense, untouchable. It is little wonder, then, that this leper pleaded with Jesus. "If you choose," he cried out, "you can make me clean" (1:40).

Reaching forth his hand, Jesus touched the leper, touched someone who had not known human touch for countless years. Only then did he reply, "I do choose. Be made clean!" No surprise to us, the man was made clean. But the real miracle, the truly profound healing, took place the moment that Jesus chose to reach out and touch the leper...before the man was clean.

This is what the Savior still does, touches us when we feel most untouchable. More than this, Jesus calls us to reach forth our hands in care and concern and deep respect, and in his Name to help those who do not feel loved to know deep inside their souls that God does indeed love them. In a spare moment during my day, as my fingers run across the smooth stones on my prayer beads and my lips utter words of hope and intercession, I am reminded that divine connection is never simply spiritual, it is also tangible, a gift I can bring to those who still cry out, "If you choose, God, you can make me clean."

—Chuck Robertson

People have been praying with beads, stones, or knots on a cord for millennia. Fingering the objects can help keep one's mind focused, and I'm interested in ways of being more centered and to bring my focus back if my mind wanders. Two women in our congregation, Kathy and Gina, make Anglican prayer beads. Kathy recently told me how she was introduced to praying with them while she was at a church retreat. She learned about the origin and meaning of the Anglican rosary beads and decided to make one for herself. She's made many since then.

Kathy beamed as she described how she loves to select the beads, feel them between her fingers and thumb, and to create something beautiful with an inner purpose. She prays as she selects each of the thirty-three beads, and as she strings one after the other.

I bought one of Kathy's Anglican rosaries. I selected one with amethyst beads that was small enough to easily fit in my pocket. Like her, I've prayed the suggested prayers and have also begun to expand its use to pray for others.

—Linda Gelbrich

We live in a technology-driven world full of devices to meet our needs or satisfy some desire. We rely on them to give us directions, manage our schedules, and keep us connected. From the first click of the morning, however, and with each subsequent click or stroke, their energy supply is being depleted. They constantly need recharging to function as designed.

We keep chargers in our homes, our cars, in our pockets, or in our purses to keep them running. We become frantic and frustrated when one can't be found, or when the battery is running low. We fear losing power.

Prayer is like those chargers. It allows us the same convenience and accessibility to God, our ultimate power source. Prayer keeps us charged and connected. It gives us power.

—Kathy H. Culmer

⋈

He was praying in a certain place, and after he had finished, one of his disciples said to him, "Lord, teach us to pray, as John taught his disciples." He said to them, "When you pray, say: Father, hallowed be your name. Your kingdom come. Give us each day our daily bread."

—LUKE 11:1-3

Our noontime collect reads, "Regard not our sins, but the faith of your Church" (*The Book of Common Prayer*, p. 107). I can really feel the church trying to live out its calling to "bear one another's burdens, and in this way, you will fulfill the law of Christ" (Galatians 6:2).

I am burdened with the long-term illness of my mother. I am burdened because of the way I treat my wife and kids when we are trying to get loaded into the car. I am burdened because intellectually, it is difficult for me to say the word virgin in the creed. I am burdened, I am burdened, I am burdened.

Our community of faith provides us with the strength to carry on. Even when we don't feel like it. Even when we didn't get enough sleep. Even when it just doesn't make sense to keep on believing, we do. Because I don't need much faith when I see the face of Christ turning around, offering me a hand saying, "Peace be with you."

Lord, I believe. Help my unbelief.

—Charles McClain

Rejoice in hope, be patient in suffering, persevere in prayer.

—ROMANS 12:12

While visiting my grandmother one hot summer day, a severe thunderstorm seemed to come out of nowhere. I was just a child then. The sound hurt my ears and the bright white bolts seemed to be aiming at the roof of Nana's one-story cottage. I had almost curled myself into a living ball of fright when she said, in her gentle Southern drawl, "Thunderstorms remind me of the power of God."

In one short sentence, she redirected my thoughts. I'm still afraid of thunderstorms, but it fills me with wonder to think that the deafening rumble is a hint of the power in God's voice. The psalmist wrote that "the God of glory thunders" (29:3), and God's voice splits cedar trees and causes oaks to writhe. Isaiah reports that the voices of seraphims were so powerful that they shook the thresholds of the great temple during the prophet's vision (6:4).

God's thunderous voice is heard just three verses into the Bible, when God says, "Let there be light." If angels' voices shook the enormous temple in Jerusalem, then imagine what the voice of God sounded like when speaking light into the heavens and earth. Everything must have writhed. Creation itself gives a vivid picture of the Trinity.

—**Susan Taylor Block**

How to pray and when to pray? When my mother died, there were no words. I found myself going through her things. Among them, I found a broken set of beads. Looking at and touching them gave me such comfort. Touching those beads kept me close to her and moved me through many painful hours.

One day, I was given a set of Anglican prayer beads by a friend with whom I shared spiritual conversations. The beads felt good in my hand and had meaning and depth. My friend explained to me that those who make the beads believe it is a prayerfully made ministry. Prayer upon prayer upon prayer goes into those beads.

The number of beads symbolize the life of Christ. The beads and cross are rich with reminders of the Holy Trinity, creation, and other markers of Christian life. At the touch of a finger, the beads bring body, soul, and spirit together.

—Karen Montagno

※

Almighty God, you proclaim your truth in every age by many voices: Direct, in our time, we pray, those who speak where many listen and write what many read; that they may do their part in making the heart of this people wise, its mind sound, and its will righteous; to the honor of Jesus Christ our Lord. Amen.

—THE BOOK OF COMMON PRAYER, P. 827

Please, God, not tonight. My baby's not ready. On the sweaty, plastic sheets of a hospital bed, I bartered with God. *I'll do anything, God. If you give my baby a few more weeks, a few more days, I will tell everyone. I will praise your name and shout from the rooftop about miracles of healing. Please.*

I prayed without ceasing through the night and over the next three weeks. Each day was a victory, a step closer to full term, a chance for the nervous system to mature and her lungs to strengthen.

First-time moms pray a lot, I suspect. I started before she was conceived as we worked with a fertility specialist. I dropped to my knees when he told us that I would likely miscarry. I prayed for the first twenty weeks until the doctor smiled. *This is why,* he said, *I'm a man of science and a man of faith.*

Madeline was born nearly five weeks early—but three weeks after the first sign of the potentially life-threatening toxemia. Neonatal specialists waited, but after a quick examination, they handed her to my husband. Our baby was healthy. And wailing.

I don't know why some prayers are answered and others seem to fall short. I don't know why my child thrived, and another mother sang a lullaby to her stillborn daughter. I don't understand the ways of God and the intersection of pain and loss. But the not knowing, the not understanding will not keep me from praying.

At her baptism, after we wiped the water from her crown and the tears from our eyes, I reached for the microphone. I didn't plan to make a speech; I'm from a restrained denomination. But God answered my prayers, and I had made a promise. I turned to the congregation. *I'd like to tell you about the power of prayer.*

—**Richelle Thompson**

JUNE

Singing

Now it is your unquestionsed desire to sing of God whom you love, but you ask me how to sing God's praises…you wish to know what praises to sing…If you desire to praise God, then live what you express. Live good lives, and you yourselves will be God's praise.
—Saint Augustine of Hippo (Sermon 34)

Those Who Sing
Pray Twice

INTRODUCTION   *Those Who Sing Pray Twice*

Behavioral biologists suggest that over five thousand different species of living creatures sing. Some of the singing species are capable not only of singing but also of composing and improvising songs. Knowing this, when we sing the words, "All nature sings and 'round me rings the music of the spheres," (*The Hymnal 1982*, p. 651), we can sing the song with a whole different understanding. Maybe this is what Saint Augustine meant when he said that people who sing pray twice. When we sing, we praise with our individual voice the God of our personal understanding but we also join our voice with the other voices in all of creation who sing out when they are joyful, searching, weeping, praising.

WAYS TO ENGAGE

Learn a new song.

Sing as part of your devotional time.

Learn to play your favorite song on the instrument of your choice.

Make a play list of your favorite songs to listen to during your quiet time this month.

Music and singing have been part of my life for as long as I can remember. I can tell you a whole chapter of my life just based around songs I learned at camp, or VBS, or James Taylor's *Greatest Hits* album. Something special and holy happens when we sing, something different from just talking. I'm sure the smart folks who study neurobiology and audiology could explain it scientifically, but for me, singing is different because it comes from your heart, out of your mouth, and into the world.

There's a special intention when we sing—even if we're singing under our breath to calm our nerves, or a little louder to calm the baby, or louder still to call a room to order. Some people are gifted with golden throats, and others of us croak like God's own precious frogs, but all of us, at one time or another have thrown back our heads and sung at the top of our lungs. In those moments of pure worship, joy, and abandon, I imagine the whole host of heaven joining in with us, singing the songs of love, joy, ongoing creation, and awe that fill the whole universe.

Even if you croak like a peeper, my prayer is that you will find a song to sing, full-throated and unashamed, even if it's in the shower, to a God who loves you beyond your wildest hopes and dreams.

—**Rachel Jones**

Everyone in my life knows that I'm a singer. I sing to myself (and to others, if I'm being honest) all day, every day. I sing "good morning" to my daughter. I sing "I'm filling up your food bowl" to my cats. I sing "please speed up, you're blocking the fast lane" to drivers in front of me on the interstate.

Everyone in my life also knows that I'm not a gifted singer. When God made this voice, the mold was broken—and with good reason. I think I used to be a good singer; at least, I was in the elementary school choir. But in my teen years, I totally lost whatever ability I had to carry a tune. In the middle school choir, I was always strategically positioned as far away from the microphones as possible, for fear my belting would actually reach the ears of the crowd. Eventually, I grew hip to the fact that I was never getting any of the solos I auditioned for, and I stopped trying.

I'm uncomfortable singing in church to this day. I've heard enough snarky comments about tone-deaf people ruining the worship experience, so I usually open the hymnal and follow along, quietly. I feel intimidated by the beautiful voices all around me. So I wait, and I walk to my car, and I sing. I sing at the top of my lungs, and I know that God hears me and smiles.

—**Holli Powell**

When my friend Jack asked me how I learned to draw and paint, I told him that I didn't. I learned to see. Jack is a musician, and while we were roommates, he showed me that the reality of being a musician isn't far from that of being a visual artist. You learn to be a musician not by technical expertise alone but by learning to listen and feel.

I was lucky enough to be encouraged and sang with numerous choirs and singing groups throughout my childhood and adolescence. But music for me was a stressful, laborious task that, while proud of the result, I never felt confident in my offering.

What Jack taught me was to listen to the unique character of my voice, to follow the rhythms that felt right in my bones, to create harmonies that made me smile, not to imitate or replicate someone else's music. In this freedom, I found myself enjoying music and liberating the music in others; I found that I had my own songs to sing.

There is freedom when you play or sing such that it feels right in the very marrow of your bones. The reality is that the chorus of creation doesn't sing with one voice. It hums with billions of voices, each carrying a song of praise only they can bring to the Creator.

—Jason Sierra

There is something powerful about music that originates in the spirit. There is also something about suffering that calls forth an almost primally sacred need to sing away suffering, or sometimes, sing into the space of suffering.

I spent one Memorial Day on Pine Ridge Reservation for a Taizé pilgrimage of trust—a gathering intended for young adults to come together in sacred space to raise voices in song with others from the Taizé tradition and persons from the Native community.

Deep into a canyon on the edge of the church property, we chanted each morning, noon, and night. Deeper into the night, we were offered the sacred expression of the Lakota people by being called with song and dance indigenous to their communities.

This offering was the first such gathering since 1973, when a standoff between the United States military and Native people fractured trust and relationships.

We healed, reconciled, and wrestled with the history of church and state, Native persons and Anglo-Americans through contemplative song. In shared community we found a way to surpass the pain of our collective pasts without ignoring the pain of history by living into the suffering and offering songs of joy and lament in equal measure.

From the canyon chants in the tradition of Taizé to the rhythms of native drums, we were called together into the midst of the sacred—without judgment, without hate, and beyond rage—into some kind of sacred beat we carved out together, amid the backdrop of the sacred Black Hills.

—Teresa Pasquale

One of the churches I work for held a Sunday morning discussion about youth and mainstream media. At one point, the conversation turned to rap music and how awful and distasteful it can sometimes seem. It was as this point that I pointed out two sides to the rap music argument: yes, some rap music is terrible and distasteful. On the other hand, rap music began as an opportunity for young people to vocalize their opinions about the reality of the world around them. Rap has been so influential throughout the last four decades that, when asked who the greatest poet of Generation X was, Noble laureate Seamus Heaney suggested Marshall Mathers, also known as rapper Eminem.

Chants, hymns, and songs have been a part of the church since its inception. They give worshipers an opportunity to praise and experience God on another level. They give depth to the words that have been spoken about God throughout millennia. Most importantly, music gives us a way to express our personal relationship with God, an opportunity to speak directly to God regarding our feelings about our life and environment and how we see God in it. And the beauty is that there is no wrong way to sing about God's love and praise in our lives.

Priest and musician John Newton wrote, "I once was lost, but now am found, was blind but now I see."

Rapper and producer Kanye West said something very similar: "I'm just trying to say the way school needs teachers, the way Kathie Lee needed Regis, that's the way I need Jesus."

—Longkee Vang

The universe's rules are based on mathematics, so it makes sense that people use math to create prayer through music. Most art, I suppose, can be expressed in mathematical terms by people who know what they are doing, but I feel that even I can comprehend numbers when I listen to music. I can hear the instrument creating vibrations; if I could slow down the vibrations, I could count them. I can number the beats, and I could conceivably measure the ratios between notes. Music makes mathematics into something that we can hear, and then we use that language to bring ourselves closer to God.

The sound of voices lifted in harmony is both an excellent metaphor for what the Christian experience should be like and a powerful prayer experience in its own right. The music elevates us, and the words combined with the music can knock us right out of the spiritual ballpark. My favorite hymns, "Not Here for High and Holy Things" and "Let All Mortal Flesh," combine haunting music with powerful images and poetry. When I worship using those hymns, every part of me prays at the same time—body, soul, mind, heart. I don't always pray easily because I tend to overthink prayers, but when I sing these hymns, prayer flows out of me freely without my thinking about it at all.

—Elizabeth Brignac

Be joyful in the LORD, all you lands;
serve the LORD with gladness and
come before his presence with a song.

—PSALM 100:1

I struggle with my faith on an almost daily basis. I'm very empathetic to atheists and humanists, though not the angry militants. They need more dietary fiber. In some of my darkest moments, certain music brings me from a point of no return. It saves me from what Dante described as hell, an endless conversation with myself.

Several of Richard Wagner's religiously themed music dramas have a significant, empowering influence on my spiritual life. Wagner, with moral and ethical challenges, possessed a brilliance to express faith, rebirth, purity, renewal, divinity, forgiveness, and redemption in the music he composed and the librettos he crafted. Wagner's *Tannhäuser* is a divine liturgy. It's another example not to limit or contain the experience of holiness within four walls on Sunday and to seek sacred inspiration in the unlikely.

Music comforts the heart and soul. It's a spiritual balm, an experience to keep in check the brain's persistent, dastardly, rational, and intellectual functions. It washes away like a soothing bath the nonsensical realities of life. What the soul feels is sometimes more important than the mind's pursuit of logic and common sense.

—Paul Jesep

During my first semester of seminary, the American composer and arranger Alice Parker was the musician-in-residence. I quickly became a fan.

We all thought we knew how to sing together. Wasn't music a part of nearly every service? But Alice taught us how to sing in a different way than I'd ever sung before. She didn't give us a sheet with words on it or a sheet with musical notations. She just walked around in front of us and sang to us and asked us to sing back to her. And we didn't just sing in unison—different sections sang different parts, and some sections came in at different times. We just followed along and sang with Alice, and sang to Alice, and sang for Alice. The result was a sense of community that had not existed when we were singing out of the hymnals. Pretty soon, Alice was opening the gates for us to sing to God, to give God thanks and praise in a new way.

We sang from our hearts, lifting them up to God with and through our voices. It was beautiful.

—Penny Nash

X

And the ransomed of the LORD shall return,
and come to Zion with singing.

—ISAIAH 35:10

Roosters were still snoozing when I perched atop a clothesline pole in our backyard singing songs from *The King and I*. I wanted to sound just like Deborah Kerr.

I was mesmerized by Kerr's British accent—a soft sound so different from my pesky Texas twang. Wanting to sound British is something I never outgrew. I went to England and earned a master's degree in voice and accent coaching. Finally, I could speak in a posh British accent—kind of. There's always a bit of the Texan drawl lurking.

But I learned something more important than a British accent during college. I discovered what the Brits call our "signature note." One famous voice coach says it's the note we cry out when we're born—a sound as individual as our fingerprints. When we're grounded in our signature note, we're centered in who we are. The stresses of life slowly disconnect us from that note.

Some days, I suspect my special note was miffed about all the stuff I'd piled on top of it. But when you meet up with your signature note again, nothing short of a miracle happens. You're reconnected with what God gave you when you were born. And when you speak or sing good words, it's like praying twice.

—Charlotte Chere Graham

We began our day joining in the daily devotions with fifteen trust officers who had 4,375 clients to manage in this particular nonprofit Carribbean office. Hands were clapping, a tambourine was playing, eyes were closed, and voices were loud. They did not need the song book. "We can touch the world and make it better; do your part, and we will touch the world," they sang heartily. While what seemed like a monsoon was pouring outside, there were smiles, warm welcomes, and lots of singing inside.

Later, we followed our guide down a muddy trail down a sloping, uneven path, into a valley with no paved roads. After two visits to homes in a barrio, two trust officers led the way back up the hill, continuing to smile, without umbrella or raincoat and their bootless feet covered with mud.

Back on the bus, the trust officers began to sing songs unfamiliar to me and not found in an Episcopal hymnal. Even in our muddy and wet conditions and across the barriers of culture and language, we found the holy tune and spirit-filled rhythm of praise. There on the bus I realized Saint Augustine of Hippo got it right when he wrote, "Singing belongs to one who loves."

—Westina Matthews

I began playing the piano at age six. Throughout elementary, middle school, and college, I've had a number of wonderful piano teachers. The one who had the most impact was Sister Emelene Matocha, a Roman Catholic nun from whom I received one-on-one instruction in college.

Sister Emelene was from Kyle, Texas, and had entered the convent at seventeen to study music. She was an exacting teacher with an affinity for Bach, and she made it clear that entering the convent at seventeen had been very, very hard. She poured that hardship into her music, and as a result, even her classical playing had the unmistakable quality of soul.

Over the years, Sister Emelene and I became close, so it was a surprise to me when she had some harsh words one day. I'd just finished playing a Bach prelude (I can't remember which)—a piece I'd practiced over and over again and was especially proud of. After a long silence, she at last said, "You need to find your soul." While my playing was technically fine, it was not soulful.

That truth hurt, but it was also transformative. How I went about finding my soul is another story for another time. Her point (now mine) is that making music is about so much more than just notes on the page. Like any good spiritual practice, making music demands nothing less than profound transformation. It forces us to find our souls and to bear them with deep love.

—**Miguel Escobar**

My grandmother was a music teacher and church organist. By the time I was two years old, I had a beautifully illustrated book of hymns for children, which included not only the obvious, "Jesus Loves Me," but also such unlikely choices as "Work, for the Night Is Coming" and "Abide with Me."

I was happy to stand up and sing these in Sunday School, and as soon as I was old enough, I joined my church's junior choir. I could hit the high notes on pitch and memorized quickly, so I was often asked to be one of the little sopranos who sang descants. I loved the sound of voices in harmony.

Youth choir, senior choir, high school and college choruses, even the Atlanta Choral Guild—if there was a singing group that could use another soprano with a small voice, I was there. And always, I sang in church choirs.

Rather rapidly, my voice got old—thinner, a little squeaky, less reliable. The pretty notes simply aren't always there at my command. I still sing in the choir, but there are times when I grieve for the lost soaring descants of my childhood voice. I do not always enjoy the sound of my own voice now. But when I'm moping about how bad I sound, the Holy Spirit chides: "Do you really think you're singing for you?" When God's the audience, every voice has a place in the choir.

—Mary W. Cox

There is glory in the strains of "Jesus Christ is Risen Today" as they triumphantly fill the sanctuary on Easter Day. And there is equal power in the measures of "For All the Saints" sung tearfully by grieving families at the funeral of a loved one. Music touches us at a deep and sacred place, a place that scientists are only now plumbing but which God has known from the beginning.

It is no wonder that the angst-ridden adolescent years are the years when music means the most to us. While we adults are tempted to yank those ever-present earbuds out of our teenagers' ears, we might instead seek to appreciate how that music is helping them find their place in the world.

The world is singing. The words of the old Coke commercial sound in my ears, "I'd like to teach the world to sing, in perfect harmony." We need to open our ears to hear it: the song of the birds, the wind, our neighbors, our children. The world's score is large enough to give us each a solo section, if only we will stop and listen to one another.

—Susan Wyper

)X(

The LORD, your God, is in your midst, a warrior who gives victory; he will rejoice over you with gladness, he will renew you in his love; he will exult over you with loud singing.

—ZEPHANIAH 3:17

My three year old sings "Happy Birthday" to someone almost daily. Whether it is actually your birthday is not important. If she wants to make you happy, out comes that song. Part of the reason she does this is to witness your pretending to blow out candles and shove cake in your face, but the biggest part of it is because she has associated this act with love. When people sing that song, it is usually followed by clapping and cheers, and in her limited understanding, there is no difference between singing "Happy Birthday" and giving a big hug.

I believe God feels the same way about songs. When you get in your car, put on your favorite song, and sing with reckless abandon, God cheers. When you sing in the shower with no music at all while making a shampoo mohawk, God claps. When you stand in a pew and sing slightly off-tune, God feels a warm embrace. There's a certain happiness that comes from singing that is both a gift from God and a gift to God.

It's hard to sing without sloughing off energy and emotion, a release as valuable as crying or screaming (which I think are two of the most beautiful types of prayer). Imagine if we all prayed with the gusto with which we sing. Imagine that chorus in heaven! I think God hopes we will pray that way.

—**Lauren Caldwell**

During their captivity and bondage, generations of African slaves sang songs called spirituals. Imagine a faith amidst oppression that fueled a desire for slaves to call out to God in song. The slaves sang other kinds of songs, but the songs to God have garnered the most interest, perhaps because they epitomized a confidence in God made manifest, even in the worst of times.

Throughout life, we see and experience suffering and pain. As we learn from the Israelites in captivity and the enslaved Africans, no matter what we are going through, we can find a way to sing to God. The spirituals remind us of the importance of singing out loud and singing out of every experience. Whether we feel alone, abandoned, hopeless, happy, victorious, or blessed, we are called to sing to God.

Researchers who study spirituals agree that the slaves sang in order to remind themselves to never stop working for their freedom, to remember that God loved them and wanted them to be free.

The person of faith who sings is called to commit actions of justice and love. The saying that the person who sings prays twice is a reminder to all of us that, every time we sing to God, we must recommit to working twice as hard for justice for all.

—Mark Bozzuti-Jones

Perhaps you've said, "I can't carry a tune in a bucket." No bucket needed. I know a vocal coach who helps people who are convinced they can't carry a tune. When I met this coach, I was sixty. I could sing but learned by sitting next to her in the church choir, September through May. Twelve years of rehearsals multiplied by forty weeks annually? About 480 lessons. Sneaking peeks to observe her, I listened carefully. I tried pulling air toward the back of my palette, as she did, not pushing it forward. Was I more listenable after I moved away? Here's hoping.

I sang heartily when other tourists were absent while I walked miles on the Isle of Iona in Scotland, and my songs were accepted by woolly sheep and Highland cattle. The congregation of animals stayed nearby, curiously tilting their heads. Borrowing hymn-tunes, I sang my own words to express grief, verses that changed intermittently to full-voiced thanks to God, our ever-present strength and comfort.

You want to sing? Find a coach, or cows and sheep. Above all, find the psalms. Take the words to heart, and you will find a tune in your soul to sing with all your heart.

—June Terry

Music has always been a major part of my life. My mother taught piano out of the home for more years than I have been alive. My father would go down to the basement and practice Bach on his organ. During the evening hours, music was a constant companion.

My first experimentation with music was singing. This is probably true for most of us. I joined my church's youth choir and took voice lessons. Today I even lend my voice to sing with the little ones at my daughter's school.

Becoming a father has a way of changing one's perspective. My daughter loves music. At only four years old, she has yet to master her own voice, but this doesn't stop her from breaking into spontaneous song at the drop of a hat. At night, I can hear her singing to her stuffed animals instead of sleeping.

Watching her love of music has helped me appreciate the musical thread in others as well. From our church soloist to parishioners around me, we each raise our voices in worship, and one's ability to sing should never get in the way of one's passion to sing. British novelist Lawrence Durrell wrote, "Music is only love looking for words." No wonder those who sing pray twice!

—Spencer Hixon

I believe God wires our bodies to acknowledge greatness in outward expression. When we glimpse who God is, when we see, hear, and feel how majestic and mighty and powerful God is, our bodies, voices, hands, and hearts can't sit still. They aren't supposed to. In Luke 19, Jesus tells the Pharisees that if the disciples were to quiet their praise, the stones themselves would cry out. If a stone can proclaim the praise of God, so can you and I.

Everything in creation confirms that our bodies are wired to promote, praise, glorify, extol, revere, bless, and worship the God who created them. Maybe you won't use your voice. It may sound like applause or a groan. It could be a laugh, a cry, a bellow, or a gasp. Maybe it will sound like a ball bouncing, fingers on a keyboard, or the ring of a telephone.

I don't know what it will look or sound like for you; I don't even know how it will always look or sound for me. But, I do know that when *El Shaddai*, the All-Sufficient God, meets us in our humanity, we can't sit still or be quiet any more than the stones can.

—Bree Combs

X

For this I will extol you, O LORD,
among the nations, and sing praises to your name.

—2 SAMUEL 22:50

Saint Augustine of Hippo once said that people who sing pray twice. My family says a prayer before every meal. When my oldest son was three, he liked to sing the Johnny Appleseed song—always with everyone holding hands—and with quite a bit of gusto, I might add. I always admired his enthusiasm, even when he wasn't too happy about the food that was coming his way.

Once, we were in a fast food restaurant. He was really excited about the food, especially the toy that came with it. We were all about to dive into burgers and fries when the little guy started yelling: "Song, Song, Song!" I tried to explain to him that a quiet prayer would be more appropriate, but he was unbending. "Song!" he yelled, drawing quite a bit of attention. So we all joined hands and sang the song, and it felt like the whole restaurant stopped and stared.

When it was over, he was so proud. A woman at the table next to us smiled, as did many others. I don't remember what we talked about or the toy that my son was given with the meal. But I do remember the day we thanked God for the food with a song—and the blessing that we received.

—Jason Leo

I love to sing, and I love to sing to Jesus. I have seen God's unlimited power firsthand. I have been healed. I have been transformed, and I have been forgiven. I sing because I am happy, and I am free. I also sing because I have a gift God has given me. It is not always easy to sing; it is not always fun, and it sometimes feels as though I am carrying people—and they are heavy.

I sing because there is no better way for me to thank God. There have been many instances in my life where, after an unpleasant or trying situation, all I can do is sing—not always words, not always songs, but sounds and melodies that come out of the situation. I have often told my music teammates that sometimes I just want to run around the church, throw myself on the ground, jump, yell, or cry as I'm singing.

They laugh and say I should, but I am often wary of others' reactions, not because I am ashamed but because I know I have a responsibility when I am leading people in worship. I am aware some people go to church expecting to be fed, entertained, or fulfilled. And when I feel weary or tired or upset because of this, I go to God and ask for God's power to be revealed in my life and for God to sing through me.

—**Sandra Montes**

When a 1960s radio station plays Roy Orbison, I am transported not just to my youth but to a realm of the ineffable and the transcendent. The titles alone, such as "I'm Hurtin'" and "Running Scared," speak to the human condition. And has there ever been a voice better suited to express our yearnings than Ray Orbison's as it reaches, reaches, and reaches for the high notes?

The whole body of Leonard Cohen's work reveals a search for meaning and connection carried out over decades. Haven't we all met—or been—"some Joseph looking for a manger"? Two of my favorite books—a murder mystery and a work on writing as a spiritual practice—share the title *How the Light Gets In*, borrowed from Cohen's haunting song, "Anthem."

Probably no singer has affected me more than jazz singer Dianne Reeves, whom I once heard in solo performance. Her very presence filled an entire auditorium of listeners transported by her powerful yet intimate voice. She brought the crowd to their feet with her feminist anthem "I Am an Endangered Species," but she also sang of her spiritual journey: "I am a curious spirit child who fell to Earth through a crack of lightning. But God, so kind and merciful, sent old souls to guide me home."

As I listen to singers such as these, I give thanks for the "old souls" of music whose voices reach out and speak to my own soul.

—**Joan Bowers**

According to my parents, I sang tunefully almost from infancy. My first solo came at age five. I joined the girls' choir at church in second grade, and, always in vestments, I never did learn to dress properly for church. In junior high, my gym teacher liked my singing and adjusted my grade accordingly. (Thank you, Lord.) At an enormous high school in a strange city, my voice helped me find a place. In college, singing beat waiting tables as a way of earning money. For more than twenty years, I made my living singing opera before turning to the dark side—music criticism.

Now, as in childhood, I sing for love, out of need, to make a connection with the Deity, and with little concern for the state of my sinuses. We have an excellent church choir with high standards, and we offer up our voices.

It's not just the act of singing, but the act of singing with others, of blending, of joining our voices in worship that makes me feel so good. The combination of the right words with the right music adds to our understanding of God. In singing, we become more than the sum of our parts and, somehow, a part of the Eternal Song.

—Sarah Bryan Miller

The bells woke me. It was 5:30 a.m., according to the tiny clock by my bed. Winter constellations hung low in the sky. Fifteen minutes till Lauds.

The retreat house bed was warm, and I was half awake. But if I missed Lauds, that beautiful early morning office that Benedictine monks have chanted for centuries, I knew I would be sorry. The chanting, I'd come to realize, had an effect on me I couldn't quite describe. Each time I chanted with the monks, I could feel it healing and uplifting me, pushing my ego out of the way so the words could pray themselves.

Singing as a spiritual discipline need not be limited to monasteries. Does the idea of such a discipline seem strange? I thought so too until one year I decided to make a Lenten discipline of learning one new hymn each week. As I practiced each day in the car, in the shower, or while walking, I began to sense that the same process I'd experienced on retreat was happening again. Even the somber hymns took me to a place of prayer, pulling me away from the day's distractions. Certain phrases would often linger, coming back to me later in the day just when I needed them.

—Kathleen M. Flanagan

They shall come and sing aloud on the height of Zion, and they shall be radiant over the goodness of the LORD.

—JEREMIAH 31:12

197

Life continues to try to teach me daily—often many times a day—how to pray for guidance, how to do the next right thing, and then how to let go of the outcome. This practice has proven time and time again to be as challenging as it is rewarding.

Most recently I have found myself having to focus especially hard on the "letting go" part. This morning, in an effort to come up with a new mantra for this exercise, I found myself thinking about the acronym for "let go of the outcome," LGOTO. When I sounded out the letters, they reminded me of the word *legato*, which I recognized as a musical term but could not remember what it meant. When I looked it up, this is what I found: In music performance and notation, *legato* (Italian for "tied together") indicates that musical notes are played or sung smoothly and connected.

Wow! How perfect!!! Yes, when I let go of the outcome and surrender the results, I am indeed tied together with something far greater and more beautiful than I could ever imagine on my own. Life goes so much more smoothly, and I am joyfully connected to the music of the universe. Oh, how I love these precious "aha" moments!

—Allison Zent Blankemeyer

*T*he *Book of Common Prayer* is over four and a half centuries old. That is pretty incredible. More incredible still is the fact that the Psalter portion of it is actually over three thousand years old! The psalms are our first hymnal, complete with 150 songs of joy and sorrow and fear and longing and praise.

The Lord is my shepherd.

My God, my God, why have you forsaken me?

I lift up my eyes to the hills; from where is my help to come?

As the deer longs for the water-brooks, so longs my soul for you, O God.

God is our refuge and strength, a very present help in trouble.

By the waters of Babylon we sat down and wept.

I will thank you because I am marvelously made!

Whether chanting a psalm alongside my fellow worshipers on a Sunday morning or leafing through *The Book of Common Prayer* and singing one to myself during the middle of the day, those ancient hymns give clear expression to the feelings deep within me. Just when I think I am all alone in whatever I am going through, just when I think that no one else can ever understand what is going on inside me, I look at the psalms and find my deepest prayers in the old words. The psalmist's words become my own. I sing, and three-thousand-year-old songs are fresh and alive once more.

—Chuck Robertson

I have friends who joke about only moving their lips, saying they can't carry a tune. But I love the idea of singing as making a joyful noise, and it's made with the instrument we carry with us.

Are there songs you have a hard time not singing? I love going to concerts where the lead singer invites the audience to sing along when a well-known song is played. Are there hymns from childhood that still bring a smile when you hear them, like, "All Things Bright and Beautiful," or "Fairest Lord Jesus"?

I remember a few years ago my husband and I joined with dozens of others one evening, all of us with candles lit. We met outside the home of a man who was to leave the next morning for cancer treatment in another state. He was weak, and both he and his wife were frightened. We began singing "You've Got a Friend," Carole King's song popularized by James Taylor, loud enough for them to hear through the door. They opened the door and heard their friends singing. They heard, "When you're down and troubled and you need a helping hand. Close your eyes and think of me and soon I will be there to brighten up even your darkest nights…you've got a friend." We sang, cried, and hugged them. It was a way of blessing them on their journey.

—Linda Gelbrich

By musical standards, my mother could not sing a note, but oh, how she loved to sing! And I loved to hear her sing. It wasn't about the sound or about the words but about the joy with which she sang. Whether standing over the sink, stirring a pot, or moving about the kitchen, the words rose up from somewhere deep within, moving her and moving along with her, as they made their way into open air.

My own joy came from knowing that she was feeling good in her soul when she sang. The songs were almost always hymns. She sang to God and about God. The freedom with which she sang and her devotion to her subject made her singing nothing short of prayer. They were her adoration, petition, and thanksgiving all rolled into song. The lyrics of the hymns just gave her the words to say. When close enough, I could sometimes feel some of what she was feeling too.

My mother had her silent prayers too, the ones she didn't say out loud or share, the ones where her eyes were closed and her lips moved quietly. Her singing was just another way of giving voice to those prayers.

Whatever the prayers of our hearts, O God, and whatever their expression, may they always be a sweet, sweet sound in your ear. Amen.

—**Kathy H. Culmer**

We are invited to a life of praise, no matter where we find ourselves. The life that we live is our song. It is our little piece of creation. Whether you swing a hammer, crack a book, cook a meal, saw a fiddle, or drive a truck, you are invited to sing your song. And it can be a new song. God offers love to you every day, new every morning in faithfulness.

If you are like me, it ends up being the little things that draw me into singing my prayers. Like sitting in my car, in the driveway, after a long day, and praying, "Lord, have mercy on me, a sinner." And the song echoes back, and instead of guilt or a wall of shame, I feel my burden lightened. Thanks be to God for the songs we sing—and the times when God sings back.

—**Charles McClain**

)(

Are any among you suffering? They should pray.
Are any cheerful? They should sing songs of praises.

—JAMES 5:13

Those Who Sing Pray Twice

I'll never forget the day I first saw Ms. Roz. I was around twelve, sitting in church with my mom. She was tall, with a dark suit and high heels. Her long, thick hair hung straight down her back. She's so elegant, I thought to myself as we stood to sing a hymn. And then, she started singing.

It seemed like the world stopped and started at the same time. I had never heard anyone sing like Roz was singing, except on a record. The notes soared up, coasting right up to God, it seemed. I just kept thinking, "This lady is not real. She's got to be some kind of star or something." She turned, smiled, and gave me the sign of peace. I was in awe.

Roz joined the choir and sang many solos. As an aspiring singer myself, I dreamed about singing like Roz. I didn't just want to sing like her, I wanted to do everything like her. She was a teacher, and she sewed; she had the ultimate fashion sense, and on top of all of that, she was beautiful. She was the epitome of everything I thought I wanted to be.

I sang in the church choir, and I had a great voice. But I could never get my voice to sound like Roz. My dreams and plans to have a career in music changed. I would never be as good as Roz.

What I did learn is that God loves *my* voice. God created it to give praise, not to sound like everyone else. No matter how good you think your voice is, remember: God uniquely designed your voice, and it's part of what makes you *you*. That means it's great!

—Miriam McKenney

I am not a morning person. It is rare that I feel like singing or writing poetry. One morning I woke up with a surprising sense of joy, and I wrote this poem. This morning was different. I woke with lifted spirits, and I took notice. This is what I wrote:

> I don't always sing
> But today like some lone bird
>   perched in a spacious place
> Morning beams
> Open the lips of my heart
> And my voice rises in song.

That day I realized that singing gave a melody to my prayer, and it was one of praise and thanksgiving! Through my voice and surprised ears, I experienced the beginning of the day in a new way. Since that day, I have learned that singing (or listening to singing) expresses the depths of my heart, gratitude, deep desires, rawness, and joy.

—Karen Montagno

Almighty and eternal God, so draw our hearts to you, so guide our minds, so fill our imaginations, so control our wills, that we may be wholly yours, utterly dedicated to you; and then use us, we pray, as you will, and always to your glory and the welfare of your people; through our Lord and Savior Jesus Christ. Amen.

—The Book of Common Prayer, p. 832-833

Journaling

Keep my commandments and live,
keep my teachings as the apple of your eye;
bind them on your fingers,
write them on the tablet of your heart.
—Proverbs 7:2-3

The Tablet of Your Heart

Writing down our thoughts, feelings, and prayers is a special kind of gift. In the grand scheme of things, written language is a fairly new way to express human thought. For millennia, the people who knew how to read and write were an exalted class—they had the power of words, the power of information. As literacy has spread, the ability to concretely share our ideas, desires, thoughts, revelations, and deepest hopes have become tangible lifelines to millions of people who might otherwise feel voiceless and alone. We hear God ask us to write things on our heart, we hear Daniel tell us about the writing on the wall, we see the black and white on the pages of our Bibles, and we marvel that those words have made it all the way down to being read by our eyes, understood in our hearts. Journaling isn't committing all your deepest and darkest thoughts to the page nor is it a dare to write down all your craziest dreams and ambitions. It's both of those things, and neither of those things. Journaling is a discipline that asks us to sit with our thoughts, write them down without judgment, and let them be.

WAYS TO ENGAGE

If you have never journaled before, start small. Begin by writing notes on a pad before or after your devotional time each day. Write about whatever comes to your head, even if you feel like it doesn't make sense.

If you're an old hand at journaling, consider keeping one that is specifically devoted to prayer requests, dreams, travel, or another topic important to you.

If you are moved by the idea of journaling, try making lists of words or ideas that you want to remember for further reflection or deeper prayer time.

When we packed up our house in Houston to move to Cincinnati, the boxes and packing tape found their way into my dreams. In a fit of anxiety, I bolted downstairs in the middle of the night to check on a box I couldn't remember labeling. I became suddenly and utterly convinced (in that three-in-the-morning way) that I had thrown away my journals—all of them, including the one I'd started when I was thirteen.

The box, predictably, was sitting in the middle of the room, top flaps open. The cool rush of relief washed over me as I saw the collection of journal spines jutting out. I picked up the little blue one and thumbed through the pages.

I can follow those lines back a long way and find myself encouraged to keep going, keep writing, keep loving, and keep recording the way God is telling a story of love in the midst of my own perfectly ordinary life.

—Rachel Jones

When I was a child, I carefully opened my journal each day, took out the same pen (one could never journal in the same notebook with different pens), and wrote out the date, followed by the words, "Dear Diary." Dear Diary. That simple framing helped me begin the complicated process of translating inner turmoil or confusion into coherent words and phrases. If I was writing a letter, then I had to explain the situation, and in order to explain the situation, I had to get my own head around what I wanted to say. Without that opening salutation, I couldn't put pen to page.

I still write most of my journal entries in the form of a letter, but today it's usually a letter to God. My journaling takes different forms—it's just as likely to be in the Evernote online application or on the back of a church bulletin as it is to be in one of many journals scattered around my home, office, and car. Thankfully, I've let go of that weird pen thing, but the framing remains the same. My most fervent, most heartfelt, most in-depth prayers have been the ones I've set down on paper (or computer screen).

—Holli Powell

Ж

Keep these words that I am commanding you today in your heart. Write them on the doorposts of your house and on your gates.
—Deuteronomy 6:6, 9

Memories are fickle things. Scientists have shown that each time we recall an event, we essentially recreate the memory. With each recreation, our memory becomes less exact, its edges rounded off, the story more coherent with the rest of our narrative lives and the context around the story less reliable.

As I reflect on my own spiritual growth, I cannot help but wonder whether the way I remember my faith as a teen is accurate. What didn't I know then? How did I think? What did I care about? With such uncertainty, it is difficult to trace the roots of my faith, to lean on any solid trunk of my personal spiritual history. The only concrete keys I have to my own spiritual history are those glimpses into my eighteen-year-old psyche provided by things I wrote: letters, essays, stories, and journals.

I write because I need to get things down on paper, because it gives me a chance to look my thoughts square in the eye and decide if I agree. Writing things down frees me from the burden of carrying the weight of my memories. I also write for my future self, so that when something feels wrong or needs re-examining, I can go back, know where it came from and re-examine it, mend or replace some element of this faith I've built over a lifetime with the care it deserves.

—Jason Sierra

When I work on a book project, there is far too much emphasis in my head on what the words I am writing will become—their mission, their intention, their goal, and their purpose. The sacredness of journaling is that its aim is the opposite. The intention is the present; it is a mindful practice to write without a goal, only with the intentionality of emotional and spiritual nakedness on the page. We are meant to be raw without distinct intention—and through this unabashed process, sacred moments are born.

I can't entirely describe why or how it happens but some of my greatest moments of sacred consolation and my wildest mystical arguments have come through the process of journaling—God weeping and shouting alongside me, in equal measure, with much greater wisdom. This is the conversation space, for God and me, in the sacred art of literary conversation.

Sometimes thought to be reserved only for self-help exercises or children's diaries, the spiritual journal has the potential to be so much more. We are called to speak into the darkness with the depths of our souls. If you write until you stop thinking about what to write next, until you cannot find a single false word standing between you and the song of your heart, then you can find God staring right back at you—in every noun, every verb, every line. God shows up in the depths of our authenticity.

So, write! Write until you find your truth, and then listen deeply and intently for God's words, writing back their reply.

—Teresa Pasquale

The art of journaling has been a staple throughout human history as a vehicle that connects current generations to previous generations. And if you examine the practice closely, you will discover there is no right or wrong way to journal. Journals are personal stories, details, or thoughts from one's own view. No outside force can invalidate what has been written down in a journal; others can only speculate and try to interpret the author's message and meanings.

When we journal, it gives us another vehicle to communicate with God. The great thing about journaling is that it doesn't have to make sense. It doesn't matter if we have the perfect word or the correct grammar to jot down. It doesn't matter if there are run-on sentences or fragments. What matters is that our hearts and minds are one, and our writings convey our deepest feelings to God, who hears our longing and comforts our souls.

—Longkee Vang

Ж

I will put my law within them,
and I will write it on their hearts;
and I will be their God, and they shall be my people.

—JEREMIAH 31:33

I have prayed, and I have journaled, but I have never kept a prayer journal. My mother, however, has done religious journaling for years, so I decided to ask her about it.

"You sit down and ask God to be with you, and then you write out all the fuss and the furor, and at the end, there's an answer," she told me.

"OK. So what else do you do?"

"That's it." There was a pause. "You write about blessings too," she added helpfully.

I remember how she used to get up very early in the morning and curl up in the old red chair and write in her journal by the light of one lamp in the silent, dark house. When it was cold, she warmed herself with an old, white blanket that she liked. Sometimes she fell asleep.

Mom is not someone who brings other people's attention to her problems. Prayer journaling as a discipline suits her. I talk out fuss and furor and pray about problems as I go. She writes her fuss and furor to God, struggles with problems, and moves on quietly. As I grow into motherhood, which lends itself to dealing with problems unobtrusively and getting up early, I find prayer journaling an increasingly attractive option. I admire my mom— tough, unflaggingly kind, endlessly curious about the world. If prayer journaling has helped her become this resilient and selfless, it is a discipline well worth trying.

—**Elizabeth Brignac**

Facebook messages, ecards, and text messages have replaced snail mail cards, handwritten letters, and the reflective nature of diary writing in long hand. I still believe in writing out and snail mailing cards and letters. At worst, I'm Victorian. At best, I'm courtly when I stamp something to send that brings a smile.

I'm mindful that all the cards, notes, and letters I've sent over the years to friends, family, and acquaintances constitute a kind of journal. For several years now, I've participated in a penpal campaign to those incarcerated in prison. And you don't need a birthday or holiday to send an "I'm thinking of you" note or card to friends and family.

Sometimes when I offer an observation or share what I think might be comforting, I hopefully encourage the recipient to be true to his or her creation as the Creator intended. Handwriting your deepest thoughts, expressions of love, or most ardent prayers is an opportunity to connect or reconnect and nurture wellness in your relationship to yourself and to God.

—Paul Jesep

I kept a diary in elementary school, the kind with the little lock and key. Of course, I lost the key to the first one. The next one didn't have a key, but I hid it in my pajama keeper under my pillow for safety. I am an experiential learner. I'm pretty sure I used colored pens and decorated the pages with hearts and flowers as I described the drama of my fourth-grade life.

Back then, I saw journaling as keeping a record of my thoughts about the things that were happening in my life. I don't think I was very introspective about those things. I was simply reliving them, enjoying going over the details again as I wrote them down. And I kept them hidden so that the recounting and reliving of them was mine alone.

Now my writing is mostly public instead of private. I keep a blog, and I write about events but also musings and wonderings. Sometimes I write to work out how I feel or where I think I might see God in my life or in a particular situation. Sometimes I rant, and sometimes I lament, and sometimes I am just bewildered.

I'm not sure it matters whether one's journal is public or private. Perhaps it's a matter of temperament. What is more important to me is the act of writing down thoughts, of gathering vague ideas and putting them into words and sentences and questions so that they have substance. Writing helps me draw closer to God by giving thoughtful voice to my fragmented worries and half-formed fears.

—Penny Nash

"If I should die before I wake..." That line from the childhood prayer put me right off keeping a journal.

Instead of a journal, I write in my life log. This morning ritual lets me put my thoughts on paper, but only I know the meaning of what I've written.

Each page in the log has three columns listed across the top of the page: love, sad, and good wishes. Each day I write the date and in each column I list the names of people, places, events, or activities I connect with the emotion described in the title.

For instance, under love I might put dancing because I love to dance and am grateful for the gift. Under sad, Baghdad because I'm heartbroken it's a city I may never see again. Good wishes is where I put the names of people I want to send a special prayer. It could be the name of someone I love or someone I should learn to love. Only I know my special connection to the name, place, activity, or event listed in each column.

My life log is a quiet time for reflecting on my life, and the secret and significance of each entry is between me and the Lord.

—**Charlotte Chere Graham**

My first diary had a pink plastic cover with Tinker Bell on the cover and a lock that could be picked with a hairpin if I lost the key. As my life progressed, I moved from diaries to journals. I have been journaling for over forty years and have at least fifty notebooks of different sizes and covers.

Somewhere along the way, I began to keep a spiritual journal—a place where I give myself both permission and time to reflect on the meaning and mysteries of life. I ask questions for which there are no immediate, apparent answers. I take notes from homilies and meditations, write down my favorite scriptures and quotes, and begin thoughts without endings. I include a prayer list for people, circumstances, and hopes.

One Sunday, I left my journal in the pew and discovered it was missing only once I was back home. I prayed that whoever found the journal would receive a blessing in an hour of need. When I went back to my parish the next day, the journal was there, and I knew my prayer had been answered, for it was opened to a page on which was written a quote by priest and writer Henri Nowen: "We need quiet time in the presence of God."

—Westina Matthews

☓

This is the covenant that I will make with them after those days, says the Lord: I will put my laws in their hearts, and I will write them on their minds.

—HEBREWS 10:16

Writing suffuses my life in ways I've not always been completely aware of. Like many people, most of my writing comes down to emails, texts, blogging, and social media posts. As a lay preacher, I also write short homilies two or three times a month. Then there are lengthier, more formal projects that I execute as part of my job: articles, speeches, project concepts, and proposals for donors. Once or twice a week, I'll also scribble a note or two in my journal at home.

Words, then, can be like breath itself: always surrounding us but not something we pay much attention to on a day-to-day basis. But in the same way we can become more aware of our breath, we can also become more aware of our words, especially in our writing.

Two pieces of writing advice have remained with me, and I think they have everything to do with being a person of faith. The first writing advice is to be respectful.

The second has to do with revising toward greater truth. Once you start looking, it's amazing how many exaggerations creep in as added color to a story, or how quickly a fast-and-loose grasp on stats becomes a means of scoring a debate point. Revising can become a time for asking ourselves hard questions about why we need to entertain with tall tales or whitewash complex realities— and can be a means of drawing closer to the God of Truth.

—**Miguel Escobar**

Haiku as journal?
    Seventeen syllables: too
    much—and not enough.

In the tradition of Japanese poetry, haiku are a response to nature; in my life, writing haiku has become a response to, well, everything. Many are paired with photographs I've taken. Some are responses to art or music, to sermons or books, or current events. Some are even what I call "snarku." (These are not holy thoughts, but they are as honest an expression of unholy feeling as Psalm 109.) A snarku:

    Don't go blessing me
    if you don't really mean it:
    My life is no sneeze!

This year I've set myself the discipline of writing at least one haiku every day. This is in part a flexing of creative muscles, but it is also a way of reflecting on my life—and sharing my reflections. You will be reading this in July, but I am writing in May. Here's a Mother's Day haiku that won't be out of place in summer or any season:

    Giving birth is just
    the first step—becoming love
    will take your whole life.

—Mary W. Cox

My experience with journaling (and I am a devotee of the discipline) is that it is easier to do when life is not going well. But it is equally, if not more fruitful when life is humming along. It is not for nothing that the psalms include both lament and exaltation. To maximize the benefit of journaling, it is important to sit with paper and pen and pour out all that's within, both grime and glory. The more we weave together lament and exaltation, the more we see that our life in God moves us from death to life, from sorrow to joy, from judgment to grace.

A favored exercise in writing groups is to take a word or the beginning of a sentence and to write it down and then keep writing, nonstop for twenty minutes. Don't pick your pen off the paper. Just keep going. And when your mind strays or stalls, return to the word, begin the sentence again, and keep writing. It's meant to loosen your mind, to turn off any internal editor that might chirp away at you, that might stop you from sharing with God all that wants to be shared.

It might be fun to use this exercise today. Take out your journal or a single sheet of paper. Put yourself in a chair at a table, maybe facing a window if you can. And at the top of the page, *On the tablet of my heart, I write...*

Twenty minutes, no stopping! Ready, set, go!

—Susan Wyper

I often wonder what you would see if you could read the tablet of my heart. Do positive traits overshadow the negative traits when written? As we move through life, we gain certain prejudices based on our experiences, and these become a way of attempting to protect ourselves from both physical and emotional harm. Some of these safeguards are based in reality and are worthy of our notice, while others are made out of fear and are detrimental to our humanity. Does God judge us based more on our thoughts or our actions?

If we fight these prejudices and try to act as if they are not a part of us, is that enough to satisfy our promise to strive for justice and peace among all people and respect the dignity of every human being? Can we keep that baptismal promise if we remove the actions, or do we also need to remove the thoughts? I struggle daily with discerning which thoughts are worthy of fear and which thoughts are just paranoia.

I like to hope that when I stand before God and my heart is read, my actions are what is written and remembered, not my thoughts. I like to hope that the good outweighs the bad and that whichever is stronger is the one that gets the ink.

—Lauren Caldwell

Journaling is good for the soul. Sometimes I journal as a way of recording the ways I experience life. Every so often, I make journaling my prayer by writing with my left hand. The journaling with my left hand makes me pay more attention to what I write, since I use my right hand for just about everything.

On a daily basis, we hear stories of horror, loss, tragedy, and death. It seems at times that life is a tale told by an idiot. However, every day we have the chance to open ourselves to the reality of God's word that brings peace, compassion, justice, healing, and life.

God's ongoing invitation to us is that we write a new chapter in the history of the world. The great invitation is to write God's love and compassion on the tablets of our hearts. We could live lives more centered on God if we invited God to write our stories, to create a gospel of our lives, and to write in us a prayer that seeks to do the will of God.

—Mark Bozzuti-Jones

〤

And the angel said to me, "Write this:
Blessed are those who are invited to the marriage supper
of the Lamb." And he said to me, "These are true words of God."

—Revelation 19:9

"Slapping a sloppy brush of thanksgiving over everything" didn't leave her deeply thankful. So wrote Ann Voskamp in *One Thousand Gifts*, the result of her friend's challenge to list a thousand God-given gifts. "Thanksgiving" became an action verb for her. Befriended by companions like Voskamp, I began a journal, recording gifts as small as a chickadee, as vast as redemption, as spontaneous as a friend's humor, as reflective as visiting hospice. And my list includes quotations about gratitude. It's too easy to sit still, and such quotes get me up to serve somehow, to spread a little bit of joy.

My thanksgiving journal has a parallel booklet with prayer requests for people enduring struggle. This list stays near the chair where I watch the news since the best way to affect the outcomes of reports is to pray. Over time, I see concrete examples of God's responsiveness. Rereading notes of past years, I replay the lifelong conversation with God: old notes lead to gratitude.

—June Terry

)(

When God finished speaking with Moses on Mount Sinai,
he gave him the two tablets of the covenant,
tablets of stone, written with the finger of God.

—Exodus 31:18

Whenever I have an important idea, I write it down. I've been doing this for over half my life. At times, I go back and read over my idea book. Sometimes, I am surprised at what I find. Old entries are like mental snapshots of the past and often bring with them more memories than I anticipated.

I used to keep a journal as well that recorded my day-to-day minutiae. It is harder to connect with these memories. It took me a while to realize that most of these focused on the negative things that happened in the day like flat tires and failed assignments. Even the strong memories are usually negative ones. There are, of course, occasional flashes of brightness, but even these were usually precursors to something unfortunate.

The same is true for our spiritual lives. It is all too easy to dwell on the things we've done wrong, the choices we shouldn't have made or didn't make. Instead, I try to record the inspirations of my spiritual life. Even if it is from something sad, the inspiration holds a wisdom I know comes from the Holy Spirit and leaves me feeling refreshed, renewed, and reflective.

—Spencer Hixon

I don't like journaling. There have been seasons in my life when I engaged in the spiritual discipline, but it was mostly because I felt pressured to do so by someone I deemed more spiritually mature. I was intrigued by my friend's devotion to the task, so I asked her about the motivation. She said her life was so crazy and hectic that journaling was her way to purposefully acknowledge what she was seeing, hearing, and believing about God and what God was doing in her life.

The problem is that we often don't take the time to reflect on what God is doing. Our spiritual eyes can stay clouded to God's. We must choose to be intentionally reflective.

Some people, like my friend, use journaling as their mode of reflection...and it can be a great one. Journaling promotes self-examination and facilitates spiritual growth through written meditation. Some people don't mind writing, but if journaling feels too overwhelming, maybe jotting lists, notions, prayers, or even just words is all you need to process and better discern God's voice.

—**Bree Combs**

I have tried the spiritual practice of journaling a few times over the years, with no real success. It's a little hard for me to find the time, and I never really feel like I have all that much to write down. I do however keep track of my daily life on small obscure pieces of paper.

Usually these scraps of paper are in need of being thrown away, so I repurpose them for my daily list of things to accomplish. I write in very small print so that I can fit everything on the scrap and then cross off items on the list as I make my way through the day. Any item that I was unable to complete goes at the top of the next day's small piece of paper. This sort of connects all of the obscure pieces of paper, which I throw into a basket on my dresser.

Sometimes I go back and read through the list. It's not really journaling, but I am always mindful of the complexity of the journey that God has called me to and the real adventure that is life with Jesus. Journaling is one way of looking back on our journey as followers of the Way, but there are other options too, and I know that there is one that will work for you. Perhaps there are some small obscure pieces of paper lying around your home.

—Jason Leo

*This book of the law shall not depart out of your mouth;
you shall meditate on it day and night, so that you may be careful
to act in accordance with all that is written in it.*

—Joshua 1:8

I like to write. Many times I have begun a journal. I have bought the essentials—a beautiful journal and pretty pens in different colors. When I go back to read these beautiful journals, I relive everything I wrote in them. Some entries are adorable, like cute anecdotes about my son, Ellis. Some are funny, and a lot are painful.

I have used journaling to heal. I recall my journal entries when I was going through an unwanted and painful divorce. I wrote, "Day 1: Will I survive?" Day 2…Day 3, 4, 5, 6, 7. Then suddenly it was Week 2, Week 3, then Month 2, then, "I can't believe I haven't written in here for almost a year…"

I pour out my heart after something painful. I write from deep within and sometimes have to be careful not to send these thoughts to people because they are too much. When I read what I have written after a devastating situation, I realize I thought I wasn't going to survive, yet somehow God pulled me through.

Somehow, God transforms my mourning into dancing, my grief into joy. Somehow, God acts. And I am left with a huge knot in my throat, knowing that I owe it all to God. So like the woman who weeps and pours precious perfume at Jesus' feet, I do that when I journal. I gather all I have and invest in an alabaster jar of gratitude. All I own I pour on Jesus. These words on each page are a testament of where Jesus found me and what God has done in and for me. I owe my sanity, my life to God.

—**Sandra Montes**

Journaling is something I do as the Spirit moves me—to capture my reactions during a retreat, to work through a personal issue, to make notes toward a more formal writing project.

Looking at notebooks from earlier years, I experience a range of emotions: "Hmm, I don't even remember feeling that." "Goodness, that issue still plagues me!" "What on earth was that about?" Occasionally there is a kernel that deserves following up—but not often.

What has proved to be more worthwhile is dragging my introverted self to a writers' group. What a motley crew my group is—someone who loves and writes fantasy; someone who works at night and creates sharp-edged satire for an online blog; several who combine a love of words with skills in art, design, and technology; and a good-humored facilitator who is working on a novel and shares her jewel-like tanka poems. I am the oldest person in this group, but neither my age nor my genre—spiritual meditation—is ever an issue.

As we share our varied offerings of prose, poetry, art, and design, we feel enveloped in an atmosphere of mutual respect and encouragement since we are all trying to accomplish the same mission: to communicate, to express ourselves, to make a difference.

The generosity of this group provides a valuable checklist for my own faith community: are we as accepting, nurturing, and encouraging?

—**Joan Bowers**

I've always been a writer, but I've never been one for journaling. I once tried keeping a diary, but between fear of sibling blackmail and revulsion at my own pathos upon calm rereading, I tore it up and buried the shreds at the bottom of the cat box. "Keep a journal!" I was urged at my first cancer diagnosis. Good idea, but I was working full time while being poisoned and just never got around to it.

After a year—almost six months of chemo, a near-death experience (the portacath did it), surgery, radiation, recovery—I tried to remember what happened when. I failed, until I realized that I did, in fact, keep a journal of sorts in my more-than-daily email correspondence with my English friend, Margaret.

Together, we prayed and wept and snarked our way through it, emerging all the stronger for sharing. When I read it, I found a detailed account of my fears and pains and unexpected joys: the kindnesses unlooked-for, the friends who stepped up, the cats who stayed by my side. I found Margaret's responses, sometimes practical, sometimes spiritual, sometimes purely funny. I found a two-sided journal, a journal of friendship through illness, far more valuable than a diary alone could ever be.

—Sarah Bryan Miller

I recently read the journals of author Louisa May Alcott. Growing up near where she spent most of her life, I've always loved her books.

Alcott started journaling as a young child, encouraged by her parents. She writes of her delight in roaming the woods, her struggles to be good, and her thoughts about God. Later entries tell of losing her beloved sister to scarlet fever, her first attempts to find work, and her fierce determination to support her family by her writing. As the Civil War begins, she records her experiences as an army nurse in Washington and her subsequent illness, which she later shapes into stories that set her on the road to fame.

It was fun to recognize where many of her characters came from, and especially how much of herself Alcott put into Jo March of *Little Women*. But I also saw how her hard work, love of family, honesty, and courage led to her later success, tempered with suffering as it was. But then, I had an objective outsider's view, which I could never bring to my own journals. No matter how much I record, I will never be able to see the complete pattern of my life. Underneath my own words of joy or sorrow, I have to trust that God is writing straight with crooked lines.

—**Kathleen M. Flanagan**

O that my words were written down!
O that they were inscribed in a book!

—Job 19:23

Two years ago, the leaves began to change color in July. I kept thinking there must be some mistake. Doug and I were enjoying our summer, and I couldn't bear the thought of it coming to an end. Fall came in just fine, and so did winter, and my fears subsided. We found new ways to spend our days. Though bundled up, we still managed to enjoy some long walks.

What I have discovered (much to my surprise) as I watch the leaves start their change during this waning summer is that I am not afraid. I can feel the truth of love driving out my fear, smoothing over the jagged edges of loss and bone-deep grief. There are days when my heart is unspeakably full of both the joy and the ache of loving this man so much.

Last night, we went to a blues festival. When the sounds got too loud, Doug and I took a walk and found some ice cream—our favorite comfort food. At one point, he asked me if I knew where Allison was. I held his hand and told him I was Allison. He looked at me with a mix of surprise and relief. We headed back home, admiring another spectacular sunset.

Later, we snuggled in Doug's bed. He kept telling me how scared he was. I thought again about those precious leaves changing colors in July and of the inevitability of all our changes. I held my beloved close and prayed, some words I said out loud and some were said only in the depths of my heart. And a miracle happened. Our comingled anxieties and fears seemed to slip away.

As I was leaving, he whispered, "Thank you. I love you." My heart swelled, and I was reminded once again that in spite of all the losses we have experienced, gratitude and love are possible—in fact, they make all things possible. Blessed am I among women.

—Allison Zent Blankemeyer

"How was your day?" "Oh, same as always....nothing special."

I am convinced that most people go through life sleepwalking. They appear as if they are alive and moving forward, but in truth they are simply going through the motions. I have always promised myself never to let that happen with me, although I know it has more often than I'd like to admit. But my heartfelt goal is to be awake and alert to whatever God is doing all around me.

This means becoming something of a spiritual detective. Like the great sleuths we encounter on the page or on screen, we must do more than see and hear...we must observe the divine footprints and fingerprints everywhere we go. This is why I have always loved writing. By recording something, somehow it becomes part of me, part of my experience. In old black-and-white movies, detectives and investigative reporters always have a pencil and pad on hand and immediately start taking notes as they come across something of importance. How much more should we who are on the lookout for God at work do likewise?

Francis of Assisi may not have been a detective, but he was most certainly awake and alert to all that God was doing around him. He once said that every day, if we open our eyes, we will see miracles. How easy it is to sleepwalk through life, but oh, what we miss along the way! To observe, to take note, to record God at work is to enter more deeply into the great adventure to which we are called and to savor every moment of life that is given us.

—Chuck Robertson

I began writing in a journal about thirty years ago. Closing my day with journaling was a discipline and an opportunity to release what that day carried. I began to conclude my journal writing with something I was grateful for that day. My sleep was more peaceful when I focused on someone's kind words rather than ruminating on being late to a meeting because of road construction. Even though I journal less regularly now, I still value the process. Writing becomes prayer.

I have taught classes on writing and health and like to begin with free writing, encouraging participants to write anything that comes to mind, to unpack burdens they may have brought with them, or just to open the door to words and to themselves. It is a struggle for some to let the writing happen, to let go of expectations or fear of judgment. Journal writing is personal, not for critique, so we're free to let the Spirit flow through us and onto the page.

—Linda Gelbrich

X

You yourselves are our letter, written on our hearts,
to be known and read by all.

—2 CORINTHIANS 3:2

Early models of the church may be found within Israel's history, according to biblical scholars. Before there were temples, priests, or prophets, Israel's identity was defined by mutual understanding of their story. How they saw and identified themselves was communicated through the stories that they heard and told. After returning from exile and facing the threat of losing their identity because of foreign occupation, Israel came to rely more and more on written documents. To preserve knowledge of who they were and where they had come from, they wrote down their story.

Other oral-culture people have faced similar challenges. Their identity and history rely upon memory and voice as well as truthful tellers to preserve them for posterity. Once the voices are silenced (or other voices have imposed themselves), they become disconnected from people and events that name and identify them, the faith that has sustained them, and the God who empowered and delivered them through the ages.

God directs the prophet in Habakkuk 2:2 to, "Write the vision; make it plain on tablets, so that a runner may read it." When we write our story, we give life and longevity to a thought, a dream, an event, the history of a people, and our encounters with God. It allows us to see clearly for ourselves and to show others what we have seen.

—**Kathy H. Culmer**

Journaling is one spiritual practice that I have found extremely helpful. Oftentimes, it is a way of ordering my thoughts and stemming the seething tide of anxiety and worry. Sometimes my journal entries are just lists of feelings or thoughts that need to live outside my head. Sometimes there is a story from my past that needs an end put to it.

Scripture can be a really good dialogue partner. There are several passages in the Bible that make me want to ask, "Why is this in here?" I can relate to the seemingly violent mood swings of the psalmists, and the beauty of the creation story makes me want to weep for Eden. I will often jot a piece of scripture down in my journal and write underneath it, as if I could reshape the rough edges or add my life story to the canon. I ask questions and cross-examine it.

The gift I give myself is the record of my struggle. This is a story inked in the life's blood of one who continues to try to know and be known by God. In my journal, I have the benefit of all the missteps, wrong turns, forgotten epiphanies, and déjà vu of the spiritual life.

—Charles McClain

During my college years, I took two Bible courses that were taught by a popular professor named Dr. Bernard Boyd. He was a Christian minister and an archaeologist, and he carried enormous knowledge inside his head. Dr. Boyd spoke so fast that we could barely keep pace while taking notes. The tone of his voice was unemotional as he discussed Bible stories, characters, and the various sources from which scripture came.

Dr. Boyd's face was a bit craggy from the many archaeological digs he participated in under Israel's hot sun. His voice was somewhat craggy too. So it was startling one day when he slowed down and suddenly began reciting the first four verses of Hosea 11 in a soft voice, laden with feeling. "When Israel was a child, I loved him....I took them up in my arms. I was to them like those who lift infants to their cheeks. I bent down to them and fed them."

Though God abhorred Israel's foray into idol worship, God forgave them, just like a parent forgives a much-loved child. Like Dr. Boyd, it is good to remember the affection God has for the descendants of Abraham and Sarah and to pray for the peace of Jerusalem.

—**Susan Taylor Block**

As child, I kept a diary. It was a colorful little book that had a lock and key. I kept it under the mattress. My diary was a place where I daily poured out my heart. There was no judgment. It was just me talking about what was important to me.

As a new parent, I was given a baby book. In that book, I wrote about the exciting and perplexing experiences of being a new parent. There are pictures along with first words and first steps. Now my children enjoy returning to those pages and sharing them. The baby book is a treasure that always offers new questions and a lot of laughter.

Writing has been the place where I have spread out my heart—stored memories and dreams. Sometimes the entries recall difficult times. They are still precious. Sitting down regularly, making time to let the contents of my life roll forward, is a prayer and a practice.

What is on the tablet of your heart today? What hidden treasure might you find and preserve?

—Karen Montagno

॥

Almighty God, whose loving hand has given us all that we possess: Grant us grace that we may honor you with our substance, and, remembering the account which we must one day give, may be faithful stewards of your bounty, through Jesus Christ our Lord. Amen.

—*THE BOOK OF COMMON PRAYER*, P. 827

Sometimes the moss has more than it can bear,
And the water falls in drips and sprinkles and splats.
We marvel at the beauty, crystal sparkles dancing across
green and blue, catching on webs and lashes.
We embrace with wonder this beauty of new balance,
the moss that gives way to water.
We snap pictures and rock in chairs and craft poems. But we do
not in iambic pentameter capture the pieces of broken lives.
For where is the beauty in brownie crumbs and slurred tongues,
In a Lonely that tugs at stiff smiles and tears that escape
unbidden? And yet. And yet.
In the stories of brokenness from people who seem so whole,
there is beauty. In crumpled Kleenex and flickered candles,
in guitar chords and belly laughs, there is beauty.
In the quiet, beauty.
And in all, there is God, who gives courage to un-Humpty
Dumpty and find new pieces to put back together again.
So I will manage my heart and unmask my soul.
I will let God write on the tablet of my heart.
I will embrace my body as a vessel for God.
I will save money, need less. I will find comfort in a job
well done, not endlessly, fruitlessly seek perfection.
I will breathe in my children, a balm for when wind
and adventure carry them away.
And when my beloved tells me I am beautiful,
I will believe him. A little.
I will listen more than I talk,
And I will give way to the water when it is more than I can bear.
To this new path, to my family and to my God,
To This, I give my heart.

—Richelle Thompson

Body Prayer

*I will thank you because I am marvelously made;
your works are wonderful, and I know it well.*
—Psalm 139:13

Marvelously Made

We may be tempted to think about our spiritual health and physical health as mutually exclusive. But God has created us as body and soul. This month, we will explore the spiritual discipline of body prayer—ways to include our bodies (or simply create a greater awareness of them) as part of our spiritual lives. Something as simple as standing or kneeling during our daily devotional time can invite us to experience a different aspect to our holy habits.

WAYS TO ENGAGE

Consider adding fifteen minutes of physical activity to your daily routine.

Use your favorite online search engine to learn more about the idea of body prayer.

Pray during your regular workout time or take this book with you to the gym.

Set aside five minutes a day to be aware of your body, to talk to God about how you are feeling, and to check in with the Holy Spirit.

A year ago, my back went out—full-on shutdown. Two weeks of insane amounts of steroids, muscle relaxers, requisite panic attacks, falling down, physical therapy, and doctors, threw me for a total loop. Things like this do not happen to me. I put my head down, rub some dirt on whatever hurts, and just keep going. But not this time. I was leveled, helpless, humbled, and frightened.

Relearning to trust my body, to be brave enough to try one more step, to believe in my legs, feet, and hands was really hard. But every day, even on the hardest days, some kind of progress was made, some burden felt lighter, some nudge of the Holy Spirit would show me a new thing I could do. I found myself being less and less fearful of my body, and more and more in awe of the way God knit me together and was making me whole again.

I hope and pray that as you journey through this last month of summer, you can stretch out your legs and arms in the warm summer light and breathe a prayer of thanksgiving for all the gifts of this life.

—**Rachel Jones**

I don't feel very marvelously made, most days. I have suffered from a chronic sleep condition most of my adult life, which leaves me fairly reliant on caffeine in heavy doses to stay functional. I weigh more than I would like, certainly more than my doctors would like. I have bad knees, which is probably caused by the weight just as it contributes to the inability to take the weight off. And as I head screaming into my late 30s, my knees and back creak and ache when I'm still too long or active too long. This body feels like a burden to be carried.

And yet? And yet. This body is a member of the Body of Christ. She has carried me to the depths of the Grand Canyon and back to the rim. She has ridden hundreds of miles on a bicycle and completed two half-marathons. She allows me to get up and down the stairs of my house and my office each day (however slowly); she has soaked up the streets of Manhattan and climbed the Great Wall of China. She grew another living, breathing human being, and she still holds that little girl tight when nightmares come calling in the middle of the night. This body is the body God gifted me with, and like the rest of God's creation, she deserves my stewardship and care. When I stop long enough to pay attention to the way my body serves me and serves God, I give myself the chance to recognize the greatness and wonder of God's creation.

—Holli Powell

Dance today. Give your body as an offering to God.
Throw your arms open to the wind and spin.
Throw your heart open to the world and let the love of the
Creator swirl through its chambers.

Plant your feet firm on the ground.
Step to the beating feet of those around you.
Plant your soul, its roots deep in the soil of this world.
Let its branches be moved by that which
            moves the deepest parts of you.

Give your hips to the swinging pendulum of the tides.
Draw the great circumference of the earth, spinning on its axis.
Let your mind be moved by the spirit, straying always from
            the extremities back to the center.
Seek her balance, around which she is ever in motion.

Stretch your toes and your fingers wide to feel the
            coolness of the air between them.
Find the places where your heart has become small
            and unmoving and let Light enter those spaces.

Bend yourself low to greet the earthworms, the snakes,
            the scurrying mice.
Jump to meet the eyes of the giraffe grazing on leafy trees,
the lemur swinging from branches, the bird glancing off the sky.
Stand to look through your own eyes.
Allow your mind the freedom of doubt and the ecstasy of faith.
You are blessed in your own unique perspective.

Rest your eyes on the broad table of the horizon.
Cover them with the blackness of the night.
Rest your soul on the altar of the most high.
Give your life to God with abandon.

—Jason Sierra

A complexity of physical ailments, at that point undiagnosed, left me in the midst of the Maundy Thursday service feeling dizzy and breathless, in excruciating pain. I wandered out into the garden. I stared up at the stars and wondered if they were the same stars Jesus gazed upon in that original garden moment.

After a long night of pain and confusion, I rose out of bed on Good Friday feeling like I might be dying. I can remember the numbness in my limbs, the dizziness in my head, the exhausting pain rippling through my body, falling to the ground in my study with my forehead touching the carpet and my arms prostrate on the ground. I remember thinking, "This is what dying feels like. God, please, save me from this feeling of death."

A half a day later, a series of doctors and a number of diagnoses led me to understand that my pain was fibromyalgia, my breathlessness was seasonally induced asthma, and the delirium caused by the strange onset of the two—nothing, however, was able to explain that sacred moment, prostrate, humble, fearful, and crying, lying on the ground in a moment that led me into relationship with Jesus in a way I had never experienced before and haven't since.

The embodiment of suffering brought me closest to God and his only begotten Son in a way that no other expression of Good Friday and Easter could ever have told me with words—it was a felt relationship, experienced first and last in my own body.

—Teresa Pasquale

Today, more than any point in history, humans are careful about what they put in and do to their bodies. It doesn't matter if you're an athlete, a parent, or a kid running down the street, we are all cautious and aware. We know that what we eat directly affects how our body processes food, which affects how we feel mentally and emotionally. But more importantly, how active we are affects us physically. Like muscle memory, if we don't use our bodies to walk, dance, shake, or move, our bodies weaken from lack of use.

Our spiritual life needs exercise as well. Doctors say that being active thirty minutes a day makes a huge difference to our physical well-being. Why not take some time to pray, volunteer with the youth group, or pray the Daily Office? Such simple practices could help us maintain our connections to the other marvelously made people in our lives.

—Longkee Vang

X

My heart, therefore, is glad, and my spirit rejoices;
my body also shall rest in hope.

—Psalm 16:9

My attitude toward the body's involvement in prayer has changed over time. In the Nicene Creed, we say that we believe in the resurrection of our bodies, but I imagine that many Christians wonder why God bothers. Christian tradition mostly approaches the body as the source of problems and temptations to sin. This approach trucks along nicely with the widely held secular notion that what lies within is the real self—that our bodies are shells that house our inner lives. I have always preferred the life of the mind, and from childhood, I rather liked the idea that our minds and souls were butterflies crammed into the ugly cocoons of our bodies.

Then my dad died. I forgot the resurrection of his body entirely; it was his soul that was important, and how could that soul's personality ever really be resurrected? We were supposed to deny ourselves, I felt, as preparation for our final loss of self. My dad might live eternally in God, but I had lost him. A kind priest gently pointed out my error. Our souls and bodies are united, he pointed out. The resurrection of the body meant the resurrection of my father's whole self. The body was an integral part of who he was.

Since then, I have tried to fight my mental habit of separating the body and the soul. When I pray, I try to remain aware that I am praying with my body (brain, voice, arms, knees) because my body is who I am rather than just a carrying case for my soul.

—Elizabeth Brignac

I refuse to go to the gym. Instead, I stand at my desk for half the day and do moderate walking. I park the car at the far end of a lot to get extra steps. In buildings, I walk down the steps, though going up gives way to the elevator.

In workshops, I emphasize wholeness. It's mind, body, and spirit. Proper care of the body empowers the soul, until it transitions from this life, to be mobile and explore. We use it to embrace creation during an evening walk by experiencing the stars and the elegant moon. If you take time to notice and don't take it for granted, celestial wonders are awe-inspiring.

Henry David Thoreau wrote that the person "who sits still in a house all the time may be the greatest vagrant of all." He said to saunter and experience the beauty in woods, meadows, mountains, and along river banks. You become a meandering river "seeking the shortest course to the sea." If you're observant, no two walks are the same. Nature changes throughout the day.

—Paul Jesep

I have long been a walker. For one thing, I can notice the world around me as I walk. I can be mindful and notice my neighbors and the birds, flowers, and weather. And I often use walking for long distances as an opportunity to get into some serious conversation with God. I get pretty grouchy if I don't get in several good walks each week.

But lately I have also returned to the practice of yoga for a different kind of body and prayer experience. As I continue to explore my contemplative side, I have turned to stretching, breathing, strengthening, and resting on a mat as another kind of prayer time. This return was prompted by a recognition that I often need to slow down. I need to breathe. I need to be physically meditative in a more intentional way.

Stretching, breathing, resting puts me into a state in which I am more naturally listening, both to my own body (which is, as Saint Paul says, a temple of the Holy Spirit) and to hearing what God may want to say to me. I'm not looking around, cataloging sights, toting up my bird list, or making to-do lists when I'm on the yoga mat. I'm breathing. I'm noticing the air touching my bare arms and feeling myself relax as the air fills my lungs and expands my diaphragm, all of which is definitely a Holy Spirit kind of activity.

Many of us have body issues. We worry about being too fat or scrawny or weak or awkward. Using my whole body to be present to God in physical but meditative prayer, however, moves me beyond those petty worries and into a place of thanksgiving to God for making me just the way I am.

—**Penny Nash**

In my world, there's a potent connection between prayer and exercise. Both are good for me, and each keeps me on the straight-and-narrow when it comes to caring for the body and life God's given me. But I didn't always connect the two.

In the memoir *Eat, Pray, Love,* the author Elizabeth Gilbert earns the nickname "Groceries." That could have been my name growing up. And living in the Southwest, my daily bread was usually a fry-up doused in white gravy with a side of chocolate meringue pie.

Back then I was as thin as a rake, so I could afford to abandon moderation and exercise when it came to eating. The same was true about my habits with prayer. God blessed me not only with a fast metabolism but also an easy life with few speed bumps. Just as I didn't see the need to control my eating or do any exercise, for a big slab of my life, I never thought much about praying and spending time with God.

I should have heeded the adage, "This too shall pass." One day Mother Nature put the brakes on my metabolism, and God decided I could do with some time at the boot camp of hard knocks. This rough patch opened me to respecting the body I was given, the wondrous gift of prayer and spending time with God every day, and the power of exercise and prayer when they are intertwined as one practice.

—**Charlotte Chere Graham**

Each year for four or five weeks, those black and orange insects called lovebugs (also known as the honeymoon fly or the kissing bug) are out in full force in the South. These lovebugs can number in the millions. One day two lovebugs landed on the windshield of my car on the passenger side where I was seated, right at my eye level, and they seemed to be holding on to each other for dear life. I have since learned that adult females live only three to four days, and the males live a little longer, and so the adult pairs remain coupled, even in flight, for up to several days. When I told my husband this, he responded, "Well, if I knew I was going to die, I'd be holding on for dear life too!"

There are some 900 thousand different kinds of living insects, one and a half million species of animals, and 422,000 known species of plants (and as many as seventeen million different scientific names are used to refer to them). There are over seven billion people with 6,500 spoken languages in the world today.

Yes, God, we are all marvelously made! Wonderful are your works, including the lovebugs who are holding on for dear life.

—Westina Matthews

〤

Do not be wise in your own eyes; fear the LORD,
and turn away from evil.
It will be a healing for your flesh
and a refreshment for your body.

—PROVERBS 3:7-8

Western Christianity has a long legacy of encouraging people to feel deeply uncomfortable in our skin. The idea that God had become enfleshed in human form was a scandal to both many Jews and Greco-Romans in early Christianity, and many of the heresies through the fourth century reveal how deeply uncomfortable many faithful leaders were with the idea that Jesus, in all his fleshy personhood, could actually be of the very same essence as God-the-Transcendent. And I haven't even begun on an early church father's view of the female body. Woman are the root of all sinfulness, a formerly concupiscent St. Augustine once insisted, shaping how Christianity has seen the bodies of over half the human population ever since.

Given this history, the fact that there are people who can be described as comfortable in their own skin is nothing short of miraculous. And if I'm honest, I must admit that I'm jealous of them. For I, like most of the people I know, fall solidly in the "deeply uncomfortable in my own skin" camp, struggling to see my body as God-given and as beloved.

My only recommendation, then, is that we encourage one another on this long journey, drawing strength from veins of our tradition that have celebrated our bodies and always being mindful of how much "deep stuff" (to use a technical term) we're wrestling with in this regard. This is a long journey for so many people, and it's one where the Good News of understanding, empathy, and compassion is sorely needed.

—Miguel Escobar

As a child, I was chubby, short, near-sighted, prone to tummy aches, and hopelessly clumsy at sports. I haven't changed much; weight is still and (always) a battle, and most athletic endeavors seem like too much effort for woefully little success. But when I retired, I no longer had the excuse of being too busy to exercise, and at just that time, the CREDO program of the Church Pension Fund introduced an online series called "Walk and Be Well." Walking didn't involve a huge investment of time or money and was something at which I couldn't possible fail—except by not doing it.

So I began to walk at least half an hour every day. I lost some weight. I rediscovered the neighborhood in which I'd been living for more than forty years—and then we moved, and I had a whole new neighborhood to discover, one I'm still discovering. I walk with a camera, which makes me look more closely at my surroundings. I meet neighbors and chat; I smile at strangers; sometimes I pray; sometimes I'm think about something I might want to write.

Some days I'm too tired, or too hot, or too cold, or my feet hurt, but I walk anyway, because walking is now an essential part of my life. This body, which I've often scorned as clumsy, unreliable, and not up to my aesthetic standards, is amazing me after seven decades: God has made me a woman who walks.

—Mary W. Cox

When Jesus sees the man lying by the Pool of Siloam, an invalid for thirty-eight years, he asks him not, "What's wrong?" but, "Do you want to be made well?" What is well? As I come to understand and reluctantly accept the limits that age brings to my enjoyment of all things exercise, to be well is to use my body to the best of its ability.

I was sure I was going to be the one whose body didn't get old, who'd be able to run the same number of miles, lift the same amount of weight, sit on my knees for the same number of happy hours as I'd always done. I was sure of it, until I wasn't.

To welcome a newborn into the world, to touch tiny hands, to count tiny toes, to watch fresh eyes take in the world is to know that we are, as the psalmist says, marvelously made. But so, too, is to listen to the wisdom of the grandfather, to hold the gnarled hands of the grandmother, to watch a hardened heart soften and open with age. There is wellness at all stages of life. And it is ours if we want it. God is in it all, and in us all, across our ages and across the ages. Take what God has given you, your marvelous self, mind, body, and spirit, and be well.

—Susan Wyper

✕

Pleasant words are like a honeycomb,
sweetness to the soul and health to the body.

—Proverbs 16:24

I've never liked yoga. It's good for the mind and body, but I'm not very flexible or in shape, which makes yoga embarrassing. I know involving your ego in yoga is a no-no, but that's easier said than done. Letting go has never been my specialty.

Despite that, I recently had the most wonderful experience in a restorative yoga class, which is basically meditative stretching. Luckily, I had no idea what I was walking into, or I might not have gone. Our teacher asked us to spend the extended time we stayed in each stretch to focus our minds on spatial awareness and where we were in the room. For some reason on that day, something clicked, and even with my eyes closed I was hyperaware of where my body was throughout the class. If I became even slightly off-center of my mat, I might as well have been upside down. I would open my eyes and adjust myself back to center as we moved from one pose to another.

The class created the most liberating feeling. My mind and my body were in perfect harmony. I can only imagine how rich my prayer life would be if I were consistently in that state while connecting with my Maker.

—**Lauren Caldwell**

In the scriptures we are reminded that God honors the body and the spirit. There is wholeness and unity in each of God's expressions of salvation. God reveals to us, in many ways, that we are temples of the living God and that the Spirit of God dwells in us (1 Corinthians 3:16). We are temple, and we are Spirit.

Increasingly, we hear about the importance of physical exercise. There is wisdom in learning to strengthen our bodies with physical exercise. In the sixteenth century, Saint Ignatius of Loyola wrote a series of meditations called "The Spiritual Exercises."

As we journey this day, let us be mindful that every human being is a child of God. How different our world would be if we saw each other as the living Body of Christ. May we remind ourselves that we are marvelously made to be the hands, feet, heart, soul, mind, and body of Christ.

—Mark Bozzuti-Jones

⊁

O God, the creator and preserver of all mankind, we humbly beseech thee for all sorts and conditions of men; that thou wouldest be pleased to make thy ways known unto them, thy saving health unto all nations....Finally, we commend to thy fatherly goodness all those who are in any ways afflicted or distressed, in mind, body, or estate; [especially those for whom our prayers are desired]; that it may please thee to comfort and relieve them according to their several necessities, giving them patience under their sufferings, and a happy issue out of all their afflictions. And this we beg for Jesus Christ's sake. Amen.

—THE BOOK OF COMMON PRAYER, P. 814-815

"Unexpectedly, I experienced the presence of God which rattled me loose." This, from my ninety-year-old friend, sober for forty years. Shaken up by a sense of God's presence, he began to be rattled loose from addiction, choosing day by day not to drink. But what was he rattled loose for?

He was rattled loose for honoring God with body, mind, and spirit, becoming a better husband, father, and resource for many, a gentleman who glorifies God by reading scripture with authenticity in church services, words read aloud and demonstrated, faithfully lived out. He has confidentially supported countless people so that they, too, could lean on God for lives of ongoing recovery. He was freed up to sound rumbling low notes, helping other basses in the church choir to praise God. And he was freed up to play Creator-initiated jazz piano.

Many of us need freedom to be rattled loose from an attachment, to let go of a memory, hurt, or fear, an object of obsession or paralyzing fear. We need to loosen the urge for control, to release ourselves from unhealthy influences. To recover daily, I need my Higher Power to rattle me loose, to grant me a prayerful body, mind, and spirit, living in courage, hope, serenity, and love.

May God free us all, giving us new spaciousness. May God help us fill the cleared space with thanksgiving and praise!

—June Terry

"On my honor, I will do my best…to keep myself physically strong, mentally awake, and morally straight."

This was something I said every week as part of the Scout oath. As I grow older, I find it, or at least the physical part, harder and harder to keep. Even though I am not elderly, I can already feel my body slowing down, wearing in places (particularly the knees). Despite this, I am still a temple to the Lord. Through my actions, I make an impact on others' lives, and through my actions, I can most fully embody the Word of God.

Physical actions can be a part of prayer. One saint would dedicate everything she did to God, from sweeping to eating. She never complained about any pain or inconvenience, instead choosing that as a sacrifice for the Lord. We would all do well to emulate her spirit of sacrifice and commitment, even if our bad knees make it difficult.

—Spencer Hixon

⋇

A new heart I will give you, and a new spirit
I will put within you; and I will remove from your body
the heart of stone and give you a heart of flesh.

—EZEKIEL 36:26

I met my youngest son for the first time in an airport. He was a chubby, wide-eyed, eight-month-old baby boy, fresh off a seventeen-hour flight from Korea. I had studied his picture for countless hours prior to that day. My eyes had traversed every inch of his sweet brown skin, but my fingers longed for the opportunity themselves. Months, weeks, and hours of waiting culminated in a lingering embrace just beyond the luggage conveyor, surrounded by weary travelers.

I could not divert my attention from this child, not even for a moment. I remember holding him, trying desperately to listen to his escort's recapitulation of the trip, but all I could think was, "Is this really happening?" Here was this child, in the flesh, whom I had longed to hold so desperately, for so long. I couldn't get to our vehicle fast enough, where I quickly stripped him down to his precious diaper. I wanted to see his toes. I needed to see his belly. My fingers traced the lines etched into his palm. My hands cupped his portly cheeks, as my lips drenched them in kisses.

This child of mine, marvelously made…not within my own womb, but within the womb of another. My senses drank in his flesh in the airport parking lot because I didn't have the opportunity at his birth. God knit this child together with purpose and intention, design and craftsmanship. I had absolutely nothing to do with it, but I was in complete and total awe of God's handiwork.

—Bree Combs

Marvelously Made

I took a test a while back and failed miserably. It was my cholesterol test. I have already forgotten the numbers, but my doctor who is half my age told me that I needed to address the situation. I have to tell you it sent me into a bit of a spiritual crisis. I didn't start immediately planning my funeral, but I did start thinking of my favorite hymn: "Come Down, O Love Divine." And my favorite scripture passages: "Nothing in all creation can separate us from the love of God." Well, maybe I did start planning my funeral.

Anyway, after talking to my doctor, we came up with a plan based on diet and exercise. Sounds awful, no? Well, the truth is, it wasn't so bad; all the numbers went down, and the doctor smiled.

The even more wonderful truth is that God has a plan for each of us. And that plan leads us, body and soul, in the footsteps of Jesus to the kingdom. Sometimes we might have to change the plan that we came up with on our own and do things differently, but it is worth it. Good things happen with God's plan. It is our promise and our hope. When we choose it, I know that God smiles, and more often than not, we all do too.

—Jason Leo

By faith, Alejandro, Laura, and Alex prayed over a dying newborn as if she were healthy. By faith the Montes family left their home to serve God in unknown countries. By faith, thousands passed through the Rio Grande as if it were dry land.

Time would fail me to tell of Alex, Thi, Lucy, Sergio, and countless others who through faith, survived wars, triumphed over an oppressive status quo, obtained promises, escaped attacks, turned weaknesses to strengths, administered justice, survived fires and car accidents, shut the mouths of accusers, became mighty in conflict, persevered in the waters of the frontera, defeated bullies, and prospered despite adversity. By faith we know where we are headed. By faith we know that where we are is not where we will stay. By faith our latter shall be greater (Haggai 2:9).

By faith no weapon formed against us will prosper. By faith we know God goes before us. By faith we leap into the darkness. By faith we sing amidst tears. By faith.

At the beginning of the year, my dad invites us all to use our bodies to summon God's new year into our life by faith.

Right now, using your hands, wipe off the old (whatever you don't want to take with you anymore) from your body. As you finish wiping, make fists and open them slowly to let go of all that has held you captive. As you hold out your open hands, receive all the good God has for you and then slowly close your hands into fists again to seize all that God is giving you. Open up your hands again to share all the good with others, starting with God. *Amen.*

—**Sandra Montes**

There I was, the bedroom door closed and sweat running down my sides, as I clung to the back of a chair and tried to get my eight-year-old feet and legs into correct ballet positions. I was trying to copy the photos and diagrams in a children's magazine featuring the legendary ballerina Maria Tallchief. Perhaps I could become a ballerina.

My next enthusiasm was for horseback riding. At about age twelve, I adored twice-weekly rides on my favorite horse, Pegasus, and tended to identify with the hard-riding Lassiter in *Riders of the Purple Sage.* Surely I could become a jockey.

What prevented me from pursuing either of these romantic job possibilities was my growing and changing body. I was never going to be the right size and shape to be a ballerina or a jockey.

My appreciation for simply being myself hasn't spoiled my love of seeing ballet when I can, and every spring when the Kentucky Derby comes around, you can be sure that I am cheering for any filly or female on the track.

God is gracious in loving us as we are. Simply trying to be a better version of my true self has proven to be a life's work without the added burden of trying to be what I am not and to do what I cannot do.

—**Joan Bowers**

When I was a child, my idea of heaven was to lounge with my books for eternity, arising only to fetch another volume.

My bookishness was compounded by physical ineptitude: when team captains chose up sides at recess, my participation was cited as a corrective for the more gifted athletes on my team. I rarely seemed to actually make it to the plate; something always happened to change the order.

As an adult, I realized that while exercise is necessary for good health, team sports are not. I started working out on my own. Finally, I hit upon the best routine for me: walking on a treadmill equipped with a device so I could read on my tablet. Exercise needn't be boring (nor humiliating) after all.

I walk early, reading the Daily Office (there's an app for that), getting centered before switching to the newspapers. As the news is frequently bleak, starting in prayer gets me through the dark but necessary spots. Thus fortified, I step forward into the day, strengthened in body, mind, and soul.

—Sarah Bryan Miller

☩

While they were eating, Jesus took a loaf of bread,
and after blessing it he broke it, gave it to the disciples,
and said, "Take, eat; this is my body."

—MATTHEW 26:26

In tai chi, I have learned experientially that what we do with our bodies affects not only our mind but also our spirits. Almost the first thing I learned was a beautiful form called "Movements of Peace." It incorporates body movements common to many different religious traditions—bowing, extending the arms, inclining the head, and raising joined hands. In one movement, we spread our fingers and bring our hands together in the shape of a heart, and as we grow more aware of our body, we can feel our pulse through our fingertips. No matter how stressed I feel, after several repetitions of this form I always find some measure of peace.

Tai chi happens to be my discipline, but many find this peace in other forms of movement, from something as structured as yoga to the simplicity of a daily morning walk. Yet some people feel a twinge of guilt about taking on a new discipline. It can be hard to make room in our schedule.

What if we thought of the time devoted to our chosen discipline as a form of peacemaking? Walking, yoga, or almost any movement can become body prayer. If our discipline makes us more peaceful, more conscious, more in tune with the pulse of our own hearts, we are sure to spread that peace to others throughout the day.

—**Kathleen M. Flanagan**

Doug and I were sitting outside a frozen yogurt place, enjoying the beautiful evening as much as our sweet treat. I finished mine before he was halfway done with his (as usual) and started rubbing his back.

A young girl, barely a teenager, walked out the door and wrapped her arms around Doug, putting her head on his shoulder. Doug smiled. I looked at the girl. I was certain she must know Doug, even though I didn't recognize her. It was a heartwarming sight, and I had no desire to interrupt.

As quickly as she appeared, she walked back inside. Doug seemed unfazed and continued to enjoy his frozen yogurt. A few minutes passed, and a woman (who must have seen the confusion in my face) walked out and said to me, "We've just come from a funeral, and we are all so sad. My daughter was watching you rub his back with such love and compassion; she simply wanted to be a part of it."

I wanted to ask who passed away, to offer my condolences, but this all happened so fast. I was almost speechless, just barely getting out, "Thank you for telling me; that was so sweet of your daughter."

The image of that sweet girl hugging Doug, of him simply being present to her and receiving what she needed to give, was beautiful to behold. This incredibly intimate moment of mutually shared affection and love, even though they were strangers, as though they sensed familiarity in each other's ache and each found comfort, gave all of our broken hearts a healing for which I am still saying prayers of thanksgiving.

—**Allison Zent Blankemeyer**

I am not what you would call a health nut. While my entire family belongs to the local gym, I am noticeably absent. Thankfully I inherited my dad's healthy genes, but you wouldn't know it at first glance. It is no surprise, then, that during my recent physical, my doctor, while admitting that my tests all show good results, said she would like me to lose a little weight without going crazy about it. Fair enough, I thought.

So I decided to become more observant about what I take in. I am not talking so much about calorie counting, but rather I started thinking about the kind of food I eat and when. As for exercise, while the gym still misses out on any membership dollars from me, I began walking more and started using the stairs at work instead of the elevator.

I have become more prayerful in my daily routine. When I am walking, I find myself more conscious of God walking with me. I look, listen, and start talking to God (not out loud, mind you, at least most of the time). And while I always used to begin meals with a quick word of grace, now I find myself taking a moment to really be thankful, for the food that makes me stronger and healthier, for those who grew it, transported, cooked, and served it, and who clean up after I am finished. And I am even more aware of those who do not have what I have.

I never expected it to happen, but living healthier has actually made me spiritually healthier as well. And that is a very good thing indeed!

—Chuck Robertson

A friend of mine loves liturgical dance. My husband is a runner, and he says running can be prayer time for him. Another friend is up early most mornings and runs before work and before traffic is heavy, saying she can listen to God as her feet hit the pavement. Children in Sunday School often learn body movement to accompany songs. All these are expressions of body prayer. But some body prayer is more subtle, like holding babies.

Recently, our daughter gave birth to twins, six weeks early. In the neonatal intensive care unit, I watched our son-in-law gently hold his tiny son in his adult hands. He radiated both pleasure and awe. When the twins arrived home, we and the other grandparents began taking turns assisting in the babies' care, and we had our own experiences of holding them close and feeding or rocking them while they held on to one of our giant fingers with their tiny baby hands.

Lyrics from a song written and sung by Carey Landry sometimes run through my head when I hold the tiny babies. It's from Isaiah 49. "I will never forget you, my people. I have carved you on the palm of my hand." The record album cover shows a child nestled into a curved hand. I first saw this a few decades ago, but I still remember the tenderness, security, and peace expressed in that illustration and in the song. I experience those feelings holding our tiny babies. It is prayer.

—Linda Gelbrich

We are made
    And being made in God's image
Yet ever being and becoming as God would have us be,
Shaped and formed and fashioned into God's likeness
More and more of God in us to see
It does not yet appear what we shall be
But when and then…our Maker's face to see
Fearfully
Wonderfully
Marvelously
Made and made perfectly
Being and becoming perfected
Daily
As more and more God shapes and takes shape in me,
Molding, making us to be what we cannot yet
But know that we shall someday see
That which God has known since before we ever came to be
More and more and more of God in me
'Til God in me should be
And God's own self God should see
Planned and purposed so to be
Since time before…and throughout all eternity
Amen.

—Kathy H. Culmer

*For as in one body we have many members, and not all the
members have the same function, so we, who are many, are one
body in Christ, and individually we are members one of another.*

—ROMANS 12:4-5

W hat does it mean to be created in the image of God?

A: It means that we are free to make choices: to love, to create, to reason, and to live in harmony with creation and with God.

(The Book of Common Prayer, p. 845)

One thing I've learned is that it matters a great deal what we think about God. Somehow much of that is bound up in the larger issue of how we think about God, in other words, how we "image" God. If a central attribute of one who has been created in the image of God is freedom, then we are free to explore that relationship in the best ways we know how. We are free to love, and if we are lucky, it's one of the first behaviors we have modeled for us. We are free to reason, to make sense of the world with the faculties available to us. And again, if we're lucky, our earliest experiences are in an environment that encourages these things.

I was and still consider myself lucky. I sometimes think most people have some experience of love and reason, but sometimes it's hard to see the marks of creation and harmony in that stamp of God's image—at least on my own soul. Through trial and error, mostly error, I set about creating God in my image or in the image of certain people who I thought might be most like my image of God at the time.

I am marvelously made with memory, reason, and skill. I challenge you to use what God has given you to recognize those who model love for us and teach us what it means to be made in the image of God.

—Charles McClain

To call my relationship with exercise tumultuous would be kind. It's always been something to do out of obligation, never desire. My spirit had never connected with my body in any intentional way. Until now.

It's taken me forty-eight years to come to the realization that God wants us to be out in the world. Here's my reasoning: God made me. God made you. God made the earth. What do those things have in common? You guessed it! God. So the logical conclusion I've come to is that if God made all of these beautiful things, sometimes those beautiful things should be together. Why is there so much beauty in the world if God didn't want us to see it and to enjoy it?

So, sure, I can walk on the treadmill. I can use my Wii Fit. I could join a gym. All of those are excellent ways to care for my body, and I encourage you to do those things. But if you're not already out there, on behalf of God let me invite you to enjoy God's kingdom here on earth. Find a beautiful park, path, trail, woods, river, or beach. Go on your own, or find a friend or partner to go with you. The keyword is GO! Where you go, God will go with you.

—**Miriam McKenney**

Psalm 139 speaks about a very present God knowing our every movement. God attends to our sitting down and rising up. How marvelous!

Each step, each word, God traces. Even in our hiding places, God is pressing upon us that we might experience the very presence of God. Even before we are born, God observes how we are slowly being formed.

The psalmist contemplates the wonder of God's artistry and wisdom. As I walk each day, I am aware of the pleasure I find in my body. The pain I feel gives me a message about changes I need to make. My eyes observe the seasons, fog rising in pillars on the river, faces of people I meet each day. My heart looks forward to seeing them again. My mind records it all.

My feet mark the changing terrain: ice, mud, cracked and packed soil, sure surfaces, stones, and uneven places—like life. My lungs fill with air. My skin registers the changing temperature, wind, and rain. All of this tells me about the intricate and beautiful creation all around me. Walking gives me such pleasure, which is all possible because such bounty falls from the hand of God. Each walk is a praise song!

—**Karen Montagno**

When you're big, it's hard to think about being marvelously made. Big girls don't get called marvelous very often. Oh, we can be smart. Witty. Friendly. Hard-working. Solid. But marvelous is an accolade reserved for the slender.

For most, the relationship with our bodies is complicated. But from my perspective, it's even harder when your body feels like a betrayal, when the outside is a total mismatch from the inside.

I've spent four decades, my life so far, in an unhealthy relationship with my body. When I was thin, I didn't know it. When I was fat, I couldn't stand it.

In the past six months, I've sought an intervention. I am working with a team of doctors, nurses, and dieticians, meeting every week to weigh and talk and map out a strategy to lose weight and gain better health. I've lost about 100 pounds, and it feels really good to wrap up in a towel after a shower, to sit in a patio chair, to walk a few blocks. I still have more work to do, but it's a great start.

For me though, the more important transformation has been in how I view my body. Instead of a burden, I am beginning to see it as a gift. These legs carried me down the aisle to the love of my life. These breasts nursed our children. These fingers are conduits from heart and brain to pen and paper, giving shape to stories and poems.

I am, for the first time, able to appreciate my body. With all of the curves and lumps, dimples and stretch marks, I am, like you, marvelously made. And loved, thanks be to God.

—Richelle Thompson

SEPTEMBER

Worship

Then he took a loaf of bread, and when he had given thanks, he broke it and gave it to them, saying, "This is my body, which is given for you. Do this in remembrance of me." And he did the same with the cup after supper, saying, "This cup that is poured out for you is the new covenant in my blood."

—LUKE 22:19-20

One Bread, One Body

We come together to tell the wonderful story of Jesus because it is the best, most life-changing story we know. We also tell each other this story over and over, down across the span of two millennia, so that we will not forget this most important story of God's love. How we choose to engage in the telling of that story isn't nearly as important as the why: we engage in the story to share and remember. Whether gathered in groups of two or three or in congregations numbering in the thousands, corporate worship calls us back to our deepest and sweetest wells of living water and bids us to drink and be satisfied.

WAYS TO ENGAGE

Visit a different church or congregation this month.

Go to a mid-week service at your congregation or other place of worship.

Invite a friend or two to share your devotional time this month.

Commit to regular attendance at your congregation and partake in Holy Eucharist.

E very workday morning at 10 a.m., something holy happens at Forward Movement. Our whole staff gathers around the conference table to read the daily devotional from *Forward Day by Day* and to share the prayer requests that our friends, subscribers, customers, and strangers offer online or over the phone. We also offer up prayers for our staff, family members, and other community concerns and joys.

This is precious time for us to share our prayers together, to bear each other's burdens, to laugh and cry together, to remember our call to discipleship, to say our prayers, and to proclaim the good news of Jesus. While my husband and I worship at the Community of the Transfiguration, the corporate worship I share with my coworkers each day is an incredible, irreplaceable slice of my daily bread. I am fed by it constantly, and the deep nourishment and comfort it gives me are profound reminders about the importance of worshiping in community.

My prayer for you is that you find yourself enriched and enfolded by such a community—that you find your place at the table, or on a pew, or in a comfy chair, and see revealed before you the hosts of heaven, dancing as one body, sharing the bread and cup.

—Rachel Jones

As soon as my daughter was able to gnaw a communion wafer with her gums, she was taking her place at God's table. She is almost six now, and she calls it, "The Bread." When she returns to the pew after attending Children's Chapel, the first thing out of her mouth is always, "Did I miss The Bread?" I reassure her, no, she did not miss the bread.

As the Holy Eucharist progresses, she gets more and more antsy, fidgeting in her seat as I stand and kneel and pray. Sometimes she'll poke my arm and ask how much longer. Now that she's old enough, I can show her in the bulletin where we are, how many more paragraphs or pages until we can stand up and walk up the aisle. She practically dances—in fact, when she was a toddler, she usually did dance. Or jump. Or run at top speed. She's growing up, so she knows to walk, but she walks with intention.

The Bread is the highlight of my daughter's worship experience. I don't know if she understands it, but let's be real here—I don't know if I understand it either. I simply know that when I stand up, walk forward, kneel, and receive this amazing gift every single week, I am in church. I kneel next to my daughter, and this body that grew her body joins the Body of Christ.

—Holli Powell

There is a line in the bulletin of the church that says something to the effect of, "Don't worry about following along exactly; let the community carry you in prayer." While the sentiment is directed at newcomers, I can think of plenty of times in my life when I couldn't follow along and needed to be carried in corporate worship.

For me, it wasn't ever really a question of knowing the words or finding my place in the right book. I was raised as an Episcopalian and know the pages of the red and blue books as well as my own phone number. For me, being carried in worship is about finding the space in my heart and soul to be present, to speak truth into the words on the page, to participate and believe.

One moment when I struggled most to follow along was shortly after I came out as queer. I found myself in desperate need of my church community and yet felt alienated by every word of the prayer book. Still, I showed up. For years I showed up and let the community carry me in prayer as I discovered new meaning, new freedom in our common worship.

The beauty is that our salvation, like our worship, is corporate. We are broken and saved as a body, the Body of Christ. Our salvation is shared. And when one part of the body is broken, the whole body carries it forward. It is never separate from, never outside. There is no outside.

—Jason Sierra

Toward the pulpit came the powerful presence of a preacher some have called the Martin Luther King Jr. of our generation, a man named the Rev. William Barber. His voice rumbled through the wooden pews and roused the sleeping giants of the stained glassed windows. He called us out of the pews and into action in the world—reminding all of us, of different traditions, races, ethnicities, and backgrounds, priests, pastors, and laypersons, that the intention of sermon-ing was for action-ing in the world.

He reminded us of the sacred tradition of prophets in the pulpit and justice-seeking in faith. He reiterated the biblical history, which called us to feed and be fed at the sacramental table as a reminder and representation of the holy in the everyday action of what we do in the world.

To be together in community calls us to carry the sacrament from the altar into the sacredness of the world. We are to be the bread of life—not just absorb it or consume it but become it in the world.

One of my favorite theologians, Richard Rohr, reminds me, "You are what you eat." If we believe in the symbolic presence of the bread of life shared in community with each other, we are also called to share that sustenance with the world, each and every day.

Our community of faith and our practice of worship reminds us of the inherent call and duty to share the common table, the bread of life in and with the world, each and every day. Let the bread not just feed us but multiply in our own lives so that it might feed the world.

—Teresa Pasquale

During the summer of my seventh-grade year, I spent almost every day farming with my grandfather. My grandpa and I would tend vegetables, harvest what was ripe, and go to the market to sell them. Out of all these experiences, our lunch time is what I remember. When we took a break and ate lunch, we had the same meal: mayonnaise and bread. Yes, I spent a whole summer eating bread and mayo, and it was delicious. Actually, honestly, I don't remember if it was that delicious, but this lunch break wasn't about replenishing energy and finding some shade. It was about sharing a meal with a man who has spent his entire life farming—and whom I love.

Every Sunday at church, I am reminded of how amazing the Body of Christ really is. How I can have a terrible week where nothing goes my way but a piece of bread can change that. Sometimes when I miss service, my week feels off. The bread that I am blessed to share with all the members of my community is good. Very good.

—Longkee Vang

✕

Speak to all the congregation of the people of Israel
and say to them: You shall be holy,
for I the LORD your God am holy.

—LEVITICUS 19:2

Why do movie theaters and concerts still exist? Many people who can afford ticket prices to see movies or attend concerts can also afford to have thousands of movies and songs delivered to them comfortably in their homes. No more cell phones going off at the worst possible times. No more dollar-per-kernel popcorn.

Community entertainment events exist because some experiences are better shared with groups than enjoyed alone. Songs that we already like become more exhilarating when the musician plays them live and the crowd's energy adds to the excitement. Comedies are funnier when the other people's laughter augments our own.

Applying this kind of energy to our faith experiences enhances them greatly. In this time of political and religious tension and individualized experiences, it is increasingly tempting to keep worship private. Going it alone means not having to compromise or be polite. We can sip coffee and wear whatever we want while we pray. But Christianity thrives on the kind of group energy that we experience in communal worship. Even persecuted Christians, for whom private prayer would be considerably safer, risk their lives to worship together. There is an energy and commitment to standing up with other Christians and proclaiming what we believe, in sharing the experience together of silently glorifying our God, an energy that we cannot experience alone. Christianity is by nature and definition a communal event; proclaiming our faith together both connects us to one another in Christ and enhances our personal faith.

—Elizabeth Brignac

Young men, bedazzled in ornate robes, walked ahead of the patriarch, a man who survived in the former Soviet Union with a Machiavellian political acumen. Pious old women crossing themselves from right to left were unceremoniously waved to step back as his holiness swung the incense burner on its chain and walked through the cathedral.

It was cultural splendor, not spiritual.

A day or two later, I was driven to western Ukraine on ancient roads used by Napoleon's troops, Nazi Germans, ancient pre-Christian tribes, and knights of yesteryear when Ukraine was a collection of principalities.

Ukraine, Europe's breadbasket, has some of the world's richest soil. It's the blackest black, not brown, and moistened with blood for thousands of years. I watched the earth's black bosom rise with each breath.

I saw women with switches guiding their geese and men preparing the black life for the spring planting of wheat. I saw hope. This was spiritual.

—Paul Jesep

B iblical scholars say that one of the oldest verses in the Bible is Exodus 15:20-21, which says: "Then the prophet Miriam, Aaron's sister, took a tambourine in her hand; and all the women went out after her with tambourines and with dancing. And Miriam sang to them: 'Sing to the LORD, for he has triumphed gloriously; horse and rider he has thrown into the sea.'" From the earliest days, getting together to praise God has been central to our identity as God's beloved people. That worship may or may not be inside a building, but it is done intentionally with others for the purpose of offering our communal thanks and praise to God.

A lot of other activities happen in churches, but they all flow from worshiping together. In corporate worship, we hear the Word of God together as a community and say our prayers together as a community, and we come to the table as a community. We sing together in praise (and sometimes lament). We wrestle with the scriptures together, and at our best, we determine how to live out our mission in the world through that wrestling.

There are lots of things one can do alone (including following Jesus), but at its heart, Christianity was formed out of a community gathered around Jesus. Jesus always expected his followers to stay together as a community. How else are we to love one another if we do not spend time with one another in prayer and at the table? Corporate worship is not all that we do as Christians (look at all the other spiritual practices that are part of this book!), but it is central to our identity.

—Penny Nash

I am an introvert. Saying that always makes me feel I need a twelve-step program to heal my addiction to spending time alone. Corporate worship is not the habitat I would naturally turn to for spiritual comfort and growth. Give me a still tree to hug, and I will feel the warm embrace of God.

But the Bible makes it very clear I must be open to corporate worship if I am to grow spiritually. God says it's not good for us to be alone (Genesis 2:18). Scripture says that corporate worship plays a crucial role in our individual sanctification and growth in conforming to the image of Christ (Romans 8:29) and that by coming together in corporate worship, we "are being transformed into the same image from one degree of glory to another" (2 Corinthians 3:18).

In other words, you must be part of a village to become a fully flowering Christian. I must trust the Lord knows what he's doing when he asks that I come together with others in corporate worship.

—Charlotte Chere Graham

Ж

I will declare your Name to my brethren;
in the midst of the congregation I will praise you.

—Psalm 22:21

I dragged myself to the 11:15 a.m. service, exhausted from work, family, and life. During the prayers of confession, I reached deep down within myself, desperately seeking an ounce of love, or of forgiveness, or of patience, or of understanding—and found nothing there. It felt as though my personal tank was reading empty. At communion, I eagerly stood in the line to receive the sacrament, intentionally choosing to stand rather than to kneel, the wafer melting in my mouth.

Take, eat; this is my Body. This is my Blood which is shed for thee.

I slurped the wine loudly from the chalice, unashamed of my need to drink deeply—and loudly—of the love of God. Perhaps I could begin to feel replenished from his blood, one sip at a time, one prayer at a time. As I knelt back at my pew, a peace that passes all understanding washed over me. I was renewed and made new by worshiping in unity with others. Thank God that in my hour of need, I was able to lean into the faith of others whose collective prayers propped me up and set me on my path again.

Eternal God, heavenly Father...Send us now into the world in peace, and grant us strength and courage to love and serve you with gladness and singleness of heart; through Christ our Lord. Amen.
                    —*The Book of Common Prayer*, p. 365

—Westina Matthews

I recently watched a documentary that made me think in new ways about cups. The documentary featured an army veteran artist, Ehren Tool, who makes and gives away ceramic cups, ones that are similar and dissimilar to the chalice at the center of our worship. These cups are imaged with complicated scenes from the artist's time in the Gulf War: the tanks and assault weapons, photographs of the violence and destruction from Kuwait, shattered bones of people he and others encountered on their tours. Like the cup we use, these cups invoke violence committed—the blood of war—but the purpose goes beyond this.

When asked why he had chosen to work on cups, Tool explained that while war can be overwhelming, cups are human-sized; they are built for human hands. Significant conversations happen over coffee cups; friendships are born and deepened over a cup of wine. He maintains that if the world is ever going to become less violent, it is going to have to begin at the scale of a human cup, with people speaking with one another about the violence we've rendered and how we're going to live differently in the future.

I can't help but think that Jesus would have agreed with this point—and that we've been given our own cup as a means for building a very different sort of world.

—**Miguel Escobar**

During the last few years we lived in Miami, Florida, our English-speaking congregation joined with a congregation that worshiped in Spanish. There were usually two Sunday services, one in each language, but knowing that we needed to become one congregation, we tried to worship together at least a few times a year. The bulletin was printed in both languages, with italics or bold print indicating which language would be used for the different parts of the liturgy. When the preacher was not bilingual, a bilingual member of one congregation or the other was drafted as interpreter of the sermon. The Lord's Prayer and the hymns were Pentecost—both languages spoken simultateously.

Sometimes our bilingual worship was well-planned and executed, and sometimes it was sloppy and awkward. But I noticed that as much as we all secretly dreaded the inevitable confusion, something amazing happened: everyone was fully present, paying careful attention to every word. It's impossible to coast through prayers on autopilot when your next response might be "Demos gracias a Dios," not "Thanks be to God!" (Or vice versa.)

There were also beautiful moments of recognition when we all understood, without knowing the words themselves, what we were doing together in the presence of God. "El Cuerpo de Cristo… The Body of Christ." No translation needed at the Lord's Table— on earth as in heaven. I am glad that our present parish has a Spanish congregation and that we sometimes worship together, using both languages; it's not easy, but it's exhilarating—and it's holy.

—Mary W. Cox

A wise old mentor once shared the secret of her long and deep faith life. "Act as if," she said. When you don't feel like you have faith enough to handle whatever comes your way, act as if you do. Faith will catch up to you.

The beginning of the program year in parish ministry is always exciting. Parishioners have returned from summer vacation, the pews are bursting, the body is strong. But within weeks, school calendars, sports schedules, and fall busy-ness will keep some folks away. And we miss them. We are all parts of the same body, and when parts are missing, the body suffers for it.

I have found that when I greet someone at the door of the church with "I'm glad to see you!", they immediately offer up an apology or excuse for their absence. I want to tell them that remark is not a comment on their absence last Sunday but rather an appreciation for their presence right now. I am truly glad to see them. As simple as that.

There is a reason, I tell our eighth-grade confirmation class, that many of our prayers begin with the first-person plural pronoun: "we" is what corporate worship is all about. It means that we carry the load one for another—so that when I can't carry it, you'll pick up my slack—whether it be a burden of time, belief, or hope.

—Susan Wyper

In middle school, I was a member of our diocesan youth commission. One year during our diocesan convention, we did a presentation that consisted of people looking under their chairs for a puzzle piece, and when they found one, they brought it to the front of the meeting space where we created a cross with the pieces. As I watched people from all corners of the room and all walks of life bring up their puzzle piece, I experienced my first example of what it means to be one member of a larger church.

While I'm sure the adults in the room were indulging us by participating in this silly exercise, to me it was very meaningful. I had always been on the outside of things in my everyday life, and this was a time when I was on the inside of something. Somehow I felt special by being a small part of the collective. It was a powerful feeling.

Christianity is constantly in a state of turmoil with one disagreement or another and that will likely never change. What must change is the brokenness it causes. It can be easy to look for the ways we are different from one another. The beauty of one holy catholic and apostolic church is that those differences are what make us beautiful and whole.

—Lauren Caldwell

⟡

Meanwhile the church throughout Judea, Galilee, and Samaria had peace and was built up. Living in the fear of the Lord and in the comfort of the Holy Spirit, it increased in numbers.

—Acts 9:31

One of the most encouraging sayings of Jesus is, "For where two or three are gathered in my name, I am there among them..." (Matthew 18:20). Our baptismal vows and our sacramental worship remind us that we are the Body of Christ at worship. Our worship gives testament to our belief in God, who calls us to pray together and to work for a world of justice and peace together.

Recently we have seen many people marching for justice. Many of these massive gatherings have been to protest the evils of racism, police brutality, and economic injustice. When we gather with others for a common cause, our voice takes on new power.

Our corporate worship reminds us that we are all God's children. This has political implications that run far deeper than we may acknowledge. Our worship demands that we see not only ourselves as the Body of Christ but also all of creation as God's family. Every Holy Eucharist is a commitment to "go in peace to love and serve the Lord." Whether gathered for peaceful protest or worship, we are one bread and one body. The radical revelation of one bread and body in the Holy Eucharist is a reminder that the world is one and that we must respect the dignity of every human being.

—Mark Bozzuti-Jones

Thinking of our reliance on one another, my mind plays a surround-sound video of worship last Sunday. The congregation and choir sang wholeheartedly along with the handbells, trumpets, a French horn, trombone, tuba, flute, and organ. No one could soar like that alone! During the Lord's Prayer, we held hands, a reminder that we need the hands of one another for mutual support in life's struggles. We shared Holy Communion, thanked God for mercy extended to us (a big bunch of sinners), and we tried to wrap our minds around faith, wanting the truth to take root in our hearts. We tried to apply grand scripture for life's nitty-gritty throughout the week. At least subconsciously, we were acknowledging our interdependence.

We need such personal soaking and shared soaring—with two or three or with dozens. Walking from the church building toward the week's routines, I was glad that every step brought me closer to returning. And I won't wait until Sunday.

—June Terry

One of the more difficult challenges facing many churches is how to bring in young adults, millennials. All too often, young people go off to college and never return to church; some return when they start having babies and want their own children to have a spiritual life. When my wife and I were first married, we fit squarely into that demographic, and we found a church that valued young married couples and babies.

We joined a group of young adults. Every week we worship together, starting with a communal meal, followed by fellowship and simple worship services. Our weekly service is a chance to get to know families who are raising children and finding strength in each others' experience with those who are growing in grace and faith.

—Spencer Hixon

Since you are eager for spiritual gifts,
strive to excel in them for building up the church.

—1 Corinthians 14:12

I think my kids fight just to drive me crazy. They will bicker over anything, argue about everything, and agree about nothing. If I'm not a referee, then I'm a traffic controller sending the kids in opposite directions just to mediate their disputes. Every now and then, I catch them in rare moments of tranquility, actually enjoying one another. Watching their love for one another is one of the greatest joys of being a parent.

I'm pretty sure God feels the same way about us. God loves watching us children set aside our differences, choose love, and pursue unity above all else. We can be a blessing to God by living in harmony with our brothers and sisters. In our homes, marriages, friendships, families, churches, workplaces, and schools, we can be tempted to choose division instead of peace.

Today, choose unity. When you are tempted to be selfish or insist on your own way, make a conscious step toward getting along. Look for opportunities to mend relationships and live at peace with everyone.

—**Bree Combs**

I like homemade bread, but I burn the water when I try to cook. My family gave me a bread machine one year for my birthday. A neighbor told me it wasn't really homemade bread if it came out of a machine. I won't tell you what I told him in response.

I volunteered at a community meal with a neighboring church. They asked for someone to make forty loaves of bread. No one raised their hand, so I did. People looked skeptical. At one point I thought my bread machine was going to explode. The guests loved the bread. There was none left over, and then they asked me to make the bread again.

We are Church because we can do more and be more together than we could ever do or be on our own. And we can know the amazing joy of being the family God intended us to be.

Sometimes miracles happen. I burn water when I try to cook, but once I made bread for more than one hundred people. Jesus performed miracles all the time, and he promised that we could too. One day your church will ask for volunteers. You should consider raising your hand. Something wonderful will happen, maybe even a miracle.

—Jason Leo

My nephew told me the other day that he is struggling with his faith. I remember being in my twenties, hearing about God, seeing my parents' example of what God's power looks like but not really understanding it.

No matter how much I tell my nephew or others about God or my experiences with God, they have to see God with their own eyes. That is why I believe going to church and being part of a faith community is so important. Sometimes it takes a lot of examples and faith stories for us to become curious about this Jesus. Sometimes it takes others' illnesses or tragedies to help us see that we have been spared by grace, not because we deserve it.

I pray for my nephew and the rest of our kids (my son and my brother's children) that they may see God with their own eyes. I pray that they continue to grow in their faith. I pray that Jesus manifests himself in a real way in their lives. I pray that they will attend a church where they can have community with others and be encouraged to seek God.

—Sandra Montes

〤

I appeal to you therefore, brothers and sisters, by the mercies of God, to present your bodies as a living sacrifice, holy and acceptable to God, which is your spiritual worship.

—ROMANS 12:1

On a trip to central Florida, the ever-present fragrance of orange blossoms reminded me of something I missed from having lived ten years in the South. There, I became accustomed to air scented with jasmine and honeysuckle, and, to this day, the scent of boxwood takes me back to one very special home in Virginia.

We now know that scent is one of the most powerful senses, particularly in evoking memories.

In the Middle Ages, fragrance also had moral associations, as in the "odor of sanctity"—the notion that the bodies of saints would smell fragrant no matter how long they had been buried.

We who believe the church to be the Body of Christ have had to confess that, at times, the church itself had a bad odor because of scandals, hurts, and hypocrisy. Those wounded by church leaders and fellow parishioners must be left with something like the odor of skunk.

As churches and as individuals, we need to ask ourselves: What is our odor out there in the neighborhood? Are we providing the scent of something that is yearned for?

At our redeemed best, we in the church can rejoice and give thanks to God who "through us spreads in every place the fragrance that comes from knowing him. For we are the aroma of Christ to God among those who are being saved" (2 Corinthians 2:14-15).

—Joan Bowers

There is nothing like being deprived of something to enhance one's appreciation of it. During the long and cold winter of 2010, while enduring months of chemotherapy, I rarely made it to church. I made do with broadcasts of Choral Evensong from the BBC over the Internet and with private communion brought from the altar by our parish priests.

The fact that I received one host from the scores consecrated that morning made a difference; it brought me closer to those who knelt together at the altar rail. Receiving alone brought home the importance of corporate worship and what I missed by not being able to attend.

No one would ever dispute the importance of individual prayer and meditation, but sometimes we overlook the central place of worshiping together, of being Christ's body. The fact is that we strengthen one another—in practice, in commitment, in inspiration—when we join our hearts together in love. Few of us can walk this long, high, and treacherous path alone, but together, fed by the Body and Blood, we uphold one another in faith so that our strength does not fail or the air become too thin.

—Sarah Bryan Miller

One windy Saturday evening in spring, we stood just outside our church's big red door. There was a chill in the air, but we warmed ourselves by the fire kindled in the brazier. We prayed a simple liturgy together, and then our deacon carefully lit the great Paschal candle from the fire. The Easter Vigil had begun.

We walked in silence down the sidewalk in a procession around the church. A sudden gust of wind whipped my acolyte's robe around my legs—and blew out the candle we had just so solemnly lit. We kept walking, and someone quietly pulled out a lighter and relit the Paschal candle.

Most of us could probably tell similar stories. We all know that the quality of our worship isn't dependent on all the details of the liturgy going just right. The candles and flowers, the bows and processions are simply symbols we use to show our love for God in ways that transcend words. We don't use them to create some perfect ritual but rather to help us forget about ourselves for a while and think about God's great love for us instead. When I leave church on Sunday, I am uplifted in a way that simply can't happen when I pray alone. Together, we have managed to create a sacred time and space of prayer. Each week, we rekindle the sacred fire—we relight each other's candles with God's help.

—Kathleen M. Flanagan

When they had prayed, the place in which they were gathered together was shaken; and they were all filled with the Holy Spirit and spoke the word of God with boldness.

—ACTS 4:31

I had the most extraordinary epiphany yesterday while I was with Doug. I had to go to a salon to get him a manicure and pedicure. His nails grow so fast, and for some reason he gets really scared when we try to cut them. He seems to trust the ladies at the salon, and I know how much he savors touch; it's his love language, so it is my pleasure and privilege to take him.

I was admiring the woman who was working with him. She was so kind, gentle, and patient. She spoke little English. I watched Doug, with his almost total inability to comprehend any spoken words, regardless of the language—and yet they communicated so beautifully with their eyes, their smiles, and their hearts.

Watching them interact, I was overwhelmed with my love for him, for her, for this world—with all its brokenness and limitations—and felt nothing but the pure perfection of that moment. I was completely free of past hurts, disappointments, judgments, and expectations that must normally influence my feelings, and I saw the world how I imagine God must see it, with only compassion and adoration.

I wonder how different we would be if we actually allowed ourselves to feel that magnificent love...how it would change us completely. I thought of how fear would vanish, and we would truly know peace. I wanted nothing more than for Doug to feel this from me, but then I realized how we all block this priceless gift, through our own dis-ease. I prayed to hold that experience in my heart and send it out into the world knowing and believing that love, above all else, has the power to heal us and make us whole.

—Allison Zent Blankemeyer

In one parish, I heard a complaint from many in the congregation that the person who baked their communion bread somehow didn't get the recipe right. The bread crumbled too easily, falling apart, unable to hold its form. Perhaps a necessary ingredient was missing or perhaps the mixture had not spent enough time baking. Whatever the case, something was needed to make a hearty, healthy loaf of bread that held together.

Not a bad analogy for the Body of Christ. How easy it is for us to fall apart, to not be able to hold ourselves together. And why? Often it is indeed an ingredient that is missing or present in too small of a quantity. This was the problem in Corinth, as Paul addressed numerous specific instances where they could have been stronger, heartier, healthier as a body if only they had been more generous in their care and respect for one another.

Paul summed it up in the magnificent, poetic utterings of 1 Corinthians 13: love is patient, love is kind, love is not jealous or conceited or proud. These words are often read at weddings, and that is appropriate. But let's not forget that these words were written for a group, for a community of followers of Jesus who were in desperate need of love in great measure. May we who are members of the Body of Christ today each take steps to ensure that we hold together by being generous in our mutual respect and appreciation and love.

—Chuck Robertson

S everal years ago, I was able to participate in the celebration of the Feast of Saint Francis in the Cathedral of Saint John the Divine in New York City. In this large cathedral filled to capacity, worshipers gathered, some with pets by their side or on their laps. On the day of the Earth Mass and Blessing of the Animals, music from the Paul Winter Consort and several choirs filled the sanctuary. Liturgical dancers enacted aspects of creation. In the Prayers of the People, we heard,

"We thank you for your creation, and pray for the earth you have given us to cherish and protect: nourish in us your love for all you have made. We are your stewards, O God." Hundreds responded by saying, "Hear our prayer" (*Prayers of the People, Form A*, The Church of Ireland).

Following Holy Communion, we said in unison the prayer attributed to Saint Francis that begins, "Lord, make us instruments of your peace...." And then animals from several area sanctuaries processed toward the altar while we were all instructed to stay seated and refrain from taking flash photos or applauding. Among those processing were a camel, yak, llama, goat, donkey, calf, monkey, peacock, and honeybees.

It was like representatives of all creation were gathered in prayer, giving thanks and receiving blessing. The voices of whale and wolf were part of the service; the voices of all the rest of us responded.

—Linda Gelbrich

When geese fly in a V formation, they are able to fly farther and higher. Each bird flies slightly above the bird in front of it, causing a reduction in wind resistance and providing an additional lift for the bird flying behind it. Geese can fly alone, but there is a lifting power that comes from flying together. They are flying as one but with the power and the thrust of many. They are simultaneously lifting one another and being lifted.

This is at least part of the power and value of corporate worship. Worshipers are able to lift one another as they are being lifted and as they are simultaneously lifting up the One who gives life and life eternal. We can worship alone, but there is an additional power that comes from worship where many hands, hearts, and voices are lifted together in adoration and in declaration of the goodness of God.

Who knows what moments of holy encounter await you there, what hidden word of hope or encouragement may fall upon your ear or touch your heart there? Who knows what hidden treasures you may find or that may find you there, in the house of prayer? Go! And, go expectantly! "These I will bring to my holy mountain, and make them joyful in my house of prayer" (Isaiah 56:7).

—Kathy H. Culmer

Our shared experience of worship forged a connection in me that has only deepened as I have become more connected to our church and to Christ. The choir and the organ fill the space like the incense that I am probably allergic to. During the eucharistic prayer, I often hear the words, "Sanctify us also," and I really believe that I am in a place where that could actually happen, and I am with people who are faithfully enduring that process.

I envision the trek down the aisle to receive the sacrament as a reoccurring journey that I walk, not only with those in attendance but also with those who have gone before and those who will come after me. That circle of receiving and returning and being sent out to "do the work [God] has given us to do" spirals up into my imagination as some sort of heavenly parade, a way for us created beings to connect to the Uncreated.

That is what our corporate worship is about. It is about living an authentic life in front of the Living God.

Charles McClain

Will you continue in the apostles' teaching and fellowship, in the breaking of the bread, and in the prayers?

I will, with God's help.

—The Book of Common Prayer, p. 304

Everyone at some time or another experiences the pain of being done wrong. Scams, hacks, identity theft, and other impersonal crimes proliferate, but it is usually the personal attack that makes our cheeks turn red. Jabs by close friends or relatives can turn the blaze into a bonfire. The psalmist says the remedy is to empty our mind of worry and anger. Then we are to refill it with delightful thoughts of God's goodness, so that God will grant us "the desires of our heart." That is quite a promise.

"Beloved, never avenge yourselves, but leave room for the wrath of God; for it is written, 'Vengeance is mine, I will repay, says the Lord'" (Romans 12:19). How does all that work? I wonder. I guess since God sees everything within everyone, like peering into a dollhouse from its open side, God knows how best to get the evildoer's attention. And with God's infinite patience, God can wait for the perfect moment to say, "Ahem." Most unfortunately of all, sometimes the offender is me—or you—or just about everyone who's ever sat in a pew. That's material for another devotion.

—Susan Taylor Block

Communion bread bakers work behind the scenes. Their ministry is a blessed gift to worship. This hands-on and sacred ministry provides spiritual food for the community each week. One piece of bread gives us the sweet taste of the Body of Christ and a foretaste of the beloved community united in Christ. In a broken world, one loaf made with loving hands, broken and shared by many, is a vision of all that unites us.

Our summer campers often get the opportunity to bake communion bread. The children plunge their hands into flour and make the sweet dough. Campers experience the great satisfaction of baking. They have an active role in feeding the Body of Christ. One loaf of bread makes them one body as it is offered during worship. As the bread is formed from flour, water, and little hands, it is a tangible symbol of our interrelatedness with God, the earth, and each other. The Body of Christ may meet in different places, but we all share one bread.

—**Karen Montagno**

✴

Be present, be present, O Jesus, our great High Priest, as you were present with your disciples, and be known to us in the breaking of bread; who live and reign with the Father and the Holy Spirit, now and for ever. Amen.

—THE BOOK OF COMMON PRAYER, P. 834

OCTOBER

Walking the Labyrinth

I am the LORD, your Holy One, the Creator of Israel, your King. Thus says the LORD, who makes a way in the sea, a path in the mighty waters, who brings out chariot and horse, army and warrior; they lie down, they cannot rise, they are extinguished, like a wick: Do not remember the former things, or consider the things of old. I am about to do a new thing; now it springs forth, do you not perceive it? I will make a way in the wilderness and rivers in the desert.

—ISAIAH 43:15-19

Make a Way Out of No Way

From the moment Adam and Eve walk into the land east of Eden, the people of God become consummate walkers. On calloused feet, the children of Israel walk over impossible obstacles. Jesus and his friends walk all over Judea, proclaiming that the kingdom of God is near. And Jesus walks across the face of troubled waters—an impossible thing that truly happened. We are a walking people.

The most practical difference between a maze and a labyrinth is that a labyrinth has no dead ends. Every turn leads you along the path—no step is wasted. This month, we are invited to spend time with the labyrinth, to ponder the ways God makes a way out of no way.

Ways to Engage

If possible, find a labyrinth near you and try walking it several times this month.

Try using a hand or finger labyrinth during your devotional time.

Every day for months, I prayed the same prayer every morning, stopped at the same stoplight, trying not to cry or throw up from the weight of what I was carrying. "Jesus, my brother, make a way out of no way. Show me the precious miracle from heaven in this garbage heap of a situation. Help me stay out of your way." On and on I prayed, begging Jesus to make a way out of no way, dogged in my tenuous belief that persistence pays off, that something would turn out right, that all things would be well.

The slow and steady work of redemption is being played out over the whole face of creation, in my life and yours; when it moves at glacial speeds, we cry out. God is always on time, even when we insist that God is late or early or has forsaken us. The constancy of the sunrise and sunset every single day assures us of God's timeliness, if not God's great goodness. Time has a different and altogether deeper meaning for God, who sees all of this—past, present, and future as now. It is impossible for us to know how to reconcile that kind of infinitude, and so we must lean into the strong arms of faith to carry us across that void of unknowing.

May you find yourself basking in the love of this on-time God, who makes a way out of no way, who carves beautiful canyons in the flesh of creation and in the flesh of our hearts, and who loves us beyond all comprehension.

—Rachel Jones

When Abraham walked up the mountain, prepared to sacrifice his beloved son Isaac, God brought a ram out of the bushes and made a way. The Israelites stood with the Red Sea in front of them and the Egyptian army at their backs, and God parted the sea and made a way. When Jesus breathed his last breath upon the cross and was buried in the tomb, seemingly ending his message and his reign on earth, God rolled away the stone and made a way.

Our faith is full of stories of God making the impossible a reality, and yet there are so many times in my own life that I have felt there was no good way forward. I might not have actually thought "not even God can fix this!", but I certainly behaved as such. But then I found a small clearing, maybe enough to get one foot down, and then another and another. Soon I was somewhere I didn't even know I could be, somewhere beyond my imagination. Every time I've felt stuck, every time I've felt alone, every time I've felt like I didn't know in which direction I was headed, God has made a way for me.

—Holli Powell

But Moses said to the people, "Do not be afraid, stand firm, and see the deliverance that the LORD will accomplish for you today; for the Egyptians whom you see today you shall never see again."

—EXODUS 14:13

As a socially reserved extrovert, I find social situations infuriating. I want nothing more than to be open and present because that is how I feel most whole. At the same time, that isn't how I was raised. I was raised among introverts for whom small talk is excruciating and large social events are exhausting. Over the last fifteen years, I've been pushing myself closer and closer to the goal of social ease. Emotionally I keep finding myself in the same frustrating place, like a spiral, slowly spinning toward a goal, toward the center.

Given the speed at which life moves, it is tempting to want to find the most direct route to a goal. Just as habits build character through repetition, change also takes frustrating repetition. With each revolution, we have the opportunity to reflect from a slightly different angle on the problem. We can gain appreciation for a certain point on the revolution by re-engaging it, for the perspective it offers and the depth it gives to the person we are becoming.

May we greet the spirals and labyrinths of our lives as opportunities to re-engage the various perspectives God offers us as we build and unbuild the people God is calling us to be. May we always be blessed by what is perhaps the most difficult habit and the most necessary to Christian life—patience.

—Jason Sierra

I t is a trait in my life that I can make the simple complicated. I take that essential journey, that never-changing cyclical path, and I distract myself with the changing dressing of my environment, with the changing seasons of life. I am distracted by how life crowds the way with ornate flowers, prickly cacti, or a complexly interwoven vine. I lose the path, I lose my way—distracted by complexities on the way to truth.

The beauty of the labyrinth is that it waits for us. It doesn't change to meet us where we are, it just waits for us to find it, to walk, step by step into the truth of our lives, and to find the sacred honesty of our soul and the genius of God at the core of the spiral's path.

How many times in my life I tried to make the journey harder and longer than it needed to be. How many times I have wanted to laugh at myself when I realize how much simpler the path could have been.

The labyrinth is the metaphor for my life—and if it is true for my life, it is likely true for all lives. We are all trying to turn the labyrinth of life into a maze—we think there are a hundred complex and dizzying ways to get to the heart of the universe and the seat of our souls, but there really is just one road in and the same road out.

See the path for what it is, not what you try to make it. Walk the labyrinth to remind yourself of the sacred simplicity in all things—which we miss when we try to make the labyrinth into the maze it never was, at all.

—Teresa Pasquale

Located in front of the lodge was the Merciful Love Labyrinth, made with the same 1930s stone that had been used to build the chapel on the sacred site. It was a beautiful, concentric circle with a path wide enough for two. The youth approached the entrance and entered. We noticed that, although the path was wide and we were the only ones walking, the youth waited to enter from the same entry point.

We asked why no one entered from different sides or started from the middle and walked out of the labyrinth. The youth told us that that's not how it's supposed to be done; there's one way in and one way out. It was at this moment that the spiritual guide on the trip reminded the youth that this was a labyrinth and not a maze. There were no tricks or dead ends here, no misdirection or strict rules. It didn't matter where we started or ended; the path we took was the important lesson.

—Longkee Vang

※

The Lord is my rock, my fortress,
and my deliverer.

—2 Samuel 22:2

Journeying takes us outside of our lives for a while, until we reach our destination and re-engage. My family visits New Orleans every year. Driving there takes a couple of days, and I find that I value those days almost as much as I do the visit itself. On the way there, after the flurry of packing and stuffing the car with luggage and making sure the children have gone to the bathroom—again, I rejoice in the sudden stillness of being in the car, the abrupt cessation of business. My state of mind relaxes to one of peace, even informal meditation, because even if I feel like I should be doing something, there isn't much business I can attend to in the car. Sure, I break up the occasional children's quarrel; I regulate screen time, but by and large, the journey enforces a temporary quietness.

I have never experienced a pilgrimage, but I picture the meditative act of walking combined with that unique peace of attending to nothing but the journey itself. Then I picture the holy purpose of the journey, taken in the footsteps of so many Christians who have walked the same path for so many years. I hope to make a pilgrimage one day.

Some people approach the labyrinth as a miniature pilgrimage—a short, holy journey away from the business of the world in the footsteps of other Christians who have traveled the same way. I love the idea of that approach. In lieu of an actual pilgrimage, I will try walking a labyrinth that way.

—**Elizabeth Brignac**

During a light snow I worked at my desk. The clock gave notice a new day had arrived. Heat and an orange glow violently pierced the cold winter night. Looking out my window, I saw a building across the parking lot from me had erupted in flames.

After making sure all my neighbors were up, I returned to my apartment (perhaps for the last time?) and wondered what to take in the minutes left. Clothes? Certain books? My grandmother's framed embroidery? Other than what I wore and the laptop, I took nothing.

Although a real possibility existed I would lose everything (thankfully my building was spared), there was something extraordinarily freeing in not being weighed down by the false security of possessions. I took an odd comfort in the possibility of starting again despite all the personal and financial hardship.

I walked into the snowy night toward a downtown hotel without thinking about the next day. I had taken this route many times on rainy, snowy, humid, and sunny days. Depending on the time of year, I could experience flowers growing in cracked pavement. I had made it my street labyrinth, occasionally challenging myself to find quiet as life swirled around me.

In the ensuing activity of sirens and fire trucks, there was peace within. Before arriving at the hotel, the gift of stillness had briefly settled over me. I actually thought about nothing for several, glorious minutes. No angst. No worry. No anxiety. I had let go.

—Paul Jesep

Last spring I went on a weeklong pilgrimage to the Isle of Iona off the coast of Scotland. One of our activities was making and walking a labyrinth on the beach.

Our leader drew the basic outline of a labyrinth, and we were tasked with decorating it—making the lines clear with rocks, kelp, sticks, and shells. We took some time to be quiet and consider what we might bring into the labyrinth, what we might want to let go of when we reached the center, and what we might bring out of it. Then slowly, one by one, we entered and began to walk.

I knew what I wanted to leave behind in the labyrinth. I wanted to leave behind my impossible standards.

So I picked up a big rock to carry into the labyrinth, big enough for me to feel the weight of it, to feel the burden of carrying it. I walked in silence, but I was very aware of the rock in my hands and how it pulled my shoulders forward to carry it.

When I reached the center, I leaned over and put down the rock. I stood there for a minute and felt myself, my soul, grow lighter. And then I straightened up and walked out, determined not to pick that rock back up again.

—Penny Nash

I love walking a labyrinth. I walk one each day, an internal labyrinth that takes me from the dawn of my day to the end. Before I begin walking the day's labyrinth, I spend ten minutes with the image of sitting in a field with God. Then for the next ten minutes, I chant my favorite prayer out loud. Finally, I sit in stillness, listening for any special instructions God may have for me.

The beauty of the labyrinth is that there are no blind alleys or dead ends. Ultimately, it's meant to welcome and facilitate our journey from birth to spiritual awakening to our passing. Through gentle dedication and acceptance of meandering twists and turns, it's a carefully designed path taking us to the center of ourselves and the Christ within each of our hearts.

I hold the image of the labyrinth close as I negotiate an everyday life that does its level best to take me down dead ends. As the labyrinth's trail takes me to the end of the day, I put my head on my pillow and say my favorite prayer one final time. Nodding off, I welcome a gentle sleep that refreshes me to the center of my being for the next day's journey.

—**Charlotte Chere Graham**

Walking up the temporary stairs over the West Side Highway—"temporary" now for more than thirteen years—to the World Financial Center, I realized how depressing and exhausting this trek can be. It is a reminder of better days and at the same time, of a dark season. No more Twin Towers, underground shopping, or Windows on the World. In that footprint we now have six new skyscrapers (including the tallest in the United States), a transportation hub, and the 9/11 Memorial Museum.

How do we let go of remembering what was once but will never be again? How is the crooked made straight? As I walked the labyrinth during a parish retreat and pondered these questions, I began to remember that there is One who lights our way, who will make a way out of no way. May we be resurrected from our past and embrace the new.

When Jesus spoke again to the people, he said, "I am the light of the world. Whoever follows me will never walk in darkness, but will have the light of life" (John 8:12).

—Westina Matthews

✗

He will deliver you from six troubles;
in seven no harm shall touch you.

—JOB 5:19

Make a Way Out of No Way **OCTOBER 11**

I recently visited the National Civil Rights Museum in Memphis, Tennessee, housed in the Lorraine Motel where Dr. Martin Luther King Jr. was assassinated. I was reminded of the legacy of this movement and especially of Dr. King's words. I noticed that throughout many of his sermons and speeches, he kept returning to the theme of "making a way out of no way."

This saying has a rich history. While it doesn't appear in the Bible, when King and others use it, they are drawing upon an American folk proverb that has deep roots in the experience of southern slaves: God will make a way out of no way, for God can do anything but fail.

There is a hope and practicality in this message that I find especially helpful today. Two days after my visit to the Lorraine Motel, Baltimore erupted in a night of rioting over the killing of Freddie Gray. Ferguson, Missouri, New York, and South Carolina have all been sites of the killing of unarmed black citizens and a sluggish (if not culpable) justice system. Add to this the retaliatory killings of police officers, and we find ourselves in a painful and perplexing situation.

Old wounds on race, once thought buried, have resurfaced with a vengeance. Many of our faith and political leaders appear dumbfounded about what to do next. In this, I'm reminded of King and others' wisdom in what appears to be hopeless situations, that the way forward begins with leaning on the God who has made a way out of no way so many times before.

—Miguel Escobar

At General Convention 2000 in Denver's Convention Center, there was space enough behind the altar to allow for a large canvas labyrinth to be laid out on the floor. Time was made available one morning for people to engage in private meditation, including the opportunity to walk the labyrinth.

Lines at the labyrinth were long, as were the rows of shoes at the labyrinth's edge, since we were asked to remove our shoes to protect the fabric. Even waiting in line was part of the journey, and the whole experience was one of great joy.

I was surprised and saddened to read that some people objected to the labyrinth behind the altar, believing it to be some kind of pagan devotional tool, forcing those who thought they were worshiping at the altar to be reverencing also some demonic power in the labyrinth behind it. What we're looking for is what we tend to see.

What do you look for when you walk a labyrinth—or walk anywhere? I have walked many labyrinths, and every path has been different. Sometimes I've found unexpected joy or insight, and sometimes I've walked out with questions I didn't know I had when I walked in. I've come to believe that the best thing to look for in the labyrinth—and in all the twisting paths of our lives—is what God wants to give us in each moment of the journey.

—Mary W. Cox

The other day, a member of our weekly Bible study asked me where I thought I was on my spiritual journey. When I pushed him as to what he meant, he said, "You know, on a scale of 1 to 180." I had a sudden visual of my car's dashboard with its various needles: one gauging fuel, from empty to full; one speed, 0 to 120 mph; another temperature, blue cold to red hot. It wasn't an image I'd ever applied to the spiritual life. "Gosh, maybe hovering just past 90," I answered. "Up to 120 some days? But I like to think of it more like a labyrinth."

While our physical lives unfold in linear time; or *chronos*, our spiritual lives experience a more circular, infinite time.

We walk a labyrinth: there are moments when we approach the center, and others when we walk away from it. We get close to the heart, and we move away from it before we come back again. But we are always on the path and our destination is secure.

Life can sometimes feel more like a maze than a labyrinth, complete with dead ends and wrong turns. With God however, the journey is a labyrinth, not a maze. Stay the course, keep the faith, run with perseverance the race set before you, for God is at its beginning, end, and every step along the way.

—Susan Wyper

It's scary to feel like you are watching a train crash and are helpless to do anything about it, especially when you're the one who will be hurt. It goes against our nature to let go and let things happen when the consequences could be deadly. I've learned that the more I try to control things, the more out of control they get. I've learned that there is no one path I can take that leads where I want it to and that the more I meander, the more likely I am to end up where I want to be. Some people see that as aimlessness, but I see it as survival.

I was given a compass by a friend of mine with the J.R.R. Tolkien quote: "Not all who wander are lost." This friend understands the greater meaning that Tolkien plays in my life, but more importantly he was naming the truth in that statement for me. Most of the time I don't feel like I have much control over what is happening in my life. In fact, I spent many years feeling like I was looking down on my body and only able to observe as things crashed around me. I suffer from Post Tramatic Stress Disorder, and things often feel like they are happening regardless of the protections I make for myself.

I know this much is true: the most direct route isn't always straight. The shortest path isn't always the easiest. And not all who wander are lost.

—**Lauren Caldwell**

Early Christians were known as people of the Way, a community whose journey was based on following Jesus Christ. In truth, walking in faith continues to describe who we are and who we are called to be. Every day we hear the invitation to follow. The path and the One we follow deepen our sense of self and of the Way, the Truth, and the Life.

Journeying with Jesus, we pay attention to his birth in a manger; walking with Jesus demands we remember the poor. We pay attention to his baptism and his being led by the Spirit. We pay attention to who we are and whose we are. Walking with Jesus demands that we walk as children of the Light. We pay attention to him preaching Good News to the poor, bringing sight to the blind, and setting the captives free. Walking with Jesus demands that we work for justice and respect the dignity of all.

Walking with God, for God, and in God is the way to abide in God, whose love remains real and unconditional. To walk with God calls us to be Good News to the poor, compassionate to others, and sources of God's healing and love.

—**Mark Bozzuti-Jones**

⋊⋉

In your righteousness, deliver me and set me free;
incline your ear to me and save me.

—Psalm 71:2

Following a labyrinth's pattern sometimes helps unscramble my jumbled thoughts. Calm may increase in approaching the path's center, as if drawing nearer to God. Or I imagine God as shepherd, guiding me "according to the integrity" of God's heart (Psalm 78:72, New American Standard Bible).

Recently, I met a woman who saw her life like the Grand Canyon rather than a level labyrinth. Her husband died after an extremely long illness, and she'd been recovering for eleven years. Magnificently recovering. She said that at the Grand Canyon, a visitor might think, "Something happened to create this canyon, something like devastation." She described cliffs, chasms, colors, and vastness—not devastation but glorious beauty. Her story revealed glory created from cataclysm, while we sensed beauty within her own person. Transformation. She had been led, according to the integrity of God's heart, from suffering into hope and courage.

In seasons of calm or pain, we may learn that a labyrinth fosters peaceful reflection. And emerging from devastation, hope becomes a fresh possibility. In either situation, God shepherds us with infinite integrity, creating on a grand, unseen scale. As we walk through it all, we may come to know ourselves better, discovering that we aren't who we thought we were, and as a result, we will come to know God more intimately.

—June Terry

When I was young, I wanted to be a paleontologist. When I went to college, I became disillusioned when I met an actual paleontologist and found out how much grant writing he did, versus the time he spent digging for dinosaurs.

Nothing can change up our plans as much as other people will. Before I met my wife, I knew what I was going to do: work at a major publishing house in New York City and in my free time, write the great American novel by the time I turned thirty. Instead, I moved to South Carolina and worked (ironically) as a grant writer. When we had our daughter, after many prayers and conversations, we decided that I would become a stay-at-home dad.

This decision was not easy. It felt like the path I had prepared for myself had been closed off, and I was left without any options. It was only after putting my trust in God that I saw the pathway prepared for me and understood in a new way the amazing grace with which God loves us.

—Spencer Hixon

X

Because he is bound to me in love, therefore will I deliver him;
I will protect him, because he knows my Name.

—PSALM 91:14

It was supposed to be the scariest haunted house in Kentucky, and as a twenty-year-old college student, I was up for anything. As the front door slammed behind me, I was immediately engulfed in darkness...sheer, utter, mind-paralyzing, frigid darkness. I held tightly to my fiancé's hand. Like cattle being herded from field to field, we shuffled our feet along the sticky floor, trying to discern each twist and turn. Suddenly, a rush of wind assaulted me, and I heard a sound so loud my entire body shuddered. Light flashed for a millisecond and fear itself came crashing down. I collapsed on the floor. I was so overcome by fear that I couldn't scream, or run, or even move. Jason was startled for a moment, but he grasped my hand, gently tugging upward. I was on the verge of a complete meltdown. He whispered, "It's OK. I am right here. Let's keep moving forward."

In that moment, a calm came over me. Jason stepped in front of me, and I buried my face in his back. I followed him through the rest of the tangled maze, focusing on the one thing I knew was certain up ahead...freedom. Minutes later, we emerged from the nightmare. Relief flooded every crevice of my being.

Sitting on that dirty floor, overcome by my situation and surroundings, I didn't have the capacity to proceed. But Jason's gentle guidance gave me the gumption to keep moving forward.

Crouching in the dark can feel safe and familiar. Occasionally, it can even feel like the only option. But God calls us into the light. Whatever your circumstances are today, let me be the voice that whispers to you, "Keep moving forward. It is going to be OK. Press on."

—Bree Combs

There is a farm near our home that has a pumpkin festival just before Halloween. The farmer and his family set up games and activities for children and families. We go every year. And we all love the corn maze—an elaborate and complicated maze of footpaths carved out in the corn fields that leave us confused and well…lost. But it is fun, and we know we are safe, and that eventually (if we can't find our way out), someone will come and get us.

It is easy to feel lost in the journey of life and to wonder if we will ever find our way. I have been so completely and utterly lost so many times in my journey that I have lost count. Half the time, it was when I was sitting in my own home. Completely and utterly lost. Praying for direction. No idea what I was doing or where I was going. Time and time again, I was given direction. Words of encouragement. A pat on the back. A phone call. A letter. An email. A text. A knock at the door. Lo and behold, I would be on my way again.

Jesus reminds us again and again that the kingdom is at hand, and all we need to do is reach out and touch it. We all get lost every once in a while. Jesus calls us to be the church, so that when we do get lost, someone can come and help us find the way again, back to the kingdom.

—Jason Leo

Once someone jokingly told me, "You think the world revolves around you, don't you?" I was about to reply with a huge smile when my son said, "Yeah, but her world revolves around me!" This is very true. My son is my pride and joy, my love and my life. I study, work, and succeed for him. I want his life to be as easy and rich as possible. I can't imagine my life without him.

I can't imagine being Jesus' mom. If I feel this way about the one who gave my life a reason, how would I feel about the One who gives everyone's life a reason? I can imagine Mary's nervousness in seeing Jesus take those first steps and the tenderness of seeing him sleep. I can imagine the pride she felt when he was playing well with friends and sadness when he would cry. But I can't imagine the joy of knowing he would save the world or the pain of knowing how he would save the world. I have tried to put myself in Mary's shoes, but they are too big to fill.

As a mother, I know firsthand the love we feel when we hear our child's name or see our child's smile. I know what it feels like to say, "This is my son!" Then I think of God saying, "This is my Son." This is my Son who heals. This is my Son who rescues. This is my Son who saves. This is my Son who forgives. This is my Son who protects. This is my Son who loves. Praise God that "This is my Son" has gone, goes, and will go with me!

—**Sandra Montes**

Over the years, I have found walking the labyrinth to be a deeply meaningful experience in a variety of places and circumstances.

The huge labyrinth on the desert floor near a Tucson, Arizona, retreat center gave me time to ponder the mysteries and responsibilities that I was entering into as a spiritual director.

At the university where I taught, I used to seek respite from campus busy-ness by walking a portable canvas labyrinth set up in the student union. With serene music playing in the background, faculty, staff, and students could join in an experience that spoke to something other than books, grades, and careers.

Yet the most personally meaningful labyrinth I have ever walked was in Rancho San Rafael in Reno, Nevada. It was not created by a church, retreat center, or college chaplains, but rather was built by a consortium of law enforcement personnel, social service agencies, friends, family, and surviving victims of crime to provide a place for meditation and healing. When I walked that labyrinth under the hot Nevada sun, I felt joined to the ancient desert fathers and mothers, to prophetic voices through the centuries who have kept calling us to love God and to love each other. As I walked that labyrinth, I acknowledged both my complicity in the evils in society and my faith that healing and reconciliation were possible.

—Joan Bowers

I once read a science fiction story positing a future in which an Earth-like Mars was home to a race of con men; they survived by exploiting the people of Earth. One of their scams raised funds for a little girl afflicted by a nameless but invariably fatal disease. Actually, it did have a name. That name is "mortality," and we all suffer from it.

The thing is, none of us are getting out of this alive. With Stage 4 cancer, I happen to possess a better idea of how long I have, and what I probably don't have to worry about (the implosion of Social Security, a world devoid of privacy, the next rebirth of bell bottoms).

In the shorter run, I continue working, singing, preaching, talking with my daughter, playing with the cats, reading for pleasure when I can get away with it. Knowing what the slightly longer run holds, I have updated my will and am culling my stuff, an effort I hope my heirs will someday appreciate.

I do not fear death, although the process of dying is cause for concern. I shall just have to trust my doctors, who have become my friends. As for what comes after, as an Anglican, it doesn't much matter to me whether the Protestants are right, and we are saved by grace alone, or if the Roman Catholic doctrine of burning away sins in purgatory holds. Either way, I'm good; the sureness of the love of God will see me through.

—Sarah Bryan Miller

The labyrinth is a metaphor for many things—a pilgrimage, our life path, our journey home to God. It is also a metaphor for the daily rhythm we experience with any practice of prayer. We get disoriented by each day's twists and turns, by what seems like endless plodding through our daily routines, but then we turn toward the center, and we remember that God is there. When we rest in our quiet time of prayer, whatever discipline we use, we bring the day's journey with us and try to lay it all down. As we walk outward again tomorrow, we will likely follow the same path, but always, even when we don't realize it, our time of prayer is sustaining us.

I went on retreat at a monastery that has a labyrinth on the grounds. I've had the chance to walk it several times. No matter how often I walk it, it never ceases to fool me. The labyrinth is disorienting. Just when I think I am nearing the center, I find myself turning toward the periphery. Sometimes when I seem farthest away, I suddenly realize I am almost at the center. I've learned to let go of figuring out where I am. As long as I keep walking, whether slowly and prayerfully or battling with distractions, I know I will finally reach the center.

—Kathleen M. Flanagan

)(

They will fight against you; but they shall not prevail against you, for I am with you, says the LORD, to deliver you.

—JEREMIAH 1:19

A few days ago, I drove Doug out to see his daughter, Jodi, and grandchildren. He no longer knows any of them specifically, but is always so happy to see their smiling faces and receive their hugs and kisses.

"This is what I want!" he exclaimed. He referred to having people (including little ones) around, laughter, happiness, and being outside. He looked at Jodi and me with such positive conviction and relief. "Can we have this?" he asked, clearly meaning that he wanted this afternoon to last permanently.

I did what I've been encouraged to do by Doug's caregivers—I lied and told him, "Yes, we can have this." More relief, more joy sparkled in his eyes. I so wish I could give Doug what he wants most of all—his life back, in full, wonderful splendor, complete with every last freedom and memory that this terrible disease has stolen from him.

Doug asked me if I would "Let Allison know." "What should I tell her?" I asked Doug. He smiled, and said, "Tell her we're here..." It was as though "here" is the place he longs to be, the place that once was, the place where he was sitting beside a pool, surrounded by people he loves and flowers and sunshine.

—Allison Zent Blankemeyer

The Song of Simeon bears the memorable line about Jesus being the "light to enlighten the Gentiles." As followers of Jesus, we are called to be light-bearers in our generation, turning seemingly perilous mazes with their indecipherable twists and turns into narrow but clear pathways of wholeness, healing, and peace. To do this, however, means keeping our eyes open to the One who guides and guards us, so that we never fall into the trap of being the blind leading the blind.

In our era of push-button technology, where the flip of a switch results in instant artificial illumination, it is important to take note of what it meant in previous times to light a torch in the dead of night, offering just enough light to find one's way through the darkness, through the valley of shadows.

At the close of the day, it is helpful indeed to take stock of the twists and turns that we have encountered, consider where our feet might have stumbled or even slipped off the path altogether, and also where God's light brought us safely through. Then we, like Simeon of old, can lay our head down in peace and declare that in the midst of the labyrinthine journey of our day and night, we have seen the Savior walking right there beside us along the way.

—**Chuck Robertson**

It happened again the other day. I heard someone call a labyrinth a maze. I tried to explain that there is no trickery or threat of being lost in a labyrinth, that it is a path to the center and back out. I too may have confused the two words before I walked a labyrinth at an adult education weekend many years ago. Several of us were so taken by the experience, we flew to San Francisco to learn more and to walk the labyrinths at Grace Cathedral.

I've seen children run on the labyrinth and almost dance along the path. One woman began attending the monthly walk after her cancer diagnosis. The path is not a straight line, just as our spiritual path tends not to be. As I step into the labyrinth and walk into the first turn, it's like a reminder to turn back to God, walk a few more steps, and turn back to God again. The path takes me closer and then it moves farther away. But when I continue to follow the path, I reach the center, and there I may experience many things, but the overall sense is peacefulness. As I turn to go out from the center, I feel renewed, and I'm carrying peace and renewal with me out to the world.

Recently I heard of an incarcerated man who asked to receive a labyrinth drawn on paper. He wanted to follow the path with his finger and with his mind. "Show me your ways, O Lord, and teach me your paths" (Psalm 25:3).

—Linda Gelbrich

" So God led the people by the roundabout way of the wilderness toward the Red Sea" (Exodus 13:18).

It appeared that the Israelites were being led from one impossible situation into another. They had been promised a land flowing with milk and honey but found themselves facing an impassable Red Sea. With the threat of annihilation by Pharaoh's army behind them and drowning in the sea before them, there appeared to be no way out for the fleeing Israelites. God, knowing the Israelites were not yet prepared for what awaited them in the Promised Land, had led them this way purposely. God would not leave them alone, however, but would be their companion through and their way out of this impossible situation, traveling with them in a pillar of cloud by day and a pillar of fire by night.

Sometimes God uses situations that seem impossible and impassable to prepare us to advance to the next phase of our journeys. While the way seemed impossible to the Israelites, it was the way chosen for them. Whether they could see it clearly or not, it was there for them. There is always a way out with God, yet sometimes that way requires that we go through the difficult and the seemingly impossible to realize it. Let us not give up hope when we face obstacles on every side but be assured that God is there to show us the way or to make a way for us.

—Kathy H. Culmer

The experience I have with the labyrinth is one of bodily surrender. You just give yourself over to the path. Even though I've walked the labyrinth dozens of times, it is fresh because I don't have to worry about where I am going. It is a prayer with your whole body. One of my mentors actually has a labyrinth in her backyard. She invites our Education for Ministry class to come and walk the labyrinth.

The labyrinth is a mirror that shows me the hidden rhythms of my life, and I sometimes feel like I'm not quite going the right way, that I'm stuck in one spot. At the same time, the labyrinth invites me to tap into a resilience and fortitude I didn't know I had access to. I become wedded to this path that I recognize has been laid before me, for my benefit.

What I find out from walking the labyrinth is not always what I expect. Surrounded by a great cloud of witnesses, my soul is encouraged and reinvigorated not only to keep going, but also to find the hidden light, the secret joy of every step.

—Charles McClain

Blessed be the God of Shadrach, Meshach, and Abednego,
who has sent his angel and delivered his servants
who trusted in him.

—Daniel 3:28

A sheperd's crook can illustrate flock mentality. When one is placed a foot high across a narrow alley, the first few sheep have to leap over the crook or staff to make their way through the alley. Then, the shepherd withdraws the staff. The remaining animals, sometimes as many as a thousand, will each leap the identical height over the imaginary staff.

Isaiah, foretelling the death of Jesus, wrote, "like a sheep that before its shearers is silent, so he did not open his mouth" (Isaiah 53:7). The bleats of the woolly creatures can get pretty loud sometimes, but their silence is deafening. When they panic, they remain quiet. Louis Irigaray, a shepherd and author, recorded the death of two hundred sheep that jumped off a jagged cliff to escape a lion that was posing no threat. As the sheep fell to the ground, they were "awesomely silent." Even at the moment of impact, there were no groans.

The psalmist, the prophets, Peter, Paul, and Jesus himself used sheep to prophesy, praise, warn, and teach. Learning more about the woolly creatures' habits enriches the passages. The potential for humanity's personal application of most of them seems infinite.

—Susan Taylor Block

The saying, "God makes a way where there ain't no way," speaks to the mysterious power of God who can reveal a path where there appears to be no option. This is an affirmation of faith. It is also a word of comfort during trial.

Recently, I was invited to walk a labyrinth. As I faced it, the labyrinth looked like a circular path that ended at a point in the middle with no new way out. I approached feeling weighted down with the cares of my life. As I entered, I felt the invitation to lay those things down. I walked and quickly started to focus on the path. I could feel the pressure dropping off with each step. When I reached the center, it felt like a place of rest. I lingered there.

How could such change happen with just a few steps? I breathed deeply. As I walked back, again step by step, I was able to take in the calm peace I felt. I reached the entry point; I did not pick up the burdens I had left there. I felt ready to return to my challenges with fresh eyes.

—Karen Montagno

𝄪

Oh, that Israel's deliverance would come out of Zion!
When the LORD restores the fortunes of his people,
Jacob will rejoice and Israel be glad.
—PSALM 14:7

When they finally found his body, it was stuffed into a manhole on a sketchy street. I didn't know him well—just met him a few times when he came to family functions with our nieces. The three of them were inseparable.

In the aftermath of his murder, I learned more about Garrett. He loved guitars and was a decent musician. He was goofy sometimes. Completely loyal. And he was adrift and dabbling in drugs.

Two small-town dealers wanted to make an example of him. He owed a hundred bucks. So they placed a fake order for pizza, and when he arrived to deliver it, they blasted him with a shotgun.

His parents were devastated. Our nieces were crushed. A whole community spun, reeling from the brutality and senselessness. Committed to making a way out of no way, his parents asked the priest to talk about drugs during their son's funeral. To tell these young people that each time they bought drugs, smoked a blunt, or took a pill, they were putting a nail in Garrett's coffin. This wasn't the time for the gloss of sweet memories. They could be next. Or Garrett's death could be a new way forward.

His parents started a foundation and sponsored support groups, recovery rallies, and battle-of-the-bands fundraisers. His mother became an outspoken advocate for tougher enforcement and gentler recovery. Last month, the family invited his friends to come and celebrate Garrett's birthday. They are young adults now, finding jobs and getting married, shouldering rent and bills and commitments, most of them making a way in the world.

Garret is forever nineteen, frozen in pictures, his face sheepish and full of possibility.

—Richelle Thompson

NOVEMBER

Acts of Compassion Stewardship

The king will answer them, "Truly I tell you,
just as you did it to one of the least of these
who are members of my family, you did it to me."
—MATTHEW 25:40

For the Least of These

INTRODUCTION   *For the Least of These*

J esus makes some of his most explicit statements about how we are to treat each other in Matthew 25. This is the way that Jesus asks us to comfort the afflicted, love the ones who are hardest to love, be present with the ones we might rather ignore or wish away, all for his sake. At the end of his life, we see Jesus as naked, hungry, lonely. If we look away from him in this most vulnerable moment, during his most profound act of love, we miss the great reconciliation of our deep sin with God's transcendental grace and forgiveness. This month, we are invited to practice compassion as part of our devotional practice, to learn to love the face of Jesus behind every face we see.

WAYS TO ENGAGE

If you volunteer at an organization, consider adding it to your personal prayer list and your parish prayer list.

If you don't regularly volunteer for your parish or another organization (and if you are able), consider setting aside some of your devotional time to discern where God may be calling you to serve. Then act on it.

Find ordinary ways to express compassion in your daily life.

Consider stewardship in light of Matthew 25. Find ways you can share your bounty—of time, money, and talents.

Jesus lets us know in real and concrete ways that hunger, thirst, strangeness, imprisonment, and loneliness are part of the human condition. Whether or not we find ourselves living out the extreme definitions of these words, we will all experience being the least of these at some point in our journey from womb to tomb. And because we are created in the very image of God, Jesus feels all of those terrible feelings right along with us. Jesus knows the pain of hunger, the torture of thirst, the abandonment of strangeness and nakedness, the ache of imprisonment, the dangerous and sonorous sound of loneliness because he felt every one of those feelings, right down to his bones. He does this in front of our eyes, and it is terrifying to see. His friends and his mother weep over him; they cannot bear to see him humiliated, treated like a creature little better than the beasts of the field.

With his life, Jesus shows us the transforming possibility of being the victim and the victor, the sufferer and the soother. The author and perfector of our tender and tenuous faith shows us that deep calls out to deep—deep compassion to deep suffering, profound acceptance to profound disconnection, radical hospitality to radical alienation.

Whether you find yourself in need or providing solace today, my prayer and hope is that you see the face of Jesus in the face of your brothers and sisters and in the face that stares back at you from the mirror.

—Rachel Jones

By the time you read this, my monthly pledge will have already come out of my bank account and gone into the church's account. It is the first bill that gets paid each month, and it's automatically done so that I don't have to debate it or second-guess it. There are a million reasons I do this, and none of them are easy to explain, but mostly, they boil down to this: my giving to the church is the most important spiritual discipline I have.

I agree 100 percent that giving doesn't always mean money—it can also mean time and talents. But I'm a CPA, and I'm a CPA who has served as both a parish and a diocesan treasurer. In the ten years I did that work, I never once encountered a congregation that didn't need funds, that didn't have to make hard decisions every year about what programs to cut or what salaries to fund because of a lack of giving. And I don't like the kingdom of God, the Body of Christ, arguing about which appendage to remove because we can't afford all of them. So I give. I may not give as generously as I should, but I give faithfully and regularly.

The church doesn't like to talk about money, but I do, and I will. Consider making a regular gift part of your spiritual discipline. Don't wait until your other bills are paid; don't wait and see how much is left at the end of the paycheck. Give first. Give from your heart. Give a gift to God.

—Holli Powell

I n today's world, or at least in twenty-first-century America, we purport to believe that all people are equal under the law, that there is no "least" among us. Even judging by material wealth or political power, I bristle at notions of individuals as lesser, needing something done "to" or "for" them. All individuals have agency and therefore a right to self-determination, right?

How then in this age and culture do we follow Jesus' command to serve God by serving others while respecting and protecting the dignity of every human being?

This work is neither easy nor quick and never simple. It is the hard work of relationship-building, self-examination, sacrifice, and listening. It is work that requires vulnerability from me. It is work that requires I be willing to be transformed. And that scares and exhausts me. But it is perhaps for this very reason that we are called to it, because part of the work of reconciling all people to one another is through our common transformation. By looking beyond ourselves in these new ways, may we find ourselves to be among the least and find Jesus very present with us in those we would serve.

—Jason Sierra

Empathy is one of the hardest curated elements of the therapist, but it is also the skill that I have found most spiritually valuable. My job is to stand in the midst of the fear, rage, anxiety, and sorrow, often with those that the world would call "the least of these"—people who have found survival in prostitution, robbery, violent offenses, and abusing as they were abused.

The least of these are different for all of us—some people, some choices, some life paths, and some inherent natures are harder to hold with love, and the natures that stretch us to the limit of love may be different for each of us. Most days people tell me they could never do what I do. But in order for me to live a life of faith and hope and grace, there is no other option. I do this work because it is the only way I know to reach outside of my selfish self and find the road to compassion.

Let us learn the way to limitless love together.

—Teresa Pasquale

For the LORD your God is God of gods and Lord of lords, the great God, mighty and awesome, who is not partial and takes no bribe, who executes justice for the orphan the widow, and who loves the strangers, providing them food and clothing. You shall also love the stranger, for you were strangers in the land of Egypt.

—DEUTERONOMY 10:17-19

Twice a year, the Episcopal churches in my town host Teens Encounter Christ. It's a retreat weekend in which high school teens come together and experience the story of Holy Week, led by various speakers and activities throughout the weekend. The most popular activity is the bologna sandwich station.

Yes, twice a year, approximately fifty young people gather for a weekend and make bologna sandwiches. It's a simple activity. There aren't any fancy machines or gadgets that help make the sandwiches any faster, just hands of young teenagers eager to change the world. And that's how miracles happen.

At the end of the weekend, the sandwiches are handed out to soup kitchens all across the city. On average, approximately 10,000 people are fed.

Sometimes, we think that service needs to be a grand gesture, constructing a Habitat for Humanity house, starting a food drive in our church communities, or flying halfway around the world to build something. But more often than not, service starts as something small: the little girl who drops coins into a Salvation Army red kettle, the parent who decides to clean up the local park for children to play in, the teens who spend a weekend making bologna sandwiches and learning more about Jesus.

—Longkee Vang

The ambitious character Paris on the TV show *The Gilmore Girls*, becomes angry in one episode because she can't work volunteer hours at a soup kitchen over Thanksgiving. "Harvard is going to be expecting Thanksgiving shelter work!" she rants. "They'll know that I called too late!" After a beat, she adds, "You know I ultimately do all these things for the good of mankind, right?"

I sometimes wonder if the ways in which we encourage young people to serve their communities—requiring service hours for honor societies, college scholarships, and so forth—really teach them what it feels like to serve. From the viewpoint of the service recipients, it might not matter why the students do the work. But if we want to teach our children to value the act of helping the community, we should begin when they are young and make service an organic part of their lives, a natural extension of their desires and talents, rather than a tacked-on college application requirement. Otherwise, we may be teaching them responsibility, but we are not giving them access to the satisfaction that results when we know we have offered our talents to help other people and that our work has made a difference.

Instead of asking our children to serve themselves in the guise of serving others, we should teach them to look outside of themselves. As they become older, we should show them continually what it feels like to extend their talents to the service of others and then trust the power of those experiences to motivate them.

—Elizabeth Brignac

Work brought me to Lower Manhattan several autumns ago. The meeting required a uniform of pin stripes and briefcase. A gentle nip accented the sun-filled day with its bright, blue sky and white, cotton candy clouds. I met Linda, a homeless, middle-age, barefoot woman, and her orange cat, Mary. Linda had white hair and a soiled face. She sat on a mat against a wall with a cup out for money, though she asked for nothing. She was ignored by the self-important, those with schedules to keep, the up-and-coming hungering to impress prospective employers, and individuals trying to cope with personal challenges, perhaps not wanting to be overwhelmed by another example of injustice.

After I passed Linda, something drew me back. I circled around and on bent knees introduced myself and learned her name. Linda immediately introduced me to Mary who rubbed against me and purred thunderously. We bonded. Unsolicited, I placed several bills in her cup. Linda beamed. I don't recall her exact words but to paraphrase, "I can take care of Mary now. She only has me. We take care of each other."

Linda looked into my eyes, which I remember as if it happened just moments ago, and sincerely asked, "Will you have enough for yourself?"

—Paul Jesep

Generosity is a powerful spiritual practice. I have learned that generosity is the best response to anxiety. When I am anxious about something, say money, the best thing I can do is give some of my money away. When I am anxious about time, I need to slow down and give away some time. When I am anxious about my possessions, I need to divest myself of some of them. I am serving money, time, and things when I let my anxiety about them drive my behavior.

A mentor told me once, "Whenever I start worrying about money, I know it's time for me to write a check." Giving money away helped him see that he had enough. He'd write a check to the church or to a charity, send it off, and then finish out his month without starving or becoming homeless. He could refrain from writing a check and experience the same result, but he would have done so by clutching fearfully at his money and living in a world defined by the scarcity principle: there's only so much, and you'd better hold on tight or there won't be enough for you.

Giving money away was his way of showing that he truly believed that God provides. In God, there is always enough, always more than enough. By regularly giving away some of what we have, we live out that belief in God's profligate generosity.

—Penny Nash

My Cairn terrier Angus died a year ago. It wasn't the first time I'd suffered a pet's passing. But my anguish over Angus nearly snuffed out my spirit. God decided I needed help. And this help came in Ricky Roo.

Ricky Roo is an orange tabby, fifteen years old who needs medications twice a day for a thyroid gone rogue. When Ricky's owner died, his younger siblings got homes straightaway. Not Ricky. No Internet ad, Twitter tweet, or YouTube video showing Ricky doing his cutest tricks captured anyone's heart.

One day, looking at the spot on the back of the sofa where Angus liked to perch, I shuddered out a choking sob. Then, suddenly, I decided I wanted a cat. Actually, it wasn't me who made that decision. It was the Holy Spirit. Left on my own, I'd have continued wallowing in my grief 24/7.

When I saw Ricky on the Internet, I knew he was my match made in heaven. His online profile description could have read: "Loving nature. Quirky personality. Adores a good cuddle. Have been patiently waiting over a year to find the purrfect long-term, committed relationship."

Ricky Roo now stretches out on the back of the sofa where Angus once rested. I had no one to bandage the wound from Angus' death. God's compassion for both of us is a daily reminder to follow the Lord's example of selfless service to those in need.

—**Charlotte Chere Graham**

I find myself saying, "I'm going on a mission trip in Africa with my church." People nod with a knowing understanding, and no further questions are asked about the trip. I suppose there are other words or phrases that provoke a similar response—9/11, Katrina, tsunami, Hurricane Sandy, a tour of duty in Afghanistan. People utter a quiet *hmmm* and allow the moment of silence to absorb the full meaning of the words.

My passport is stamped with two visas. In four days, I will begin taking malaria pills. *Oh Lord, where are you taking me, and why?*

O God, our heavenly Father, whose glory fills the whole creation, and whose presence we find wherever we go: Preserve us as we travel; surround us with your loving care; protect us from every danger; and bring us in safety to our journey's end. *Amen.*
                    —adapted from *The Book of Common Prayer*, p. 831

—Westina Matthews

ᚷ

Contribute to the needs of the saints;
extend hospitality to strangers.

—ROMANS 12:13

Walking around Brooklyn, I came across a sign that revealed a sentiment that seems to lie just beneath the surface. The sign was above an old garage and was dedicated to the memory of the firefighters who had died in the terrorist attacks of September 11. It originally read "We will not forget them," but someone had used spray paint to cross out the word "forget" and replaced it with "forgive."

We will not forgive them.

The original focused on the firefighters lost. The new version is focused only on "them"—an unnervingly sweeping term if there ever was one.

Standing on that empty street in Brooklyn, I was struck by how much hurt and rage so many of us carry around inside, festering in an unwillingness to forgive. I've also been struck by what a profound act of service it is to help people pick apart the tight knot of hurt that can become the crushing center of their lives. We oftentimes think of forgiveness as a grace from God, but I think it's instructive that one of Jesus' most scandalous acts was his taking on the power to forgive. Will we be equally scandalous in following this example of compassionate service?

—**Miguel Escobar**

M y husband volunteers as a hospital chaplain.

He frequently says, "I was supposed to be there today." Then he tells me about praying with a family faced with a hard and heartbreaking decision, or a patient who needed information, or a WWII veteran who wanted to tell his story and loved telling it to an appreciative audience—my husband is a military history buff. Mainly, he tells me about people who simply needed to be heard; the heart of his ministry is giving undivided attention.

We often think that ministries of service can only mean participating in organized programs of giving and helping, but ministry can also mean simply being there—for family, friends, or strangers. My husband's experiences have made me more aware of the times when I was "supposed to be there," to lend a hand, or say a word—or not say anything at all. Sometimes we can recognize—at least in hindsight—that we were able to make a difference because we were uniquely qualified, but more often, we were simply available.

Watch for the places where you're "supposed to be."

—Mary W. Cox

Years ago, I was walking the streets of Boston with a childhood friend. We had each just had children of our own. The two boys, James and John, (our very own sons of Thunder) were running ahead, her John dressed in immaculate and ironed clothes, my James in sweatpants with torn knees and a ratty T-shirt.

I said, casually, "Look at John, he's so perfectly dressed while James is a complete ragamuffin." She turned and answered, seriously, "You don't mind that James is a ragamuffin because you know he doesn't have to be." She was absolutely right. James had a drawer full of perfectly fine pants at home, a circumstance I blithely took as presumption, not privilege. I was properly chastened.

It is important that we recognize our privilege, whatever form it takes: economic, educational, physical. Most of us are privileged in one way or another. Our task is to identify that privilege and then put it to use in the service of others. "As you did it to one of the least of these," Jesus says, "you did it to me." Whatever it is you find yourself blessed with this day—be it time, money, patience, humor—share that blessing.

—Susan Wyper

ℵ

*You shall not strip your vineyard bare, or gather the fallen grapes
of your vineyard; you shall leave them for the poor and alien:
I am the LORD your God.*

—LEVITICUS 19:10

The problem I have with the stewardship talk is that it frames time, talent, and treasure as things we are giving away. If we drink one less Starbucks, we could give that money to the church. Can we miss church this week and help in the nursery? Can we give up our Saturday and help with the grounds? Stewardship is always framed like we are giving up something good for something less fun.

Let's be honest, when stripped down, that's exactly what stewardship is. We're being asked to go without so that the church can fulfill its mission and God's vision can be realized on earth. The problem I have is that it isn't a very enticing proposition. We are selfish creatures (and become more that way every day). As we talk about stewardship, can we reframe this biblical truth as gift and not a hardship?

I would love to hear the benefits of stewardship—the things we gain. By giving we won't get Starbucks this week, but we will get to meet a new person at coffee hour. You won't be at the worship service this week, but you will snuggle babies. You won't get to spend Saturday relaxing on the couch, but you will spend it working outside with friends. Everything we give up is an opportunity to gain something else. Do we spend too much time focusing on what we might lose and not enough time on what we gain?

—Lauren Caldwell

The spiritual path is one that encourages us to find ways to serve, offer compassion, and practice stewardship. Jesus modeled the act of service and kindness in his healing, in his words, and in the examples he set. He reminded his disciples that he came among them as one who serves.

Part of being deliberate in our acts of service is to find ways to pay attention to the places and people who need our compassion and service. Do we want to serve those who experience racism? Get to know them. Do we want to end violence, especially domestic violence? Get to know those who experience violence.

The mystery of Jesus' Incarnation is not that mysterious after all; it is the proclamation of God that God's love is deliberate and contextual.

May we grow in our practice of kindness and service by being more effective stewards of our time, talent, treasure, and presence.

—Mark Bozzuti-Jones

X

For the needy shall not always be forgotten,
and the hope of the poor shall not perish for ever.

—PSALM 9:18

As a nurse, I took care of a comatose man who awoke weeks later knowing my voice and remembering things I'd said. And I knew a teacher of nursing who, after she endured cardiac arrest, told her students precisely what they had said during her resuscitation. It's no surprise then that, in God's strength, I sang softly to my husband during his coma and death.

Since stewardship means committing to God all we are and have, we are stewards of our voices, which can serve as instruments for compassion. Whom do you know who may be confused because of illness, someone who might yearn for the sound of a remembered voice? Whom do you know who's lonely or irreversibly limited, someone who would be encouraged by the love of your voice? And if conversation is tough, how about reading aloud?

Speak words to someone whose life has become limited. Visit the woman who has lost so much initiative that you must do most of the talking. Sit with the man who doesn't even open his eyes. It's called ministry, stewardship, and compassion. Christ, absolutely unlimited and infinitely compassionate, accepts your care as given to him, and thanks you on behalf of his voiceless loved ones.

—June Terry

One year early in my library career, I headed to San Francisco for a conference. I'd never been. I had heard so many amazing things about this city, and I couldn't wait to get downtown to ride the trolley and do all of the touristy things you do when you go to San Francisco.

Homeless people lined the streets. I've lived and worked in big cities before, so homelessness was nothing new, but this was different. I had never seen so many in one place before, other than at a shelter. I stepped aside and watched what was happening around me. People were begging, sleeping, talking, and living—while people walked over them and around them. It was as if they were invisible. The scene made a huge impact on me. I couldn't get it out of my mind.

A few weeks later, I was home visiting my parents. I brought it up to my mom, who was a public health nurse. I asked her, "How do you help people when there are so many in need? How do you help people when you don't know what they will do with the money? More importantly, how do you live with yourself when you don't help?"

She sighed deeply and said: "Miriam, you just have to follow your heart. If your heart tells you to help someone, help them. Right then, help them. Know what that feels like. If you don't get that feeling, don't help the person. Don't question your own judgment. There'll be someone else whom you'll want to help soon enough. Just trust that God will guide you to the answer that's right for you." More than twenty years later, I'm still taking her advice. Thanks, Mom.

—**Miriam McKenney**

I absolutely despise housework. I hate cleaning toilets. I abhor vacuuming. I vehemently detest dusting. And I loathe washing windows. Who am I kidding? I haven't washed a window in ten years. I guess we know why. The only thing I like about cleaning is the feeling of accomplishment when it's done. Unfortunately, because I dislike the process so heartily, I find lots of reasons to procrastinate the job. This doesn't help the situation, however. Postponing cleaning only delays the inevitable, making the job even more miserable to complete when I finally pick up a broom.

I recently read a blog offering great advice for people who feel overwhelmed by the thought of cleaning an entire house in one day. She recommended breaking the job into parts and addressing one task every day. For example, on Mondays she suggests dusting the house. Then on Tuesdays, she advises cleaning toilets. Wednesdays are for vacuuming, and so on and so forth. She theorizes that breaking one large job into several smaller jobs makes the enterprise more manageable. And she was right! I still hate cleaning, but addressing one mission per day keeps me focused and prevents the tendency to feel overwhelmed and quit altogether. My new mantra...I can't clean everything today, but I can clean something!

It's easy to feel like we are too small to make a difference. We can't change the world, but we can change our little corner of it. Don't let the size of the challenge discourage you. Think of one thing you can do today to make a difference. As my pastor would say, "You can't help everybody, but you can help somebody!" You could even clean my toilet on Tuesday, if you want...

—Bree Combs

The church I attend recently placed a statue on the property. The statue is a park bench with a homeless man asleep on it. It is so realistic that people have assumed the man is real. A close look reveals the homeless man is Jesus, the wounds on his feet visible and obvious.

The statue, not surprisingly, generated a significant response from the congregation and the community. Some people found it profoundly moving and very beautiful. Others demanded its removal and moved on to another parish. I observed the responses with curiosity and fascination. One day, a member of our parish, a mother with a son, came by and placed canned goods underneath the statue. I asked her why she did that. She responded "Well, I felt I had to do something."

Acts of compassion and mercy are at the heart of the Christian movement. And I am mindful, and thankful, that in many ways Jesus is more than able to bring about acts of compassion and mercy. I am surprised that there is still so much controversy surrounding these efforts, but I am thankful that people still have the strength and courage to reach out in love. I pray that we all might reach out in love and that the kingdom keeps getting a little closer. For everyone.

—Jason Leo

I think I am an extrovert until I am in a room full of people I do not know. I would rather nobody talk to me and remain unnoticed, alone. However, when I see someone who does not know anybody, I go to them and give them a big smile, welcoming them.

I learned from my parents to be welcoming. They smile a lot, ask a lot of questions, and always want to feed people. They are genuine, and it comes naturally to them. It is a gift. They have hosted people in our house as far back as I can remember. They welcome people the way I imagine Christ welcomes me.

I have seen my mom hug people others wouldn't touch. I have seen my dad feed people who can never feed him in return. I have seen my parents invite strangers to stay in their home for days. They give and don't expect anything in return. And during all this, they don't have to say anything about God's love or quote scripture because their actions are a living Bible.

In church, I have seen my dad surprise people because he will say, from the altar, "I haven't seen you in a few weeks, where have you been? Let's have a meal and talk!" They don't think they are noticed or missed. Isn't that how we are with Christ at times? We go away to take care of some things and don't realize Christ is always there—ready to welcome us, ready to take us back in, ready to love on us.

—Sandra Montes

The seat at the bus shelter is hard, slippery, red plastic, a mere six inches or so wide and sloping to the front. Such a seat can't possibly accommodate a squirming child, a baby needing a diaper change, an elderly woman's grocery bags, or (what the designers were no doubt trying to prevent) a homeless person lying down for a rest. My husband and I shake our heads in wonder at how modern engineering and design companies have conspired with urban planners to remove any notion of comfort from what we usually think of as a bench.

Over the years, we have viewed similar-looking wooden seats in medieval churches across England: narrow ledges that could be tipped up for monks to lean against during long church services. Called *misericords* (from the Latin word for "mercy," *misericordia*), those seats were at least intended to provide some comfort for people who felt they should be standing, and the varied and whimsical wooden carvings under the seats attest to a rich folk culture imbued with humor and a recognition of human foibles and frailty.

We moderns may hope for a "wideness in God's mercy" for ourselves, but what we often provide for others is as hard, narrow, and uncomfortable as the seats at London bus stops.

—Joan Bowers

X

Those who oppress the poor insult their Maker,
but those who are kind to the needy honor him.

—Proverbs 14:31

My suburban parish participates in several outside ministries that take our concerns beyond and invite us to become genuinely involved in our community. One of these opportunities is to assist with the weekly meal at a parish in the city. In a gentrified neighborhood, St. John's is surrounded by need of many kinds. Each Saturday, a local bakery donates day-old bread for people to take home; volunteers cook and assemble a healthy meal.

I'm pretty useless as far as this sort of practical thing goes. I can't stand and stir for long, and neuropathy in my fingers makes me tediously cautious with sharp objects. But I can collect bags for toting the bread, dress salads, and wipe down tables. And I can make conversation.

Making conversation turns out to be a big part of this ministry— sitting and chatting with diners. It's not always comfortable, but it's not about comfort. It's about connecting and about remembering that we are connected. It's about finding things we have in common, and about finding common ground, even when that ground sometimes feels a little rocky. Feeding the hungry isn't just about food but about feeding the need for human connection. And that is a two-way street.

—Sarah Bryan Miller

I wasn't sure what to expect when I volunteered for the Choice Food Pantry. I imagined there would be plenty of manual labor—sorting cans, stocking shelves, helping to unload the truck that brought the local bakery's day-old bread. But the first day I came, I was assigned to be one of the people who accompanied clients. Instead of receiving bags of food, the clients would walk through the pantry and choose what they needed, thus ensuring two important things—they chose what they needed, not what someone else thought they might need, and they had the dignity of being given a choice. My job was to explain their options (they could take a certain number of items from each section) and to answer questions.

Many who came to the food pantry had never dreamed they would need to visit a place like this just to put food on the table. We were trained to be friendly, to take away the strangeness of the situation, to chat as if we were just two friends shopping together. I gradually realized I'd been given the opportunity for an unexpected ministry. I was giving not so much my time— only a few hours a week, after all—as my presence.

It is important to give money, when we can, to support corporal acts of mercy. But the word "corporal" means "of the body." We also need to see the faces of those we serve.

—**Kathleen. M. Flanagan**

Doug and I were recently on a volunteer outing to Matthew 25, a local nonprofit.

While talking with another volunteer, Doug began tugging gently on my arm, trying to secure my attention. "I got it," said Doug. I turned to face him, asking, "What, sweetie?" With the utter innocence of a three-year-old, he held up the product of a thorough investigation of his nostrils. Along with countless other things, Alzheimer's has stolen his grasp of social cues and etiquette. "Let's go find a tissue," I said, gently taking hold of his other hand, letting Heather know we would be right back.

We can respond to people or events in a thousand different ways—tears, laughter, repulsion, judgment, avoidance, and outright rejection. Or we can pause and choose to walk in love, the way that God loves us; we can choose to react with humility and grace, putting aside judgment and shame. This is what Alzheimer's is teaching me. God does not laugh at us—although God must surely laugh along with us. God isn't repulsed by our behavior, but God does come alongside of us, pouring out love and compassion, reaching out hands of healing and grace, glimpsing the kingdom of heaven.

—**Allison Zent Blankemeyer**

Around Thanksgiving, I cannot help but think of a biblical model of stewardship: Barnabas in the book of Acts. He appears at the end of chapter four, almost an afterthought, as one who sells property and brings the proceeds to the apostles.

But it is the subsequent appearances of Barnabas, "the encourager," that truly show his generous spirit. In chapter nine, at a critical moment following the conversion of Saul of Tarsus (whom the apostles refuse even to meet because of their fears about him) along comes Barnabas, assuring the others that it is OK to welcome him.

Two chapters later, Barnabas appears again as the apostles' emissary to Antioch. Described as "a good man," Barnabas rejoices in what he sees and immediately goes off to Tarsus to look for Saul. Finding him, Barnabas trains him as an apprentice. That "dangerous" newcomer would, of course, go on to transform the world as Paul the Apostle.

But that might never have happened if it had not been for Barnabas, a quiet encourager, a faithful steward of others, whose generosity of spirit led him to reach out a hand to one whom everyone else avoided. As night falls, I come to God in prayer and ask, "To whom today did I reach out…and how might I be a Barnabas to someone tomorrow?"

—Chuck Robertson

On Thanksgiving last year my husband and I were guests of our daughter and son-in-law in the kitchen of the cathedral where preparation was being made to serve a traditional Thanksgiving dinner to more than five-hundred people. People waited patiently in a long line for the doors to open. Some were in wheelchairs, some leaned on walkers, and others stood under the eves trying to stay out of the misty rain.

Inside, well over forty volunteers busied themselves setting tables, covering them with white tablecloths and bowls of fruit. Others were ready to scoop food onto plates, and some were at the door to greet the guests. Our job was to quickly scrape plates after the diners had eaten. We placed plates, glasses, and silverware on trays for the dishwashing crews, where freshly washed dishes were readied again for the food line.

Like instruments in an orchestra playing their parts, each job was necessary, and all were related to bringing a festive and filling meal to those in need. The reward was watching people relax at tables in an atmosphere of hospitality. It felt like the kingdom of God in that room. Everyone who was hungry had a place at the table, and everyone's plate was full.

—Linda Gelbrich

Jesus said to him, "If you wish to be perfect,
go, sell your possessions, and give the money to the poor,
and you will have treasure in heaven; then come, follow me.

—MATTHEW 19:21

There is an old story of a wise woman traveling along a mountain road when she finds a precious stone in a stream. While its worth was unknown to her, she knew the stone was of great value. The woman placed the stone in her bag along with the food she carried. The next day she met another traveler who was hungry and offered to share her food with him. When she opened her bag, the hungry traveler saw the precious stone and asked her to give it to him, which she did without hesitation. The traveler went on his way, rejoicing in his good fortune. He was certain the stone would provide him enough money to be secure for the rest of his life.

A few days later, the man went looking for the wise woman to return the stone. He said to her, "I've been thinking, and I know how valuable this stone is, but I am giving it back in hope that you can give me something even more precious. Please, give me what you have within you that enabled you to give me this precious stone so freely."

Our giving is the means by which we extend the hand and the love of God to others that they may seek for themselves what we have already found.

—**Kathy H. Culmer**

And I speak to you in a parable saying, "The kingdom of God is as if a family's home was destroyed by a tragic fire. Their hearts beat in their chests, racing to see what had become of their stuff. They wondered how the peace of God seemed to have shrunk and passed miles above their understanding. But you were already there. You were there when you came down the street when you heard the sirens. You were there when you organized meals to be delivered. You were there when you gave the children toys to play with and spent time with them while parents rushed to find a place to live. You were there when you passed an envelope around. You were there when you bought clothes and delivered them to a small hotel room, full of shaky gladness and a burgeoning singleness of broken hearts."

In case you didn't know—parables can be a little obtuse sometimes—that was me and my family. Our house burned on Thanksgiving Day, 2013. The days and weeks following brought an experience of lavish giving and generosity of God's people that was at times almost embarrassingly over and above what we thought we could take. Through all the changes, some still ongoing, our community, rooted in the love of God and the fellowship of the Holy Spirit, remained our anchor.

—**Charles McClain**

Moses and Paul lived amidst shouts and whispers. Moses, leader and prophet, spoke regularly to the assembled twelve tribes of Israel. Such amplitude would take a lot of lung power, but the messages were often tender. He tells the Israelites that to be obedient, they need not travel to heaven or cross the sea to learn how. All they have to do is recognize the intimate way in which God hovers over us, paying special attention to what we say and where our feelings lie.

Paul, terror of the early church turned trailblazing missionary, spoke to countless audiences. We can only imagine the fervor of his delivery as he explained and reproved. In Romans 10:8, Paul paraphrased Moses' tender words, "The word is near you, on your lips and in your heart."

Moses and Paul served as mighty spokespersons for God—all the while listening for the sound of the still small voice.

—Susan Taylor Block

Almighty and most merciful God, we remember before you all poor and neglected persons whom it would be easy for us to forget: the homeless and the destitute, the old and the sick, and all who have none to care for them. Help us to heal those who are broken in body or spirit, and to turn their sorrow into joy. Grant this, Father, for the love of your Son, who for our sake became poor, Jesus Christ our Lord. Amen.

—THE BOOK OF COMMON PRAYER, P. 826

Summer gatherings are such glorious occasions—sun, friends, and food. I was especially happy to be able to take two friends to share a birthday gathering with other friends. The tent, music, food, conversations, and salutations made for a perfect summer day.

During the drive back home, I noticed that the car was registering a problem. White smoke began to pour from under the hood, so I pulled over on the median. The car refused to go any farther, and there we were on the side of the road as the car smoked!

I frantically called for help as my friends stood outside in the summer sun. We could feel the pull of traffic wheezing by. There was no place for them to get out of the sun or sit down. It was a helpless feeling.

As I dialed and prayed for help, a black SUV pulled up behind us. A woman got out and said, "God told me to turn around and help you." She took my friends to a nearby restaurant and waited with them as family members came to get them.

I waited for roadside assistance in wonder and thanksgiving. She did not know us, and we did not know her. That Sunday the gospel reading was about the good Samaritan.

—Karen Montagno

DECEMBER

Sketching
Drawing
Doodling

Honor everyone. Love the family of believers.
—1 Peter 2:17

Bind Us Together With Love

L ong before we learned to read and write, people drew pictures on cave walls. They drew stories telling of mass migrations and memorable hunts. As our stories deepened, telling us more about life than simply how to stay alive, people began painting their most important stories on pieces of wood, stone, and canvas. Stained glass windows told the story of Jesus in blazing Technicolor centuries before widespread literacy or television became common place. This month we are invited to explore the spiritual discipline of sketching, doodling, or drawing—to see where our scratches and scribbles might take us on our journey toward the heart of Jesus. And as we encounter Jesus, we might see how God has "drawn" us, as individuals and communities, binding us together in God's love.

WAYS TO ENGAGE

Try doodling for five minutes before or after your devotional time.

Sketch out drawings of the people or situations on your prayer list.

If drawing or doodling seem intimidating, try assembling a collage of photos or magazine clippings related to the people or situations on your prayer list.

Use color to express your feelings and prayers.

As we gazed into the camera lens, all I could think about was how happy I was that we were all in a picture together. Well, not all of us. My father and grandfather were missing—would always be missing from every picture, from now on. Various cousins were absent due to sundry life events—first day of school for a child, doctor appointments for spouses, chemo treatments. But most of us were there, jam-packed into Granny's living room.

We juggled photo albums, the honey-baked ham on the counter, cell phones, car keys, and calls from work. Avoiding all conversations not related to the weather or the general health of everyone, we had one of those unremarkable Southern-funerals-turned-family-reunion that makes for uninteresting gossip because everyone simply got along.

Bound together by love, we celebrated my grandfather's life, and the life of our family as fully as can be done on this side of heaven. We laughed, we cried, and we thanked God for our beautiful, colorful, and (depending on which cousin was talking) crazy family. We are tied together by so much more than mathematical chance, DNA, or shared memories. Love covers and binds multitudes. Thanks be to God.

—Rachel Jones

In chapter 3 of Paul's letter to the Colossians, he begins by telling the recipients of the letter that as followers of Jesus, they have effectively stripped off their old clothes (the clothes of the world) and put on new clothes. He goes on to describe those clothes:

"Clothe yourselves with compassion, kindness, humility, meekness, and patience....Above all, clothe yourselves with love, which binds everything together in perfect harmony" (Colossians 3:12,14).

At first read, this seemed daunting to me. I'm not nearly peaceful enough for what Paul has in mind. I can be impatient, unkind, and all those other things—in the course of one commute! But then it clicked. I don't have to wake up as a patient, humble, loving, compassionate person. I make the choice, every day, every hour, every minute, to put on these clothes.

Love is a choice. Kindness is an action. Patience is a verb. (Well, not technically, but you know what I mean.) They will know we are Christians by our love...not by our tender feelings but by our outer appearance. Our clothes. How are we behaving? How do we show that we are following Christ? Maybe it's time to change our clothes.

—Holli Powell

I put my blue crayon to the paper and draw a single curvy line, "A wave." My mother draws a second line, parallel to mine and green, connecting at one end. "A blade of grass." I add a red-forked tongue, "It's a snake!"

This is how I learned to draw: with freedom and an open mind, one line at a time, no vision for the end product, always transforming, always becoming. This is also how I learned to build relationships, to build love, one small act at a time, one kind or true word, always transforming, always becoming.

But it's hard for me not to get in my own way. I want to jump to the end. I want the drawing or the relationship to look a certain way, to fit into a certain mold. But the beauty is that it's the little lines, the hatching, the erased mistakes, the accidental brush strokes that make a drawing or a painting sing. It's the time spent capturing and recapturing the details. These are the marks that bind an image together with the reality it is meant to capture.

Similarly, I find it is the details of how I love and am loved that bind me to others, the daily acts, the attention to the nuances of words and actions. May I always find the patience to draw them with openness and care.

—Jason Sierra

I am a lady of tattoos. I know this is a generational pastime—for previous generations and even tribal traditions it was the warriors who covered their bodies in the symbols of their story and the memories of their battles etched in their flesh. For many people I know tattoos are a way of storytelling the struggles, suffering, and joys of life in ways that commemorate the beauty of each moment; they tell the stories of our wars, both the battles won and the battles lost, etched in the hieroglyphics of flesh.

Secretly, in notebooks, I drew in pencil and pen, without right angles and away from the eyes of my art teachers. There was something fantastical and magical about drawing wordless stories. I had no use for them, no purpose for the secret hieroglyphics of my life, until I came upon the art of tattoo.

Every carving on my skin came from a sacred moment—sometimes a joy, sometimes a sadness, sometimes the impression of a feeling engraved in a certain moment of my life. While my human cave drawings may not speak to everyone and may cause derision from some, they have always been deeply rooted in spiritual practice and the sacred experience of commemorating moments when experience and imagination met in my very flesh.

Every image has its own story. The stories of my life are written across my body. They are interpretable; they are both clandestine and flagrant. They are where my present moment meets memory. They are holy—to me, if not to anyone else.

Find the beauty in the world—in the sadness and the joy—and commemorate it in some way, as your soul feels drawn, draw it out on the world. There is no wrong way to do it.

—Teresa Pasquale

There is nothing like being able to express ourselves anywhere and anytime on the go. How often have we been in a meeting, taking notes, when we suddenly start drawing something on the corner of the paper? Or when we're outside eating lunch, and use our napkin as a canvas to quickly sketch the flower bed next to us?

Doodling is quick and easy and can be anything your mind comes up with—just like prayer. There are formal times and places to pray, like during church or at a ceremony. But there are informal times as well: when we're driving, walking, or staring off blankly. Whatever our prayer and wherever we may be, it is still being offered by us and heard by God. God doesn't measure the importance of a prayer by how big or small it is; God knows that all our prayers need to be heard.

Whether we are sculptors, painters, or doodlers, we should always remember the importance of expressing our inner thoughts. Sometimes doodling is a way to remember something or make the time go by quicker. Other times, it can be an escape for us to dream however we want to dream.

—Longkee Vang

)(

Take your father and your households and come to me,
so that I may give you the best of the land of Egypt,
and you may enjoy the fat of the land.

—GENESIS 45:18

My husband and I once had a dog named Cadie. Part basset hound and part who-knows-what, she was red and solid with long, soft ears, a tongue that often seemed too long for her mouth, and a substantial tail that whipped us in the legs when she was excited. Despite a strong tendency toward obduracy inherited from her hound forebears, Cadie was a loving and beloved member of our household.

One day, as I watched Cadie sleeping on our bed with the sun streaming in on her, I was moved to sketch her. The process of trying to capture her personality and her peace in that moment focused me completely on Cadie: how she curved her long body in on itself, the blackness of her nose against her fur; the odd angles at which her legs stuck out. I worked on drawing her for a long time from different perspectives. After I put away the sketchbook, I was surprised at how much I had valued the experience, how paying such concentrated attention to Cadie had helped me appreciate her.

I have tried continually to bring that level of focus to the people, animals, even places that I love, but it isn't easy to pay that much focused attention in this busy world. This experience taught me that, regardless of skill (I am no artist), using a medium like art or writing helps me value my life's great blessings as they deserve.

—**Elizabeth Brignac**

Dad has a natural gift for drawing. He survived Nazi forced labor and later supported his family in the hard life of a welder, never thinking of himself as (or given the chance to become) an artist.

During a visit, I saw one of his simple drawings on a standard sheet of white paper. With permission, and observing his expressions of puzzlement, I took it with me. It became a framed gift for my brother who proudly displays it in his classroom.

Throughout childhood I remember Dad, a humble and usually quiet man, explaining that pen, paper, and pencil were a luxury in eastern Europe. In one piece, I vaguely recollect a modest thatched home and farm animals, probably destroyed in the war. Sometimes he included a church or faces of people. This art may have been cathartic, offering limited closure.

Icons can remind me of Dad. Using and writing icons can enhance one's spiritual life. In them we nurture our faith journey or experience the iconographer's sojourn through shapes, colors, and images.

—Paul Jesep

I doodle when I'm on the phone at my desk. I doodle in meetings. I doodle on my to-do list and my church bulletin. I do it to help me focus as I try to listen, but it's not a spiritual practice for me. I have a colleague, though, who draws meditations. During Lent last year, he drew several of them each month. They were creation-based drawings, focusing on the beauty of the earth. I was amazed at how he was able to make a stream look like a holy mystery.

I think that drawing meditations is something the world needs a lot more of. Folks have different ways of learning, different ways of accessing information, emotions, ideas. Accessing the spiritual not just through art but through intentional visual meditations makes a lot of sense to me. After all, we often engage children in therapeutic art, asking them to draw the things that worry them or to draw how they feel about something. Why not do that as grown-ups, too? Those who are gifted might well find meditative art a way of deepening their own spiritual lives, and others of us would appreciate their sharing so that we might deepen our own.

—**Penny Nash**

Picasso was quite the sketcher and doodler. Me? Not so much. Mrs. Brown, my second-grade teacher, reckoned my prowess in drawing so puny that it likely eradicated any chance I had of making a successful mark later in life. That's when my love affair with words began.

At first I doodled words with letters that had curvy, pretty shapes. Sometimes I'd even make the reckless move of drawing a smiling face inside a letter. Of course, the words I strung together only spoke gibberish. I was going for a "look," not intelligible sentences. I was careful to keep these doodles from the stink-eye of Mrs. Brown. I didn't want her belittling my unfettered fun.

I still doodle like this in meetings. But I've upped the stakes for myself. I work to design sentences that are both physically interesting to the eye and express a sentiment that is equally appealing. And sometimes I doodle pleasing sentences others have written, like this:

"Beloved, let us love one another, because love is from God" (1 John 4:7).

—**Charlotte Chere Graham**

I remember eagerly waiting to bring out the Advent calendar, a sure sign that Christmas was not far away. Each morning, we gathered after breakfast to open a window and see what surprise was waiting behind the numbered cardboard door. After dinner, my sister and I sat at the kitchen table. Surrounded by red and green construction paper, glue, crayons, paste, scissors, and glitter, we would make our own special holiday cards to give to loved ones, all the while singing our favorite Christmas carols. These cards accompanied the handmade gifts we exchanged on Christmas Day, binding us together with love.

Long gone are the days when Advent is the time for fasting, praying, and preparation. Sadly, the season has been almost totally replaced by an emphasis on shopping, gifts, and parties. As Christians, we must remember that Jesus is the reason for the season. It is the season to wait with great expectation for the miracle of the birth of the one who is our greatest example of God's love.

—Westina Matthews

X

Those who trouble their households will inherit wind,
and the fool will be servant to the wise.

—PROVERBS 11:29

One of my favorite moments in the Gospel of John is when Jesus kneels down and draws in the ground before answering a tough question from the Pharisees. In John 8, the scribes and Pharisees have just caught a woman in the very act of adultery and have dragged her out to serve as a kind of test. They and the gathered crowd want to see if Jesus will condemn her to be stoned to death in accordance with the law. Surprisingly, however, Jesus' response is to kneel down and scrawl something in the ground, a doodle that we never get to see or read.

What was Jesus doing down there in such a tense moment? How did that moment of drawing in the sand help him see the woman's situation in a different way?

When Jesus stands up from his drawing, he tells the crowd that the person without sin should cast the first stone. When he then tells the woman that he does not condemn her, it's clear that he and the crowd have been transformed.

In this case, pausing to draw was really about learning to see the woman's situation in a new light.

—**Miguel Escobar**

Today is the Feast of Our Lady of Guadalupe, commemorating the appearance of the Virgin Mary to Juan Diego in 1531. The Virgin of Guadalupe is revered throughout much of Latin America, and Juan Diego is now included in the calendar of saints in The Episcopal Church.

When I think of Our Lady of Guadalupe, I think of the Rev. Mary Moreno Richardson and the holy work she is doing through the Guadalupe Art Program. Through art, immigrant mothers and children, incarcerated women, victims of human trafficking and domestic violence, and children in foster care are all given an opportunity to see themselves as beautiful and holy. They paint images of themselves in the iconic form of Guadalupe, surrounded by her corona.

I saw some of these powerful paintings and briefly met some of the artists more than a dozen years ago when Richardson introduced them and her program, which was then relatively new, at an Episcopal Communicators meeting in Los Angeles. Several of the poised young women, holding their paintings, led us in a procession to the Roman Catholic Cathedral of Our Lady of the Angels. When I think of Our Lady of Guadalupe, I give thanks for the transformation that she—and Mary Moreno Richardson—are making possible in the lives of women and children who so urgently need to be protected, nurtured, and convinced of their own infinite value.

—Mary W. Cox

I read recently that the path to creativity passes through boredom. It is in that antsy and uncomfortable place that creativity sets up shop. I wonder: do we allow ourselves the luxury of boredom anymore?

I think about classrooms filled with students with laptops open, frantically taking notes. The problem with laptop note-taking is that we are tempted to be a stenographer, not a student. We try to take down everything with no filter, no interpretation of what is important. Doodling helps students find that. We doodle in the margin until, aha!, we hear something important. Now there are no margins to doodle in, no paper to fold into planes, or doves, or cootie catchers.

Let yourself doodle and draw and fold origami cranes. Let yourself be bored. Doodling frees your mind to think freely. To open itself to today's offering. Boredom, it turns out, is not very far from prayer. And by letting yourself think freely, by letting yourself get bored, you just might be inviting God in. And if you invite God in, God will come. And then, mark my words, you will be anything but bored!

—**Susan Wyper**

※

So then you are no longer strangers and aliens,
but you are citizens with the saints and also members of the
household of God.
—Ephesians 2:19

For months, the top position on the bestseller's book list at Amazon was a grown-up coloring book. Millions of books have been sold that allow grown-ups to do something that we have been encouraging children to do for centuries. I'm always looking for a way to detox from my day by doing something mindless. I usually settle on TV or a game app on my phone. Those are probably the two most common ways that our society unwinds.

So what is this new fascination with coloring? I think there's a feeling of great accomplishment when we connect with the arts. Not all of us possess the talents needed to create something beautiful…unless we are coloring. All coloring requires is crayons or pencils.

Coloring allows us to be creative without the intimidation of a blank page or the pressure of having to learn something new. It releases our egos and allows us to have fun. It is a form of meditation that takes no practice or discipline. You can't fail. You can't be bad at it. Why wouldn't you want to spend time doing something like that?

—**Lauren Caldwell**

Human beings are all created by God, but we are all unique. There are days when we experience how different we all are, and we may well wonder if God created all of us.

One of the greatest spiritual tasks facing our world today is to celebrate our differences. Of course, we are all wonderfully made, and we are all called to celebrate that.

Saint Paul writes that in God there is no longer Jew, gentile, slave, free, man, or woman, but we are all one in Christ. We are all God's work of art. The commandment of Jesus to love one another springs from this understanding of our unique lives before God.

I have a friend who signs all of her artwork not with her name but with the words, "I Love You." I imagine that in the heart and on the soul of every human being, there is a similar signature from God: I Love You. As different as we are, we are bound together through God's love. We are God's design, and nothing will take us away from God.

—Mark Bozzuti-Jones

X

If you remember that your brother or sister has something against you, leave your gift there before the altar and go; first be reconciled to your brother or sister, and then come and offer your gift.

—Matthew 5:23-24

Like thousands of people of many faiths who visit the National Cathedral in Washington, DC, I wandered at leisure. Taking in the beauty couldn't be done hastily, and I needed leisure for praying in peaceful quietness. In the past, I had gathered there with others in worship services, and I remembered their presence, but this day was to allow God-given beauty to heal me.

Beauty, peace, quiet? No—hard-hatted workers, racket, scaffolding! Though I'd known the cathedral was being repaired following an earthquake, reconstruction was at an earlier stage than I'd expected. Still, sunlight streamed through stained glass windows; a few small chapels invited generous blessing.

Moving toward an exit, I read a sign about the earthquake's occurrence in August 2011. Gasp! The earth had shifted under me too that August, when my husband died. Just before my 2014 pilgrimage to the cathedral, I had somersaulted backward into excruciating grief. I needed God's individualized, warm-hearted, grace-filled restoration.

Identifying with the cathedral's brokenness, I turned for another glimpse of the nave, remembering Psalm 23. Words of beauty and quiet peace, words that convey the healing process for us all, words that support our patient waiting without judgment while others are slowly being repaired. Facing brokenness, individually and in community, God lovingly restores us again and again. We're in this together.

—June Terry

When I was growing up, my sister loved to show my brother and me how to draw. She grew up to be an actual artist and graphic designer. I was never very good at drawing. She bought me books on how to draw, painted figurines with me, and even gave me a set of good art pencils. Still, my drawings are hardly more than stick figures.

Art runs in our family. My grandmother was a painter. Everyone in the family plays at least one instrument and can sing fairly well. And I am a writer.

Despite my lack of drawing skills, I'm not disheartened. I love to create. In the end, it's not about the art but the act. Thanks be to God.

—Spencer Hixon

)(

Sow for yourselves righteousness; reap steadfast love; break up your fallow ground; for it is time to seek the LORD, that he may come and rain righteousness upon you.

—HOSEA 10:12

I used to be a kindergarten teacher. It was a job filled with laughter, joy, questions, madness, and snot...lots and lots of snot! Children at that age are so loving and curious. One minute, they are hugging you around the leg and the next minute they are wandering into the school boiler room, completely oblivious to their whereabouts. They are like bloodhounds who can catch the slightest scent of adventure and exploit. Their inquisitive natures lead them in haphazard directions that rarely involve the original destination.

To solve this problem, a fellow teacher invented a device known as the Kid Train...OK, that's really just a fancy name for a long rope. Basically, when we prepared to venture from one destination to another, I would yell, "All aboard!! Time to ride the Kid Train!" Every five-year-old in the room would quickly grab hold of the rope. Then I would lead the train down the hallway. The students knew they had to keep one hand on the train at all times, otherwise they would fall off and suffer a child-sized consequence, like time-out or extra school work. That rope worked beautifully as a tool to keep them all moving in the same direction. As long as they held tightly to the rope, everyone ended up in the right place at the right time—nothing short of miraculous by any standard.

—Bree Combs

I attended a retreat at a convent recently. The first day was a little rough. I'm not a quiet contemplative in any way, shape, or form. Late in the night, the nuns gather for prayers. They pray for a lot of people. The sick, the poor, the hungry, prisoners… it's a pretty long list. And then out of nowhere, the nun leading the prayers prayed for all clergy venturing out into the night for pastoral emergencies. I looked up. What did she just say?

For twenty-three years, I have been a phone call away from visiting the sick and dying in the middle of the night, and I always assumed that no one knew and that few cared. It's just part of the job, right? And here were these nuns who had been praying for me the whole time. It was profoundly moving and downright humbling. An epiphany. Another reminder of why God invented Church.

So I want you to know something. No matter where you are in your journey, there are people praying for you. We really are all in this together. All the time. There are people praying for you right now. I promise. For me, this has made all the difference. I hope it does for you as well.

—Jason Leo

Has God looked favorably on you? Can you proclaim, "This is what the Lord has done for me"? I became a single parent through divorce when my son was very young. As a priest's daughter, I was, in many people's eyes, a disgrace, a failure. They did not know what was going on in my life, and yet, they judged me. Some out loud, some with very disappointed looks; some withdrew their friendship; some made fun of me; some avoided me, and some who were my friends became exclusively my ex-husband's friends. I'm not sure which was most painful.

Sometimes I allowed all of this to almost break me. On top of the pain of abuse, shattered dreams, and judgment, I wondered at times if God was also disappointed in me. But with every goal that I reach and cross off my long list, I feel God's approval. I know God looks favorably on me through scholarships, career successes, opportunities, and accomplishments. I know God has taken away the disgrace others ascribed to me, and I will proclaim at every step: "This is what the Lord has done for me!"

—Sandra Montes

)(

Above all, clothe yourselves with love,
which binds everything together in perfect harmony.

—Colossians 3:14

a fit of New Year resolution cleaning out, ...d I emptied closets and donated items to a ...ssuming I had pulled down another possible ...e top shelf of our guest room closet, I instead ...ding a handmade baby quilt in pinks, blues, greens, and yellows, completely finished except for the binding and tufting. The skeins of yarn for the tufting were right there on top of the quilt.

When had I last checked out that closet shelf? When had I made that quilt? And even more disturbing—how could I have forgotten making it? I realized that I must have made the quilt at least ten years earlier in a church quilting group. A friend of mine reminded me that there had been an intense one-day workshop and that several of us non-regular quilters had almost completed a baby quilt that day. I had put the quilt aside and forgotten all about it. My friend, initially amused at my forgetfulness, confessed she couldn't remember what she had done with her own quilt. We both laughed.

I try not to assume that life experiences provide one-dimensional morals to my story. Had I been too busy over the years? Probably. Should I have cleaned closets more often? Possibly. Yet I was also thankful that here, in my hands, was the perfect gift to send a beloved niece who had just had her fourth child.

—Joan Bowers

The days have been increasingly abbreviated, the dark arriving steadily earlier. Now they begin to lengthen: yesterday we marked the solstice, the shortest day of the year.

Thousands of years ago, our ancestors spent the winter months in a state of semi-hibernation, expending as little energy as they could in the time of scarce food and waning light. My guess is that this is the season when cave paintings were made: marvelous art that follows the contours of stone walls, with vivid images of animals that almost seem to breathe in the dim glow of torches.

We drive away the darkness with the brightness of lights that don't go away, at least as long as they're plugged in. They can seem a little garish, especially now: this is a time, for most of us, of frantic preparations for Christmas, with demands on our time, energy, and finances converging in ways that tend to fray the ties that bind.

It's a good time to take a deep breath, to remember why we do the things we do and the people for whom we do them, to recall the light that will be revealed as the days slowly lengthen, and the Light that was revealed at Christmas: the Light that illuminates our lives with a brilliance that can never end.

—Sarah Bryan Miller

I am lucky to have a marvelous artist for a friend. She loves people and animals and will often draw affectionate portraits of her family, pets, and friends. Yet her greatest passion is for drawing and painting scenes from nature. An avid traveler, she has brought back stunning landscapes of mountains, sea, and fields from her wanderings.

One year, though, she went on a family trip to a fine old city, with many buildings that were centuries old. There were lovely old trees and many parks, but no broad stretches of land that opened up vistas or allowed her to be inspired by scenery. Undaunted, she kept her sketchbook with her all the time, keeping a careful lookout for anything that might attract her artist's eye. Soon she discovered that many of the older buildings had fascinating details she'd never noticed. Suddenly the city seemed alive with images. Breathtakingly delicate flowers were carved around the borders of a portal. Whimsical faces, surrounded by garlands, peeped down from the corners of an old library. Wreaths, animals, and geometric patterns intertwined around the doors of old public buildings.

My friend couldn't wait to get home. She knew she would see her own town now in an entirely different way. Her discipline of careful looking had opened up a new world.

Even if we are not artists, we can train ourselves to see like one. Our love of beauty—in nature and in art—is an echo of our love for God.

—**Kathleen Flanagan**

While we were holding hands and walking around the lake at our favorite park, I said to Doug, "I sure do love you, sweetie." He looked at me, a little surprised. Smiling shyly, he asked, "You do?" I said, "Yep. More than anything!" Then, I asked him if he'd like to get married, and with excitement, he said, "Sure!" It didn't matter to me that he didn't know who I was, or that we were already married. I simply loved the idea that he would marry me all over again, just like that.

Later that night, it took us three separate tries to help him get out of my car. He'd forgotten how to make his body do this familiar activity. About ten minutes or so after we'd finally made it out of the car and into the building, we were sitting down and talking. He was trying so hard to ask me a question; I listened intently for the slightest clue. I thought I caught sounds like "chillen" and "sill" and watched his hand indicate he was speaking about something small in size. "Oh my goodness! Am I still working with children?" I wish you could have seen his face light up with excitement.

The joy we felt for having broken through the Alzheimer's "code" was truly extraordinary. "Thank me!" he said. "You are welcome, sweetheart," I said, kissing him. "You are so welcome! Thank me, too!" And we both laughed.

I thought about how Doug found a way to peer through the fog of his disease to communicate with me and about how I found a way to understand him. Love never gives up.

—**Allision Zent Blankemeyer**

It is worth asking what God looks like, and even more, it is worth remembering the answer we are given on this particular day. In Jesus, we find a picture of God that might be completely unexpected: not the all-powerful king and judge but rather a poor, humble child, one more likely to be found today (as then) in tenements and tents than in palaces and mansions.

But the real question is what image of God people will see when they look to you and to me. What picture are we drawing? Will they see a God who is quick to punish and judge? Will they see an image of a frowning, even angry deity? As long as we begin each day with worry and end each night with regret, we fail to draw a picture of a God who loves so deeply, so truly, so unconditionally that Love Divine actually came and walked among us, Emmanuel, God with us.

This night, after the presents have been exchanged and the celebrations have ceased, how good it could be for me to take some paper and a pen or pencil and draw a picture of God, even if only for myself. What picture will emerge?

—**Chuck Robertson**

I sometimes assist in leading a retreat during Advent or Lent. I work with a parishioner, Cammie, who creates an interesting retreat environment by setting up stations at tables with optional activities to engage people in a variety of ways. At one table, she places pens, colored pencils, plain paper, journal books, and pages with uncolored mandalas.

One person says she enjoys the retreat because the activities give her hands something to do. Without that, she says she can't settle into the experience. Some stay at the table a long time, selecting colors and then thoughtfully coloring a mandala pattern. Others take pens and paper, and while listening to quiet music, write or sketch.

Whether it is the free-flowing color from our pencils, the focused filling in of spaces in a mandala, or just a release of energy as we doodle, something happens. Our minds become less cluttered; we're more relaxed, centered, and open. No critic has been speaking to us—so we can listen. We are co-creating and we are blessed.

—Linda Gelbrich

)X(

An angel of the Lord appeared to him in a dream and said, "Joseph, son of David, do not be afraid to take Mary as your wife, for the child conceived in her is from the Holy Spirit. She will bear a son, and you are to name him Jesus, for he will save his people from their sins.

—MATTHEW 1:20-21

In an Aesop fable, a certain father had five sons who were always arguing with each other. Nothing he said could convince them to stop, so one day he decided to teach them a lesson. He had them bring him a bundle of sticks. He handed each son a single stick and told him to break it, which each did easily. Then he handed the bundle to each one and had him try to break the bundle, which none could do. Finally the father explained, "You are like these sticks. When you stand together, you are strong and can accomplish much, but when you are divided, it is easy for your enemies to break you."

There is strength in unity. Individuals, families, and communities are stronger when they are united. Love is the binding agent that gives the bundle its strength and power and that makes it unbreakable. Without love, Jesus knew his disciples would not be able to continue the work he had begun, so he commanded them and us to love one another. It is love that connects us to Christ, to one another, and to Christ's will for us.

Help us, O God, to love generously, intentionally, and unconditionally. Bind us with cords of love that cannot be broken, with love that holds us but does not hold us in captivity, love that binds us but also sets us free. Amen.

—**Kathy H. Culmer**

B ind us together, Lord…Bind us together with love.

Bondage, at best, sounds like something we left behind in the nineteenth century for the most part, and, at worst, something related to addiction and the grip that it can have on some of our brothers and sisters. How could being bound be a positive experience?

When the instrument of our bondage is love, we are invited to change our perspective. Each thread represents a relationship and the effort and care that it takes to maintain it. The paradox we find when we choose to live in community is that these webs can be simultaneously extremely strong and incredibly fragile. That is the paradox of love. When we face the unthinkable, it is often the love of a friend, family member, or church community that sustains us.

I am reminded of Jesus' words, "No one has greater love than this, to lay down one's life for one's friends" (John 15:13). We lay down our lives a little bit at a time. We make choices about how we spend our time, who we associate with, what we spend our money on. Every day, the struggle is lost and won with little choices.

Dying for a cause, even the gospel, is not a choice that most people will ever have to make. But all the other little choices add up. I want to choose love, and with God's help I intend to maintain my presence in the bonds of love.

—**Charles McClain**

The Bible tells us little about the years between Jesus' infancy and his life as an adult. Thankfully, Luke added a few details. Jesus had failed to join his parents after they observed Passover at the great temple in Jerusalem. Several days later, Mary and Joseph discovered him, engrossed in scholarly talk with the temple's greatest scholars. His knowledge and inquiries astounded the Jewish leaders.

A year shy of his bar mitzvah, Jesus was still considered a boy. So, as a mere child, Jesus upended the teaching sessions at the temple. Mary chided her prodigy for causing such worry, to which he issued his well-known, self-defining answer: "Did you not know that I must be in my Father's house?" (Luke 2:49).

Some Bible teachers leave the story there, but something of great importance follows. "Then he went down with them, and came to Nazareth, and was obedient to them" (Luke 2:51). Not only had Jesus walked gracefully away from his new and rare status, but he also tucked himself back into home life in Nazareth. Subsequent manifestations of Jesus' humility would reach their apex at Golgotha.

—**Susan Taylor Block**

ꗌ

The steadfast love of the LORD never ceases,
his mercies never come to an end;
they are new every morning; great is your faithfulness.

—LAMENTATIONS 3:22 & 23

Picasso, Rembrandt, and Monet have nothing on the artwork on my refrigerator. Splashes of color, bold lines, scratchy figures are my art treasures. These proud renderings my children put up even now say, "This is us! This is what we did today. This is who we are today."

My inner critic has kept me from making my own contribution to the art gallery. But lately, I have discovered the freedom of just letting my hand travel across the paper. I have regained the joy I had as a child when I just let color scribble-scrabble across the paper. I was not looking for perfection but expression.

Recently one art teacher captured that for me again by suggesting I take off my glasses and draw or paint. I thought, "Now I can't see anything!" He challenged me. "You can see light, shadow, lines, and color." What fun to play like a child and send them my pictures!

—Karen Montagno

𝄃

Many waters cannot quench love,
neither can floods drown it.

—SONG OF SOLOMON 8:7

I've always been a bit ambivalent about New Year's Eve. On the one hand, it seems silly to celebrate flipping a calendar page. Dates and years are just things that we've made up to organize God's good time. On the other hand, this provides a chance for a party. More than that, the end of one year and the beginning of another gives us a chance to take stock of ourselves and our world.

Usually about the middle of December, the news channels and Internet fill up with review articles about the year we're about to leave behind. "Top 10 News Stories" or "Celebrities We Lost This Year" or whatever. There are also usually a few articles about how to work on New Year's resolutions.

Perhaps there is a great gift on this day. Before the party starts, maybe we could set aside a few moments for personal reflection. What gifts have I received in the past year? What challenges have I faced? What have I done well? How have I fallen short? The point of this end-of-year reflection is not to beat ourselves up. Rather it is to be honest about our shortcomings.

Jesus has promised us an easy yoke. That does not mean we have no burden, but rather that by God's grace we have help. Putting up a new blank calendar on the wall is as good of an excuse as any to realize that each day is a blank slate. God gives us many opportunities to start over, to turn afresh to follow Jesus. Maybe this New Year's Eve is just the right time for a new start.

—**Scott Gunn**

CONTRIBUTORS

Abiding with God

ALLISON ZENT BLANKEMEYER worked for many years in the textile industry before earning her master's degree in Montessori education. She taught for fifteen years and then retired early to be a full-time caregiver to her husband and mother, who both have Alzheimer's.

April 24, May 24, June 24, July 24, August 24,
September 24, October 24, November 24, December 24

SUSAN TAYLOR BLOCK is a native and resident of Wilmington, North Carolina, where she works as a freelance writer. Though most of her writings are on the topic of Wilmington's rich history, she has published light verse, heavy verse, cartoon texts, and essays as well. Spending time with her two grown daughters is Susan's greatest delight.

January 29, February 29, April 29, May 29, July 29,
September 29, October 29, December 29

JOAN BOWERS is a spiritual director and writer who lives in New Hampshire. She is a companion in The Society of the Companions of the Holy Cross. The SCHC operates Adelynrood, a retreat and conference center near Newburyport, Massachusetts, where Joan loves to spend time. She values good friends and good conversation!

January 21, February 21, March 21, April 21, May 21,
June 21, July 21, August 21, September 21, October 21,
November 21, December 21

THE REV. MARK BOZZUTI-JONES is the priest for pastoral care and nurture at Trinity Wall Street in New York City. Trained in the Jesuit tradition and discipline, Mark's work in pastoral care, liturgics, spiritual direction, Christian formation, and group facilitation keep him engaged in actively spreading the gospel of Jesus.

January 15, February 15, March 15, April 15, May 15,
June 15, July 15, August 15, September 15, October 15,
November 15, December 15

Contributors

ELIZABETH BRIGNAC is a freelance writer and the mother of two adventurous boys. She writes and edits material for ChurchNext, an online Episcopal Christian education company. A cradle Episcopalian and priest's kid, she grew up steeped in the middle way in New Orleans, Louisiana, and has spent most of her adult life in Cary, North Carolina.

January 6, February 6, March 6, April 6, May 6,
June 6, July 6, August 6, September 6, October 6,
November 6, December 6

LAUREN CALDWELL is a writer, advocate, mother, and wife living in Atlanta, Georgia. A cradle Episcopalian, Lauren is devoted to deep conversations about Jesus, hospitality, and kindness.

January 14, February 14, March 14, April 14, May 14,
June 14, July 14, August 14, September 14, October 14,
November 14, December 14

BREE COMBS is a blessed mama, a treasured wife, and a grateful daughter of the Most High King. She loves writing, cooking, reading, and eating macaroni and cheese more than any person should. She lives on a farm in Kentucky, but her soul craves salty ocean air with every breath she takes.

January 18, February 18, March 18, April 18, May 18,
June 18, July 18, August 18, September 18, October 18,
November 18, December 18

MARY W. COX retired in 2012 as director of communications for the Episcopal Diocese of Southeast Florida. She lives in Charlotte, North Carolina, where she and her husband enjoy singing in the choir at the Church of the Holy Comforter. She writes light verse and haiku and takes a camera on her daily walks, practicing to become a more skilled photographer.

January 12, February 12, March 12, April 12, May 12,
June 12, July 12, August 12, September 12, October 12,
November 12, December 12

KATHY H. CULMER is a storyteller, teacher, and writer. A member of St. James' Episcopal Church in Houston, Texas, Kathy serves as a lector, worship leader, and director of religious education. Kathy is a former mission funding coordinator for the Episcopal Diocese of Texas, is the editor of a collection of personal narratives called *Yes, Jesus Loves Me: 31 Love Stories* and author of the January 2014 meditations for *Forward Day by Day*.

January 27, February 27, March 27, April 27, May 27,
June 27, July 27, August 27, September 27, October 27,
November 27, December 27

MIGUEL ESCOBAR serves as senior program director of Leadership Resources at Episcopal Church Foundation (ECF). A lay Episcopalian, he is a man of many practices, regularly making bread, playing piano, writing, and drawing from Brooklyn, New York. He received his Master of Divinity degree from Union Theological Seminary in 2007.

January 11, February 11, March 11, April 11, May 11,
June 11, July 11, August 11, September 11, October 11,
November 11, December 11

KATHLEEN FLANAGAN is a native New Englander who currently lives in Cincinnati, Ohio. She has worked in libraries and religious publishing for much of her life, and has published poems and essays on spiritual themes. She holds a Master of Divinity degree and has been a Benedictine oblate since 2008.

January 23, February 23, March 23, April 23, May 23,
June 23, July 23, August 23, September 23, October 23,
November 23, December 23

CARL FOSNAUGH is a member of Saint Matthew's Episcopal Church in Westerville, Ohio. He is currently pursuing a Master of Divinity degree from Bexley-Seabury seminary and licensure to teach social studies in middle and high schools. Carl is an associate of the Community of the Transfiguration and a former member of Brendan's Crossing, an intentional young adult community in the Episcopal Diocese of Southern Ohio.

January 31, March 31

Contributors

LINDA GELBRICH is a retired clinical social worker who worked as a therapist and educator in integrative medicine focusing on mind/body/spirit health. A spiritual director, formation facilitator, poet, writer, and grandmother, Linda is also an active member of the laity at the Church of the Good Samaritan in Corvallis, Oregon, where she lives with her husband, Keith. She loves music, birding, designing and producing notecards, and hiking, especially in the red-rock country of the southwestern United States.

January 26, February 26, March 26, April 26, May 26, June 26, July 26, August 26, September 26, October 26, November 26, December 26

CHARLOTTE CHERE GRAHAM is the founder and chief voice fanatic of 360 Speaking LLC. She guides people in uncovering their Signature Note. Charlotte's first book, *Inside the Light—Hope & Transformation*, was recently published. You can read more from Charlotte by visiting her blog at charlottecheregraham.com.

January 9, February 9, March 9, April 9, May 9, June 9, July 9, August 9, September 9, October 9, November 9, December 9

THE REV. CANON SCOTT GUNN is executive director at Forward Movement and canon to Christ Church Cathedral in the Episcopal Diocese of Southern Ohio. He is passionate about proclaiming the good news of Jesus Christ for our time. An avid technophile, he is a blogger and social media devotee. When not at home in Cincinnati, Ohio, he is traveling throughout the church as a speaker and workshop leader.

December 31

SPENCER HIXON is a stay-at-home dad and aspiring author who lives near the University of Notre Dame. When not wrangling his daughter, he spends his time working on his first novel, fixing up his house, playing the guitar, and wearing interesting hats. Some of his short stories are available for viewing on his blog at yetanotherwritersblog.blogspot.com.

January 17, February 17, March 17, May 17, June 17, July 17, August 17, September 17, October 17, December 17

THE REV. PAUL P. JESEP identifies as a Sophiologist, believing Holy Sophia (Divine Wisdom) is the Holy Spirit. He is an Eastern Orthodox priest and a New York attorney specializing in ethics, compliance, and public policy. He also serves as a corporate chaplain working with professionals on ways to integrate their public lives and spiritual understandings. Paul is author of the book, *Lost Sense of Self & the Ethics Crisis*.

> *January 7, February 7, March 7, April 7, May 7, June 7,*
> *July 7, August 7, September 7, October 7, November 7,*
> *December 7*

RACHEL JONES loves Jesus, her husband, Bob Dylan, the book of Jeremiah, and Texas barbecue. Her hobbies include playing music, practicing yoga, squeezing her friends' chubby babies, and looking for her car keys. Rachel is the associate editor for Forward Movement. She and her husband reside in Cincinnati, Ohio.

> *January 1, February 1, March 1, April 1, May 1,*
> *June 1, July 1, August 1, September 1, October 1,*
> *November 1, December 1*

THE REV. JASON LEO is the rector of Calvary Episcopal Church in Cincinnati, Ohio. Married to the fragrant and lovely Jeanne, they have three beautiful children. When not preaching or presiding, Jason enjoys spending time at the Procter Center, the camp and conference center for the Episcopal Diocese of Southern Ohio.

> *January 19, February 19, March 19, April 19, May 19,*
> *June 19, July 19, August 19, September 19, October 19,*
> *November 19, December 19*

CHARLES MCCLAIN lives in Sewanee, Tennessee, where he enjoys life with his wife, Janna, and two children, Samson and Vera. He enjoys writing poetry, playing the guitar, sitting on the back porch, and organizing a campaign to make "And also with y'all!" a recognized appropriate liturgical response for the worldwide Anglican Communion.

> *January 28, February 28, March 28, April 28, May 28,*
> *June 28, July 28, August 28, September 28, October 28,*
> *November 28, December 28*

Contributors

MIRIAM MCKENNEY is wife to David, and mom to Nia, Kaia, and Jaiya. A lifelong Episcopalian, she currently works as the development director at Forward Movement after a twenty-year career as a librarian.

March 29, April 17, June 29, August 29, November 17

WESTINA MATTHEWS is a retired corporate executive, author, inspirational speaker, retreat leader, and spiritual director whose practice reflects contemplative living through "holy listening." A member of Trinity Wall Street, she teaches contemplative spiritual direction at General Theological Seminary as an adjunct professor.

*January 10, February 10, March 10, April 10, May 10,
June 10, July 10, August 10, September 10, October 10,
November 10, December 10*

SARAH BRYAN MILLER is a member of St. Peter's Episcopal Church in St. Louis, Missouri, where she sings in the choir, serves as a lector and licensed preacher, and runs a blog. A former professional opera singer based in Chicago, she joined the St. Louis Post-Dispatch as classical music critic in 1998. Bryan lives in west St. Louis County with her younger daughter, a college student, and a brace of cats.

*January 22, February 22, March 22, April 22, May 22,
June 22, July 22, August 22, September 22, October 22,
November 22, December 22*

THE REV. KAREN B. MONTAGNO is an Episcopal priest and director of congregational resources and training for the Diocese of Massachusetts. Karen finds joy in ministry that connects her in deep ways with others. She has three adult children and being a part of their lives is more than rewarding. Gardening, cooking, camping, and relaxing with friends is big fun for her. Two cats keep her guessing about what life is up to next.

*January 30, March 30, April 30, May 30, June 30,
July 30, August 30, September 30, October 30,
November 30, December 30*

SANDRA T. MONTES is a doctoral student at the University of Houston. Her projected graduation date is spring, 2016. Her passions include family, music, writing, movies, and traveling. She serves as a lay leader at Iglesia Episcopal San Mateo in Houston, Texas. She is a teacher and a consultant for Episcopal Church Foundation.

> *January 20, February 20, March 20, April 20, May 20, June 20, July 20, August 20, September 20, October 20, November 20, December 20*

THE REV. RHODA S. MONTGOMERY serves as the rector of St. Thomas in College Station, Texas. She has also served churches in Austin and Houston. Prior to her life as an ordained person, Rhoda was the live-in resident manager and bereavement care coordinator for the Austin Ronald McDonald House. She and her husband, Rob, love Texas football and long country drives.

> *January 24, February 24, March 24*

THE REV. PENNY NASH is proud to serve as associate rector at St. Stephen's Episcopal Church in Richmond, Virginia. An amateur photographer, she posts her photographs along with prayers and reflections on her blog, "One Cannot Have Too Large a Party" at penelopepiscopal.blogspot.com.

> *January 8, February 8, March 8, April 8, May 8, June 8, July 8, August 8, September 8, October 8, November 8, December 8*

TERESA B. PASQUALE is co-facilitator of Seekers Dinner Church at St. Paul's Episcopal Church in Delray Beach, Florida; she is also co-founder and clinical director of RECO Intensive, an addiction recovery center. She is the author of *Mending Broken* and *Sacred Wounds* and co-curates the "Emerging Voices" blog at patheos.com. She loves to teach, preach, speak, and facilitate dialogue as well as practice connecting contemplation and action and healing and reconciliation.

> *January 4, February 4, March 4, April 4, May 4, June 4, July 4, August 4, September 4, October 4, November 4, December 4*

Contributors

HOLLI POWELL is an active lay Episcopalian who occasionally preaches. She records a weekly podcast called "The Collect Call," during which she and her co-host discuss the appointed collects of the week and how they interface with our daily lives. In discharging the duties of her day job, she serves as the finance director for a nonprofit organization working in Appalachia. She and her daughter attend Christ Church Cathedral in Lexington, Kentucky.

January 2, February 2, March 2, April 2, May 2,
June 2, July 2, August 2, September 2, October 2,
November 2, December 2

THE REV. CANON CHUCK ROBERTSON is canon to the presiding bishop of The Episcopal Church and distinguished visiting professor at General Theological Seminary. A member of the Council on Foreign Relations, he also serves on the board of the *Anglican Theological Review* and as general editor of the *Studies in Episcopal & Anglican Theology* series. Chuck has authored over a dozen books, including his recent *Barnabas vs. Paul* and *The Book of Common Prayer: A Spiritual Treasure Chest*.

January 3, February 25, March 25, April 25, May 25,
June 25, July 25, August 25, September 25, October 25,
November 25, December 25

JASON SIERRA is a lifelong Episcopalian living and working in Washington, DC. He has a passion for vocational discernment and leadership development and especially explored that during his four and a half years working for The Episcopal Church. He likes to create pretty things and enjoy the pretty things God has already created.

January 25, February 3, March 3, April 3, May 3,
June 3, July 3, August 3, September 3, October 3,
November 3, December 3

JUNE TERRY taught nurses in South Africa for ten years before returning to the United States. She earned a master's degree in New Testament and met her late husband when they worked as seminary administrators. She has served as a nursing home chaplain and is active in The Society of the Companions of the Holy Cross and in her Rhode Island parish. She is thankful for friends, dogs, music, and the ocean.

> *January 16, February 16, March 16, April 16, May 16, June 16, July 16, August 16, September 16, October 16, November 16, December 16*

RICHELLE THOMPSON serves as deputy director and managing editor at Forward Movement. Her passion for hearing and telling stories and writing in a way that moves people has guided her vocation, first as a newspaper reporter, then as director of communications for the Episcopal Diocese of Southern Ohio, and continuing with her ministry at Forward Movement. She and her husband, an Episcopal priest, have two children, a horse, a dog, and a rabbit. They all live in God's country in Northern Kentucky.

> *May 31, July 31, August 31, October 31*

LONGKEE VANG is a youth minister and young adult facilitator in the Episcopal Diocese of Minnesota. He also works for a nonprofit organization located on the east side of St. Paul. When he's not recruiting youth to attend mission trips, he enjoys hiking and playing the video game *Just Dance.*

> *January 5, February 5, March 5, April 5, May 5, June 5, July 5, August 5, September 5, October 5, November 5, December 5*

THE REV. SUSAN WYPER is an Episcopal priest who currently serves as associate rector of St. Matthew's Church in Bedford, New York. She strives to live her life by having an inquiring and discerning heart, the courage to will and to persevere, a spirit to know and to love God, and the gift of joy and wonder in all God's works. She and her husband live in Darien, Connecticut, where they raised three wonderful sons.

> *January 13, February 13, March 13, April 13, May 13, June 13, July 13, August 13, September 13, October 13, November 13, December 13*

About Forward Movement

Forward Movement is committed to inspiring disciples and empowering evangelists. While we produce great resources like this book, Forward Movement is not a publishing company. We are a ministry.

Our mission is to support you in your spiritual journey, to help you grow as a follower of Jesus Christ. Publishing books, daily reflections, studies for small groups, and online resources is an important way that we live out this ministry. More than a half million people read our daily devotions through *Forward Day by Day*, which is also available in Spanish (*Adelante Día a Día*) and Braille, online, as a podcast, and as an app for smartphones or tablets. It is mailed to more than fifty countries, and we donate nearly 30,000 copies each quarter to prisons, hospitals, and nursing homes. We actively seek partners across the Church and look for ways to provide resources that inspire and challenge.

A ministry of The Episcopal Church for eighty years, Forward Movement is a nonprofit organization funded by sales of resources and gifts from generous donors. To learn more about Forward Movement and our resources, please visit us at www.forwardmovement.org or www.adelanteenelcamino.org.

We are delighted to be doing this work and invite your prayers and support.